CURRENTS of CONTRAST

life in southern Africa's two oceans

To my parents, for their love, kindness and unwavering support.
THOMAS P. PESCHAK

To Emily and Francisca, my friends, and to my family in Chile — especially my parents
Pedro and Raquel who taught us to love and respect the sea at a very young age.
CLAUDIO VELÁSQUEZ ROJAS

CURRENTS of CONTRAST

life in southern Africa's two oceans

Thomas P. Peschak

**photography by Thomas P. Peschak
and Claudio Velásquez Rojas**

CONTENTS

Author's note 7   Forewords 8
Acknowledgements 11   Introduction 12

PART ONE
THE REALM OF THE BENGUELA 29

1 GREAT WHITE SHARK
misunderstood predator 30

2 KELP
the golden forest 48

3 JACKALS, LIONS AND HYENAS
fishing for a living 62

4 SEABIRDS
dwellers of the ocean sky 72

5 SOUTHERN RIGHT WHALE
the journey 90

6 LIMPETS
a life between the tides 104

PART TWO
THE REALM OF THE AGULHAS 119

7 SARDINE RUN
the greatest shoal on Earth 120

8 KNYSNA SEAHORSE
creature of the blue lagoon 130

9 THE TEMBE-THONGA
people of the sea and lakes 136

10 SEA TURTLES
prehistoric survivors 154

11 CORAL REEFS
rainforests of the sea 166

12 THE COELACANTH
a fish that time forgot 184

Glossary 194
Selected bibliography 195
Index 197

The years 2002 and 2003 were a whirlwind tour of southern Africa's coast and oceans; a time when I did little else but sleep, eat and breathe in the presence of salty ocean air, from the remote reaches of Namibia's Skeleton Coast to the tropical coral reefs of wildest northern Mozambique.

Author's note

The challenge in writing and photographing this book was not just to portray the marine environments of Namibia, South Africa and Mozambique accurately and comprehensively – but also evocatively. To condense this boiling cauldron of life into some 200 pages and a few hundred images was a daunting prospect. The greatest difficulty was not so much which species, habitats, ecological processes or conservation issues to include, but which to omit.

To cover them all would have resulted in many volumes, so I had to be selective. Topics were chosen with the aim of showcasing marine biology and ecology that is uniquely southern African. Lions that feed on whales, baboons that hunt mussels and limpets, the sardine run and the Knysna seahorse occur nowhere else on Earth. While great white sharks, southern right whales, kelp forests, limpets, seabirds, coral reefs, sea turtles and coelacanths are also found in the oceans of other continents, the ecology, behaviour and conservation issues featured here are specific to southern Africa.

World-renowned wildlife biologist George B. Schaller once wrote: 'Pen and camera are weapons against oblivion; they can create awareness for that which may soon be lost forever.' These poignant and powerful words have echoed in my head over the last two years, during which writing and photographing this book have occupied my heart, mind and soul.

To those who are already enchanted by the blue wilderness right at our doorstep, this book aims to strengthen the bond and promote further understanding of its ecosystems and creatures. For the uninitiated, it hopes to transform the oceans from a deep, dark menacing place, home of man-eating sharks and deadly, toxic creatures to a beautiful playground of life worthy of respect and protection.

Baba Dioum, the Senegalese philosopher, said: 'In the end we will conserve only what we love, we will love only what we understand, we will understand only what we are taught.' Every person who gains an understanding of and love for the oceans will bring us one step closer to putting a permanent end to the destructive activities of trawlers, long-liners and poachers.

Until fairly recently, the bulk of the region's marine biological knowledge lay hidden in the scientific literature, which, while making exciting reading for marine biologists, excluded other ocean enthusiasts and laypeople. This changed when George and Margo Branch's *The Living Shores of Southern Africa* appeared in 1981. A hit with a wide audience, this instant classic went through 12 impressions before going out of print. Much has changed in southern African marine science over the last 24 years, however. Scientific discoveries are made on an almost monthly basis, new species are discovered and some that were once common now face possible extinction. Ecological theories that have stood the test of time have been disproved, theories that lurked on the scientific fringes for years have gained repute, and scientific methods that are commonly utilized today would have seemed outlandish 10 years ago and unthinkable 20 years ago.

The time has come for a new look at the natural history of southern Africa's oceans and at the drama of life that pulses within them. Combining popular science and wildlife photography, *Currents of Contrast* aims to bring readers southern Africa's most exciting marine discoveries with a strong focus on research findings made in the last quarter of a century – from the biology of the smallest limpet to the behaviour of the great white shark.

Enjoy the journey – I did.

THOMAS P. PESCHAK
Marine Biology Research Institute
University of Cape Town
2005

Foreword

Three of the passions in my life have been: the sea and its occupants; capturing these with a camera; and the postgraduate students who have been the lifeblood of my research. Vicariously, I rejoice in this book because it embraces all three: the magic of the sea, written and superbly photographed by two people who started as students and became colleagues and friends.

The very title – *Currents of Contrast* – focuses immediately on why our country is so extraordinary from an oceanographic perspective. Nowhere else in the world embraces two oceans of such extremes. In summer, it is possible to luxuriate in waters of 22 °C in False Bay on the Cape Peninsula, and then to hop over the short neck to the west coast where the southeasterly winds will be driving surface water away, drawing up nutrient-rich waters to bathe the coast in an icy 12 °C. And with these physical contrasts comes a remarkable diversity of life, interacting in ways that are as fascinating as they are difficult to conserve. Such is the salty world with which scientists and managers grapple, at times exhilarated by the exuberance of life and at others challenged by the complexity of these interactions.

This book vividly records triumphant success stories of conservation, disasters-in-the-making such as the catastrophic declines in abalone caused by poaching, and the excitement of studies that unravel the intricacies of the sea. At its heart, it reveals two great truths: that understanding entire ecosystems and gaining the co-operation of human beings are vital if we are to succeed in conserving our remarkable coast.

It has been my privilege to spend a lifetime studying the sea. *Currents of Contrast* distils the essence of the sea with a saturation of spectacular photography and a text that demands to be read, absorbed and applied, transmitting that privilege and its incumbent responsibilities to you, the reader.

GEORGE BRANCH
Professor of Marine Biology and Zoology,
University of Cape Town
2005

FROM LEFT TO RIGHT: A ghost crab forages on a beach along Namibia's Skeleton Coast. Argenville's limpets occupy the lower reaches of the inter-tidal rocky shore and form dense bands adjacent to kelp beds. A woman returns from gathering shellfish on a Mozambican tidal flat. A loggerhead turtle crawls back into the sea after an exhausting night of egg-laying.

Foreword - WWF-SA

Two very different currents flank the southern African subregion. Yet they share one important commonality: the economic, cultural, spiritual, social and physical wellbeing of millions of southern Africans are closely linked to the health of these ecosystems.

The economic importance of these ecosystems is without doubt. It is estimated that total goods and services provided by South African coastal ecosystems amount to some 35% of the national gross domestic product. Most importantly, coastal tourism in South Africa is estimated to be worth some R20 billion. In neighbouring Namibia and Mozambique, coastal tourism is also among the fastest growing economic sectors.

The importance of the coastal ecosystems to the healthy livelihoods of Africans is equally apparent, with an estimated 40% of Africa's population deriving its livelihood from marine and coastal ecosystems, and more than 30% of South Africans living within 60 km of the coast.

For some, our coasts and marine ecosystems are places of great cultural and spiritual importance. For others, the ocean is simply an inspirational place. Some live their entire lives under the magnetic attraction that draws them to play on its waves, plunge beneath its surface, or simply meander along its shores in the presence of its calming effect. These cultural, spiritual and recreational values are also important to the overall wellbeing of the people who live near, or visit, our shores.

Clearly our oceans are a place of great value for the wellbeing of humans. Why then are our global oceans in such a poor state? It is equally apparent that our oceans are subject to many different and often overlapping uses. Traditional sectoral management has led to conflicting and competing management objectives, leading to the phenomenon known as the *tragedy of commons* – where each resource user seeks to maximize his or her short-term gains in order to out-compete other resource users, leading to the ultimate collapse of the resource and the demise of all the users. In short, sectoral management of our oceans has failed dismally, and its continued use threatens to destroy our marine ecosystems.

Modern marine conservation and fisheries managers are in agreement that a more holistic and ecosystem-based approach to the management of our oceans is needed. Such a management style seeks to manage the ecosystem as a whole with the ultimate aim of maintaining the integrity of the ecosystem itself. Most importantly, such a management regime should benefit from the participation of a wide array of stakeholders. Who then are the stakeholders in the management of our marine ecosystems? The White Paper on A Marine Fisheries Policy for South Africa is quite clear that our marine resources and ecosystems are 'a national asset and heritage of *all its people* and should be managed and developed for the benefit of present and future generations in the country as a whole'. Clearly all South Africans have a say in building a future in which our marine ecosystems are preserved for the long-term economic, social and environmental benefit of all. This is also the vision of the new Marine Programme of the World Wide Fund for Nature South Africa (WWF-SA).

Like its subject matter, *Currents of Contrast* is an inspirational book. We have no doubt that Thomas Peschak will succeed in converting many occasional users into veritable marine junkies. Yet this book also equips its readers with knowledge and, in many cases, will provide the spark of intrigue that will drive readers to acquire further knowledge. Knowledge and passion are a powerful combination. It is our sincere hope that this book will inspire and equip its readers to become positive and constructive participants in the conservation of our precious marine ecosystems.

Dr Deon Nel
WWF-SA Marine Programme Manager
Cape Town
2005

Ms Aaniyah Omardien
WWF-SA Marine Programme Assistant Manager
Cape Town
2005

9

ANTI-CLOCKWISE FROM TOP LEFT: A lionfish. Medicines from the sea — compounds chemically isolated from sea fans and corals have resulted in the development of new medicines. At sunrise a sangoma apprentice journeys to the ocean to take part in a ritual in which she will take on some of the sea's power. The unmistakable dorsal fin of a great white shark. During the day coral polyps remain hidden inside the colony's skeleton.

CURRENTS of
CONTRAST

Acknowledgements

Photographing and writing *Currents of Contrast* was such a major undertaking that I would never have successfully completed it without the great generosity, enthusiasm and knowledge of the many people whose paths crossed mine on my many journeys: Michael Scholl (White Shark Trust), Michael Rutzen, Jenna Cains, Frankie Rutzen, Morne Hardenberg, Ivan Rutzen, Rea Hardenberg, Lindi van Rooyen (Shark Diving Unlimited), Mike Meyer, crew of the *Sardinops* (Marine and Coastal Management), Dr Ramon Bonfil (Wildlife Conservation Society), Wilfred Chivell, Yvonne Kamp (Dyer Islands Cruises), Danie and Riette Bennet (Advantage Tours & Charters), Prof. Vic Peddemors (University of KZN), Mark & Gayle Addison (Blue Wilderness), Pat Green (National Geographic), Peter Timm (Triton Dive Charters), Darryl, Clive, Michelle and Debby (Wilderness Safaris, Rocktail Bay), Dave van Smeerdijk, Damon, Steffie (Wilderness Safaris, Namibia), Ingrid Wiesel (Namib Desert Brown Hyena Project), Lise Hansen, Dr Flip Stander (Predator Conservation Trust), Jim Morrell (Knysna Estuarine Aquarium), John Paterson (Ministry of Environment and Tourism, Namibia), Peet Joubert, Gavin Bell, Justin Buchmann (SAN Parks), Dr Jean Harris, Jeff Gaisford, Hayden Ferguson, Richard Penn-Sawyers, Cedric Coetzee, Dr Scotty Kyle (Ezemvelo KZN Wildlife), Ronnie Brereton-Stiles, Gugu Zama (Green Trust), Andrew Newby, Victor Ngubane, Songimvelo Committee, the people of Kosi Bay, Craig Spencer, Monique van Wyk, Johan Erasmus (Overstrand Nature Conservation), Mike and Linda (Seawatch), Steve, Andrew and Dan (Ocean Optics, London), Mike, Andrew, Steve, Donovan, Tracy and the rest of the team (ORMS, Cape Town).

Ronnie Brereton-Stiles and Claire Wilcox proofread and commented on an early version of the manuscript. Pippa Parker, Janice Evans, Lynda Harvey, Emily Bowles (Struik) and Roxanne Reid took my words, photographs and vision and superbly created the book you hold in your hands today. Thank you for exceeding even my wildest expectations.

I wish to record my deep appreciation to Prof. George Branch, Prof. Charles Griffiths, Prof. Vic Peddemors, Dr Bernhard Riegl, Dr Kerry Sink and Michael C. Scholl for reviewing and advising me on many of the chapters in this book.

Thanks also to WWF South Africa, especially Dr Deon Nel and Aaniyah Omardien, for providing me with a grant to complete essential parts of this book and to George Branch, not only for his kind foreword but also for his inspiring words, insights and friendship over the last five years.

Special thanks are due to a group of people who have been there for me through thick and thin, good times and bad: my parents, my brother Alex and my close friends Craig Spencer, Ronnie Brereton-Stiles, Clovelly Lawrence, Michael & Tracy Scholl, Michael Rutzen, Jenna Cains, and Monique van Wyk.

THOMAS P. PESCHAK

The gathering of photographic material involved the collaboration and support of many people and institutions. The following stand out in particular, in alphabetical order: Carl Gustaf Lundin (IUCN Global Marine Programme), José Pereira and Nelson Da Silva (and the crew of MALAGAS II), Michelle Shortt (Ocean View & Masiphumelele Fishing), Dr Mick O'Toole (BCLME), NAMDEB, Port Nolloth Municipality, Vilanculos Coastal Wildlife Sanctuary, West Coast National Park and the Zoology Department of the University of Cape Town.

CLAUDIO VELÁSQUEZ ROJAS

INTRODUCTION

CURRENTS of
CONTRAST

ABOVE: Looking northwards from Cape Point, Africa's southwesternmost tip, the Atlantic Ocean flanks the Peninsula on the left and right. Contrary to popular belief, this is not the meeting point of the two oceans.

OPPOSITE: A baboon on the beach, a scene unique to the southern African coast.

Some 200 million years before the dawn of the present-day Africa, South America, Antarctica and Australia lay fused together, forming the large supercontinent known as Gondwanaland. The southern African coast and oceans were only born during violent episodes of tectonic upheaval 177 to 89 million years ago. In the early Cretaceous period Madagascar, Australia and Antarctica broke free from Africa and drifted to the east, and the newly formed marine basin became the Indian Ocean. Continental drift liberated Africa from South America only during the mid-Cretaceous period, creating between them the body of water that was destined to become the Atlantic Ocean.

Today, southern Africa's coast is the meeting place of two ocean giants – the cold Benguela current of the Atlantic Ocean and the warm Agulhas current of the Indian Ocean. They clash fiercely at the continent's southern tip, dividing the region into two contrasting marine ecosystems that rank among the richest, most biologically diverse and oceanographically complex on the planet.

The Atlantic Ocean, with its awesome productivity and abundance of animal and plant biomass, borders the subcontinent's western flank, while the Indian Ocean that lies on the east has an ecological signature of great biodiversity. For centuries scientists have tried to locate the exact battleground of these two oceans, but it now appears that it is a dynamic and diffuse border centred on the Agulhas bank, a relatively shallow part of the continental shelf that extends about 200 km offshore from Africa's southernmost tip.

The southern African coast twists and turns for well over 6 500 km, passing through three countries: Namibia, South Africa and Mozambique. From the Kunene River mouth in the arid western reaches of the subcontinent, where green turtles, Nile crocodiles and seabirds mingle beside ever-restless dunes, the coast stretches all the way to the mosquito-infested delta of the mighty Zambezi River, where tropical mangrove swamps thrive. Although not strictly part of southern Africa, the coast of northern Mozambique and its extensive fringing coral reefs are nonetheless included here because Mozambique is a country firmly rooted in southern rather than East Africa.

From east to west, the seas of southern Africa stretch from the edge of the East African tropics to the cool, temperate waters of the Cape and on to the southern border of tropical west Africa. This steep gradient of latitudinal change has led to the creation of one of the most varied marine environments on Earth. Here, kelp forests, inter-tidal rocky and sandy shores, offshore bird islands, temperate and tropical estuaries, coral reefs, seagrass beds, mangrove forests, deep-sea canyons and many other marine habitats are found.

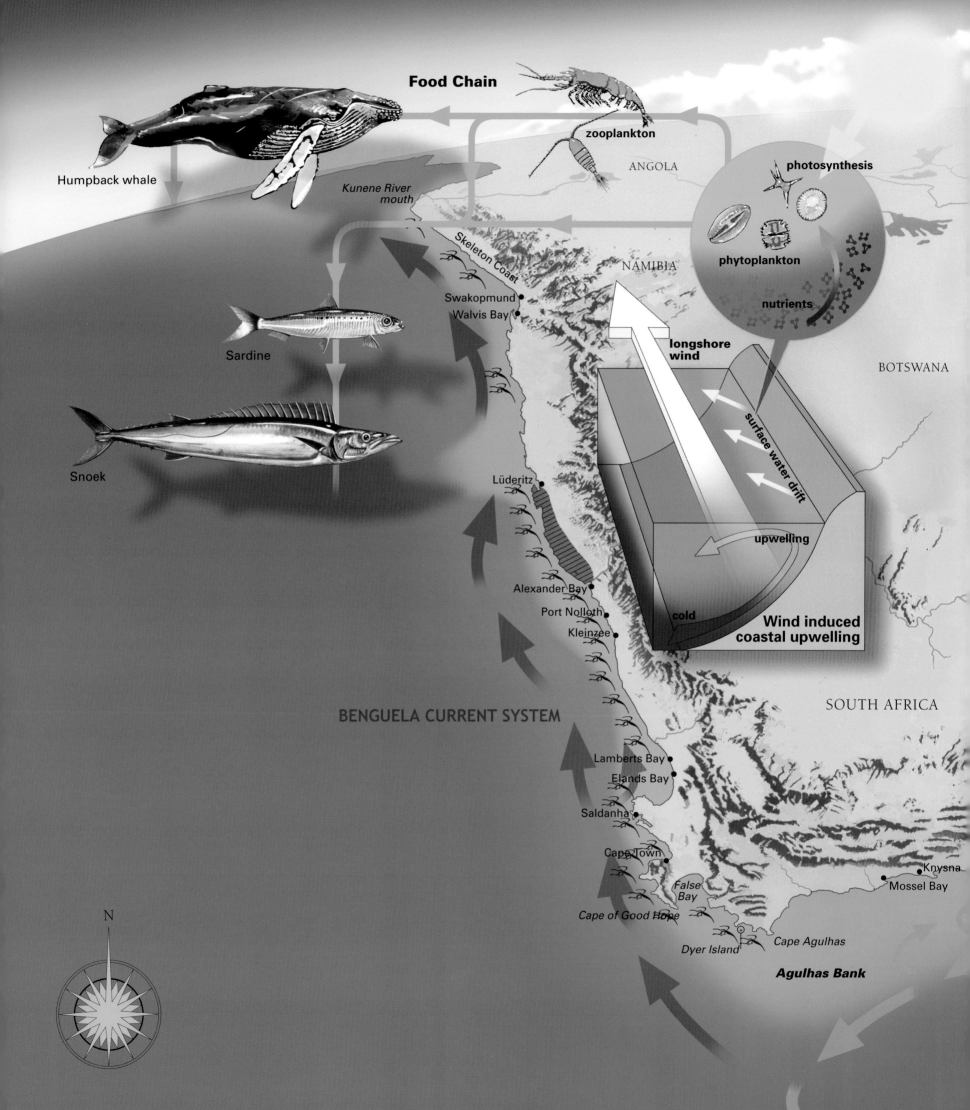

Food Chain

Humpback whale

zooplankton

ANGOLA

photosynthesis

Kunene River mouth

NAMIBIA

phytoplankton

nutrients

Skeleton Coast

Swakopmund

Walvis Bay

Sardine

BOTSWANA

longshore wind

surface water drift

Snoek

Lüderitz

upwelling

Alexander Bay

Port Nolloth

Kleinzee

cold

Wind induced coastal upwelling

BENGUELA CURRENT SYSTEM

SOUTH AFRICA

Lamberts Bay

Elands Bay

Saldanha

Cape Town

Knysna

False Bay

Mossel Bay

Cape of Good Hope

Dyer Island

Cape Agulhas

Agulhas Bank

N

ZAMBIA

Zambezi Delta

Primeiro Archipelago *Segundo Archipelago* *Quirimbas Archipelago*

Beira

Bazaruto Archipelago

MOZAMBIQUE

Inhambane

Maputo

North Equatorial Current

Equatorial Counter Current

South Equatorial Current

South Indian Ocean Current

Mozambique Current

Maputo

Agulhas Current

Antarctic Circumpolar Current

Kosi Bay

Sodwana Bay

St Lucia

Richards Bay

Umhlanga Rocks
Durban

Scottburgh

Port Shepstone
Port Edward
Port St Johns

AGULHAS CURRENT

East London

Port Alfred
Port Elizabeth
Cape St Francis

SOUTHERN AFRICA

ocean currents and
marine ecosystems

Kelp forest

Coral reef

Upwelling zone

**Sperrgebiet
Restricted zone**

The Benguela current has been in existence for just under two million years.

THE BENGUELA UPWELLING SYSTEM

The Benguela current in its present state has probably been in existence for less than two million years, although its ancestor probably evolved off the Namibian coast 12 million years ago.

Its origins lie at the southeastern corner of the South Atlantic circulation, a gyre (or circular ocean current) of water that flows anti-clockwise between South America and Africa. The Benguela is not just a jet that transports water in a northwesterly direction along the coast; it is influenced by coastal topography and driven primarily by southeasterly winds that blow year-round in the north and mainly during the summer months in the south. The Earth's rotation deflects the current's surface waters to the left of their original path, driving them offshore in a westerly direction. This warm inshore water is then replaced by cold water drawn up from depths of as much as 300 m. During a southeasterly gale, the water can well up at speeds of up to 12 m per minute and the temperature can plummet from 16 °C to 8 °C in a matter of hours, turning the water from murky green to translucent azure.

Upwelling cells are not evenly distributed; indeed, two distinct major centres of upwelling and eight minor ones can be recognised along the 2 000 km-long west coast. Maximum upwelling occurs where southeasterly winds are consistently strong and the contin-

A Heaviside's dolphin leaping. This is southern Africa's only endemic cetacean and it occurs only in the waters of the Benguela current.

CURRENTS of CONTRAST

FAR RIGHT: Sandy beaches dominate southern Africa's west coast, but in places steep cliffs plunge into the Atlantic, such as here along Namibia's desert coast.

RIGHT TOP: Exposed to fierce storms and waves, southern Africa's west coast is a ship graveyard. In fact, Namibia's Skeleton Coast received its name from the profusion of shipwrecks that lie there.

RIGHT BOTTOM: A wild, west coast shore showing its gentler, more sedate side.

BELOW: At dusk flamingos gather on mudflats near Walvis Bay, one of the few sheltered locations along the exposed Benguela coast.

ental shelf is narrow and deep – a suite of conditions that are met at Cape Frio, Lüderitz, Hondeklip Bay, Cape Columbine and along the west side of the Cape Peninsula. Centres of upwelling can also be found along the southwest coast between Cape Hangklip and Cape Agulhas, and isolated cells have been known to occur as far east as Port Elizabeth.

Upwelled water is initially devoid of plant life but very rich in nutrients, having sat below the photic zone (the zone of surface water penetrated by light) for a long time. Once reunited with the sun's rays, there is an explosion of life. Phytoplankton, or free-swimming algae, burst into bloom and the vast kelp forests that carpet rocky reefs soak up the fertilizing nitrates from the water. Together, phytoplankton and kelp forests lay the foundation for all life in the Benguela system and their high levels of primary productivity attract grazers, filter feeders and carnivores of all kinds.

In the Benguela food web, small planktonic animals called zooplankton dine on phytoplankton and are, in turn, eaten by vast schools of sardines and anchovies. Hundreds of thousands of Cape fur seals, dense aggregations of tuna, and flocks of several species of seabird fill the top predator slots to feed on the schools of silvery fishes. The kelp forests provide both food and shelter, supporting rich beds of abalone and high densities of west coast rock lobsters. Pieces of drift kelp and small particulate matter are also exported onto the rocky shores, where they nourish intertidal invertebrates such as mussels and limpets.

The Cape Cross seal colony at the edge of the Namib Desert, a thin sliver of life nearly drowned out by the emptiness that surrounds it for hundreds of miles in all directions.

The true desolation of the desert coast is most apparent from the air.

A typical west coast scene: cold sea, granite boulders and Cape cormorants.

A solitary mangrove tree outlined against the setting sun in Mozambique.

THE AGULHAS AND MOZAMBIQUE CURRENTS

The south equatorial current is a huge gyre that sits in the centre of the Indian Ocean and circulates water in an anti-clockwise direction between Africa, Asia and western Australia. At its westerly end it splits off into the Mozambique current – which flows between the west coast of Madagascar and the African mainland – and the East Madagascar current, which flows around the east side of the island.

Originally, it was believed that these two warm-water currents merged to form the Agulhas current off southern Mozambique, but recent research has shown that the contribution they make is minimal. The bulk of Agulhas water actually originates in the southwestern Indian Ocean sub-gyre. At its headwaters off the coast of southern Mozambique, the waters of the Agulhas current are gin clear and poor in nutrients, while the sea's surface temperature can reach highs of 28 °C. Just like a river, the Agulhas flows southwards along the edge of the continental shelf, its main stream being 60–100 km wide.

A split-level view of a mangrove stand in the Eastern Cape. This forest at Wavecrest is among Africa's most southerly.

Where the continental shelf is at its narrowest, near Port St Johns, the surface current can reach speeds of 2.6 m per second, one of the fastest-flowing currents on the planet, transporting 4 800 million cubic metres of water per minute. At a depth of 2 500 m, however, current speeds are much slower, just a few centimetres per second.

At Cape Padrone between Port Alfred and Port Elizabeth, the continental shelf widens and the current is forced away from the coast. This is the point that many oceanographers consider to be the border between the northern and southern sections of the Agulhas. When the current finally reaches the Agulhas Bank, it turns back on itself and begins to flow in a northeasterly direction. At this point, oceanographers call it the Agulhas return current. At the southern edge of the Agulhas, the water temperature is dramatically lower than at its northern limit, with highs of around just 21 °C in summer and regular winter lows of 16 °C.

Here, localised upwelling and wind- and wave-induced mixing of the shallow waters of the Agulhas Bank create richer nutrient conditions. While the productivity and biomass levels are always much lower than in the adjacent Benguela system, they are higher than in the northern section of the Agulhas. The western side of the Agulhas Bank is firmly rooted in the Benguela system of the Atlantic, while the eastern side lies in the clutches of the Indian Ocean. At times, however, the Agulhas current triumphs over the Benguela, transporting warm water as far west as Cape Point; at other times, the Agulhas bids a hasty retreat and cold water envelops the coast east of Cape Agulhas, dropping water temperatures to chilling single-digit figures.

OPPOSITE: Central Mozambique's Bazaruto Archipelago — islands among a maze of shallow sandbanks and seagrass beds. (INSET) Fishing dhows moored off the coast of Mozambique, waiting for the tide to come in.

RIGHT TOP: Brightly coloured starfish, *Protoreaster lincki*, stranded at low tide on a tropical sandbank.
(RIGHT MIDDLE) Luminescent green zooanthids are a characteristic feature of East Coast rocky shores.
(RIGHT BOTTOM) An octopus, *Octopus vulgaris*, searches rock pools at low tide for crabs and molluscs.

BELOW: The fish kraals of Kosi Bay are southern Africa's last remaining indigenous fishing structures still in use.

BIOGEOGRAPHY AND BIODIVERSITY

While the Benguela upwelling system and the Agulhas/Mozambique current divide the region into its two primary systems, the physical oceanography and biology within each of these two systems also vary tremendously. There is broad agreement that there are, in fact, four distinct marine provinces in southern Africa. The first, the cool temperate west coast province, occupies the whole of the Benguela region. The other three – the warm temperate south coast, the subtropical east coast, and the tropical east coast provinces – are found in the Agulhas/Mozambique region. The exact boundaries of these 'provinces' are the source of ongoing debate among marine scientists but are believed to lie somewhere in the general vicinity of the Kunene River, Cape Point, between East London and Durban, and to the north of Maputo in south/central Mozambique respectively.

Further subdivisions of the main provinces have been suggested, based primarily on biogeographical research carried out on certain groups of flora and fauna. For example, in terms of benthic marine invertebrates (i.e. those that live on the seabed), the cool temperate west coast marine province can be divided into the Namib subprovince and the Namaqua subprovince, lying north and south of Lüderitz respectively. This is also the case for seaweeds. In addition, a southwestern Cape subprovince (between Cape Columbine and Cape Point) and a southwest coast transition (between Cape Point and Cape Agulhas) have been recognised.

In terrestrial terms, South Africa has been identified as one of the 'hottest' of the world's biodiversity hotspots. It is the third most biologically diverse country in the world, playing host to over 18 625 described plants and 70 000-plus species of terrestrial and freshwater invertebrates.

So how does the marine fauna and flora measure up to such superlatives? To date, more than 11 100 marine organisms have been described here, accounting for some 15% of the world's coastal marine species. There are also 2 150 species of fish, including at least 100 species of shark and 64 ray species. In addition, southern Africa is home to more than 850 species of seaweed, which compares well with the record of 1 000 species for any known region in the world. There are over 50 genera of hard coral, including hundreds of species on the coral reefs and in the coral communities of the east coast. Furthermore, southern Africa is home to 8 species of mangrove, 13 species of seagrass and more than 40 species of marine mammal, including 25 species of whale and 12 species of dolphin. Five species of turtles and one species of sea snake also occur here.

Most southern African marine taxonomic groups show a general increase in species diversity from west to east. On the west coast, for example, fewer than 100 species of fish occur, while at Kosi Bay on the east there are almost 1 000 species. This high diversity along the east coast is partly due to a much higher range of inshore habitats, but also marks the start of the extraordinarily rich Indo-Pacific marine fauna and flora.

For benthic marine invertebrates and seaweeds the pattern is similar, but diversity peaks around Port Elizabeth and Durban, and actually decreases northwards, probably partly a result of less sampling effort in that region. There are, however, some major exceptions to the east coast diversity peak, and groups such as amphipods (small crustaceans) and intertidal klipfish have their diversity peaks in the cool temperate regions. This is because amphipods have a cold-water affinity and klipfish are believed to have sub-Antarctic origins.

In southern Africa, levels of endemism are generally highest along the south coast and lowest along the northern section of the east coast. In total, 31% of the marine fauna is endemic; for instance, 227 species of coastal fish occur nowhere else in the world. At just 15%, the levels of endemism are lowest along the KwaZulu-Natal coast, where the bulk of the fish fauna consists of western Indian Ocean species that can be encountered anywhere from the Seychelles to Madagascar, Mauritius and Kenya.

The cliffs of Cape Point plunge straight into the icy waters of the Atlantic.

CURRENTS of CONTRAST

MAN AND OCEAN

Archaeological evidence points to southern Africa as the place where humans first began to exploit the oceans for food. Some 125 000 years ago, during the Middle Stone Age, the ancestors of the present-day San hunter-gatherers occasionally harvested mussels, limpets and whelks from rocky shores near their coastal cave shelters at Klassies River mouth in the Eastern Cape.

However, marine exploitation seems to have been more prevalent in the Late Stone Age. During the Late Holocene, the San were joined along the west and south coast by Khoi-Khoi pastoralists, a herder people who kept goats and cattle. In addition to vast quantities of rocky shore fauna (shell middens as large as 30 000 cubic metres have been found), these two groups also scavenged meat, blubber and bones from beached whales and dolphins, hunted seabirds and seal pups, and rafted on logs to offshore islands to collect penguin eggs. They were the first to exploit the subtidal realm (the part permanently covered by water), catching fish with tidal traps made from boulders and with hand lines and spears. They would wade into deep pools for west coast rock lobster and even dive for abalone using the ribs of large antelopes to prise the shellfish from the rocky reef.

Dramatic changes occurred in the lives of southern Africa's indigenous populations during colonial times. The Khoi-Khoi and San were substantially reduced in numbers by colonial raids, introduced diseases and their assimilation into colonial society. Within 50 to 100 years of European colonization, the marine hunter-gatherer lifestyle along the west and south coasts had practically disappeared.

This image is the only known photographic record of the Benguela coast's last marine hunter-gatherers, the Topnar.

Adept with a spear from a very young age, Tembe-Thonga boys hunt for fish in the reed-lined shallows of the Kosi Estuary.

From sardines to tuna — fishermen in vessels great and small ply southern Africa's two oceans in pursuit of a bountiful harvest.

Yet one group inhabiting the remote desert coast of Namibia continued to harvest the riches of the Benguela well into the 20th century. The Topnar people used to live along the coast near the delta of the Kuiseb River, where they would spear fish in the shallow lagoons, hunt seabirds with bows and arrows on offshore sand spits, and dig mussels and clams from the sandy beaches. The Topnar people are still around today, though they no longer live close to the sea and most have embraced a modern way of life in the city of Walvis Bay. Those who continue a traditional lifestyle have moved many kilometres up the dry riverbed, where they survive by gathering wild nara melons and herding goats.

Today, 125 000 years of traditional subsistence harvesting have come to an end and the arid west coast of the Benguela remains largely uninhabited. Instead, nearly all fishing activities along this coast are of a large-scale commercial nature. In 1997 alone, more than 5 000 commercial fishing vessels plied South African waters, most of them in the Benguela region. South African marine fisheries are worth an estimated two billion rand each year and the total annual catch currently amounts to just over half a million tons. Of this, 150 000 tons consist of hake trawled from the sea floor, while 280 000 tons are pilchards and anchovies scooped from the water column by purse seiners, who use a net to encircle schools of fish. Invertebrates, too, are harvested: several thousand tons of squid are jigged every year and 2 000 tons of rock lobster are caught in traps.

Today, mariculture, the farming of marine organisms, has become a large industry in southern Africa and every year up to 3 000 tons of Mediterranean mussels, many hundreds of tons of abalone and four million oysters are farmed.

The nature of marine exploitation along the east coast, in the realm of the Agulhas current, is very different. When the Khoi-Khoi arrived at the Cape, the Nguni people settled in the north of the present Eastern Cape and KwaZulu-Natal. Here, however, colonialism did not put an end to the marine hunter-gatherer lifestyle, and it persists in a modified form to this day. The coastal Xhosa, Zulu, Tembe-Thonga and various Mozambican tribes still harvest intertidal and other marine resources in much the same way as the prehistoric inhabitants of the continent did.

However, not all interactions between humans and marine life are exploitative. In recent years, marine ecotourism has experienced a significant increase in popularity all across southern Africa, with activities including cage diving with great white sharks, whale watching in the Cape, swimming with dolphins in southern Mozambique, following the sardine run in KwaZulu-Natal and scuba diving on Sodwana's coral reefs. Every year overseas and local tourists spend millions of dollars on these and other marine ecotourism activities and in the process ensure that many marine animals are worth more alive, swimming free in their natural habitats, than they would be in fishing nets or on plates in restaurants.

MARINE CONSERVATION

Southern Africa has largely been spared the ravages that marine pollution has wrought upon many of the world's oceans. Instead, the greatest threat to its marine biodiversity is overfishing, including the near extermination of the southern right whale through whaling, the drastic initial overfishing of pelagic stocks and the rampant poaching of abalone. Marine conservation is, however, far from a lost cause and, in many cases, South Africa is a world leader. Its

Coming home from the sea. A Mozambican fisherman returns to his village at dusk.

important sea turtle nesting grounds on the east coast have been under strict protection since the late 1960s, while in 1991 South Africa became the first country in the world to protect the great white shark. In recent years, even the once depleted southern right whales and some pelagic fish have made significant comebacks.

Oceans cover more than 70% of our planet's surface, yet less than 1% of them are protected in reserves (by comparison, 10% of land is protected in parks). This is ironic since marine protected areas (MPAs) are probably among the most powerful weapons in our arsenal to protect marine biodiversity. Not only do they promote the good health of species within their boundaries but they can also replenish depleted fish stocks beyond their borders. South Africa currently has the most sophisticated network of marine reserves in Africa and today 18% of its coastline is under formal protection. Still lacking, however, are larger offshore MPAs that specifically protect habitats under threat from large-scale commercial fishing. Only by giving offshore ecosystems and important fish stocks protection can we ensure the sustainability of many of southern Africa's fisheries.

MPAs are only as good as the structures put in place to manage them and, at present, some of southern Africa's marine reserves are falling far short of their potential, existing only on paper, and offering little or no protection to any species, habitat or fishery. One of the greatest challenges of marine conservation in southern Africa will be to ensure that all MPAs are well resourced, sufficiently staffed and effectively managed for the greater good of all stakeholders.

MARINE RESEARCH

Southern African marine science began in earnest only in 1895, when Dr J.D.F. Gilchrist was appointed as the first government marine biologist. In addition to establishing the fishing potential of the Agulhas Bank, he also collated measurements of sea temperature and salinity, as well as taking plankton samples, first from around the Cape coast and later from as far afield as Maputo and Walvis Bay.

Dr Keppel Barnard was appointed curator of marine invertebrates at the South African Museum in 1907, later becoming its director. In addition to being a superb taxonomist, he single-handedly catalogued Gilchrist's vigorous collecting efforts of earlier years and launched daring expeditions into the dark corners of Natal and Mozambique. He left a legacy of three major monographs on southern African marine fauna -- works on fishes, crustaceans and molluscs that are still consulted regularly today.

In 1931 Dr T.A. Stephenson became the chair of zoology at the University of Cape Town and began the first systematic surveys of the rocky shore fauna of southern Africa, aiming to prove his theory that sea temperature and ocean currents govern the distribution of intertidal life.

Southern African marine biology really stepped into the limelight in 1939 with Prof. J.L.B. Smith's discovery of the coelacanth, a fish thought to have become extinct 70 million years earlier. Years later, after amassing an impressive data set on the fish fauna of the region, he published *The Sea Fishes of Southern Africa*, which at the time was the most comprehensive book on fishes of any region of the world.

At the end of World War II, Dr John Day replaced Stephenson as head of zoology at the University of Cape Town. He pursued his predecessor's work on the distribution of fauna and flora into the subtidal and estuarine realms using boat-based grabs, trawls and echo sounders. At the same time, diving technology was used to carry out the first subtidal survey of False Bay's benthic fauna and from the 1960s it became a frequently employed marine biological research technique. Marine research was also being carried out along the east coast, which was the setting in the early 1960s for research carried out at the Natal Anti-Sharks Board (today the Natal Sharks Board) on the causes and prevention of shark attacks. Also in the 1960s, along the remote shores of Maputaland, Dr George Hughes began his pioneering study of nesting loggerhead and leatherback turtles that is still running to this day.

Other talented scientists also emerged. Dr Peter Best began his study on the southern right whale and Profs Alec Brown and Anton McLachlan made South Africa a world leader in sandy beach ecology. On the west coast, a detailed study of the kelp forest was begun under the leadership of Profs John Field and Charles Griffiths. Together with a team of more than 20 scientists, they not only surveyed the kelp-bed fauna and flora, but studied energy flow and constructed the most sophisticated and detailed models of marine food webs to date. At the same time, Prof. George Branch was carrying out groundbreaking research on rocky shores, becoming the world's foremost expert on limpets. He is probably best known for his book, *The Living Shores of Southern Africa*, co-authored with his marine biologist wife Margo in 1981. The book was a landmark publication that for the first time unchained southern African marine research from heavy jargon and made its fascinating findings accessible to the public.

As southern African marine science approaches its 110th anniversary, a glance into various scientific journals shows that it has come a long way:

☐ Satellite transmitters have been fitted to Cape fur seals, Cape gannets, white sharks, southern right whales and turtles to plot their movement along the coast and in the oceans.

☐ After 50 years of searching, a living population of coelacanths has finally been discovered in South Africa, right under our noses, in fairly shallow water at Sodwana Bay.

☐ The coral reefs along the east coast, which remained neglected for so long, have finally received the research interest they deserve.

☐ The conservation of the marine environment continues to become increasingly central to research, and we have finally begun to look beyond the direct impact of fishing on certain target species and have adopted a broader ecosystem approach.

☐ In laboratories, sponges, ascidians (sea squirts) and bryozoans (moss animals) are being screened for chemical compounds that could one day be used to develop new and more effective medicines to treat cancer and Aids.

☐ The traditional knowledge of the oceans and estuaries held by southern Africa's indigenous inhabitants is finally being recorded, and not a minute too soon. The knowledgeable elders are ageing and many have already taken much wisdom to the grave.

The beginning of the 21st century is an exciting time to be a marine biologist in southern Africa. Although what we know about life in the oceans and along the coast has filled many thousands of research papers, what we do not yet know could potentially fill tens of thousands more.

PART ONE

THE REALM OF THE BENGUELA

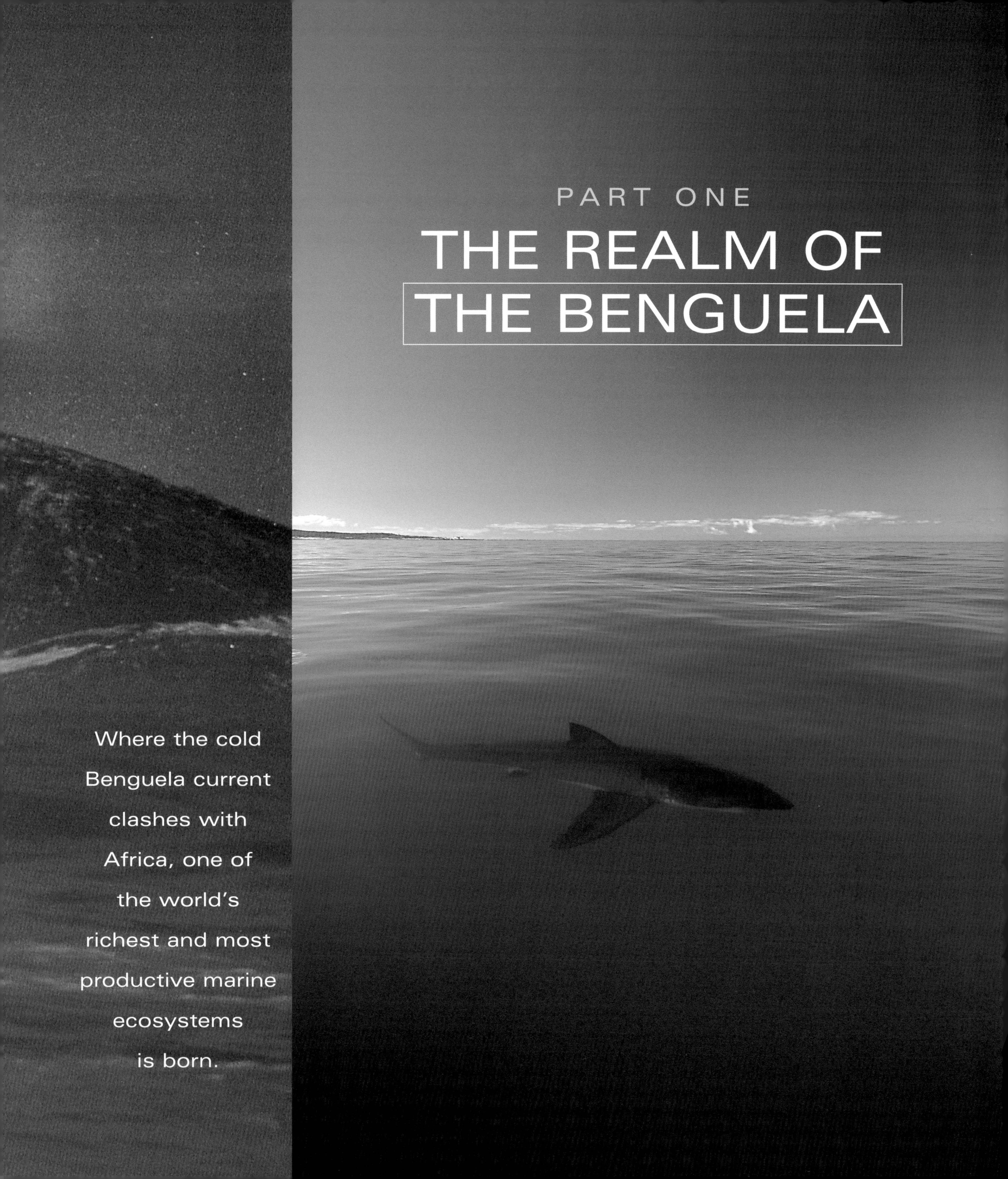

Where the cold Benguela current clashes with Africa, one of the world's richest and most productive marine ecosystems is born.

GREAT WHITE SHARK

misunderstood predator

till low in the eastern sky, the sun's morning rays have yet to penetrate and flood the ocean around Dyer Island with light. Beneath the tranquil surface, menacing shapes glide like shadows through the depths.

This pocket of temperate ocean off South Africa's coast is one of the last strongholds of the ocean's ultimate apex predator, the great white shark. At a time when most large terrestrial carnivores occur only in reserves and national parks, where barriers often restrict and confine their movements, the white shark still roams free. It does not respect international boundaries nor has it been tamed or kept in captivity. It is the ultimate symbol of wildness.

Those privileged enough to have encountered this predator in the wild describe it as curious, powerful, sleek, cautious, intelligent, even playful – a far cry from the ruthless killing machine portrayed in the film *Jaws*. Yet many still consider the great white to be that monster. On a hot summer's day in January 1998, an injured and disorientated white shark was observed floundering in shallow water off a popular bathing beach at the northeastern edge of False Bay. Instead of an armada of helpers coming to its aid, as would be expected in the plight of a stranded whale or dolphin, crowds of seaside sun worshippers picked up metal rods and beat it to death.

This chapter aims to reveals the white shark's true natural history, hoping to turn hate into awe and fear into fascination.

WHITE SHARK BASICS

Sharks first appeared on the prehistoric marine apex predator circuit in the Devonian period, somewhere between 400 and 350 million years ago. During the 100 million years that followed, they diversified until they occupied almost every ecological niche in the oceans. This period is known as the age of sharks.

The great white is believed to have evolved during the Palaeocene or early Eocene, and two competing theories exist over the identity of its direct ancestor. One proposes that it evolved from *Carcharodon megalodon*, a 16 m giant that lived in prehistoric seas around 100 million years ago. The other theory suggests it evolved from the long extinct mako shark *Isurus hastalis*.

The great white and all other sharks belong to the class Chondrichthyes, a group of fish whose skeletons are entirely made up of cartilage instead of bone. At present, eight orders of shark are recognized. The great white belongs to the Lamniformes and is part of the Lamnidae family, which includes the mako, salmon and porbeagle sharks. First described by Linnaeus in 1758, the great white is a heavy-bodied shark. Its snout is conical, almost blunt and dorsally flattened. Inside is the most formidable jaw in the animal kingdom, fitted with 26 triangular, coarsely serrated teeth in the upper jaw and 24 more slender pointed teeth in the lower jaw. The lower teeth are designed for stabbing and impaling prey, while the upper teeth evolved to cut and saw off large chunks of flesh. Behind the teeth is a conveyor belt of 'spares' that move to the front whenever a tooth is lost.

The white shark's common name comes from its distinctive white underbelly, though the colour of the dorsal surface can vary from slaty-grey to dark olive green. This pattern of dark on top and light beneath – called counter-shading – allows the shark to blend in with the dark seafloor when viewed from above and with the light-drenched surface waters from the side or below.

The maximum length of white sharks in southern Africa is somewhere between 5.5 and 6.5 m, with the largest confirmed specimen – caught three nautical miles off Danger Point, just west of Dyer Island – measuring a whopping 5.9 m.

The great white shark's scientific name, *Carcharodon carcharias*, translates into English as the Jagged-Toothed One.

DISTRIBUTION

The great white shark's centre of distribution lies in southern Africa's temperate seas. It dwells in the waters of the continental shelf, ranging from the surface to depths of more than 1 000 m. Some individuals do, however, enter tropical waters as proven by the capture of a 5 m female off Mauritius and an enormous 6.4 m pregnant specimen off Kenya.

Mapping the distribution of a secretive underwater dweller like the great white is not an easy task, and most stretches of coast have never been systematically surveyed. Most distribution data comes from commercial and recreational catch records (prior to the species' 1991 protection), catches in the shark nets off the KwaZulu-Natal coast and shark attack incidence reports, as well as incidental sightings reported by divers and surfers. The most northwesterly reports of great white sharks in southern Africa come from the Cape Cross seal colony in northern Namibia. At the northeastern extreme, they have been encountered by scuba divers on the coral reefs of Maputaland and southern Mozambique.

White sharks are not evenly distributed across their range and their numbers tend to be highest near seal colonies and offshore banks where fish, dolphins and whales abound. They seem to occur in especially high concentrations at Seal Island (False Bay), Dyer Island, Quoin Point, Struis Bay, Seal Island (Mossel Bay) and Bird Island in Algoa Bay. Frequent catches in the shark nets also show great whites to be relatively common along the KwaZulu-Natal coast.

BIOLOGY AND ECOLOGY

Rigorous scientific research on the biology and ecology of the great white shark has only been carried out at four locations in southern Africa. Most work has focused on Dyer and Seal islands off the Cape coast, two of the most infamous white shark hotspots in southern Africa. Dyer is a small island, 1.5 km long and 0.5 km wide, which lies 5 km to the east of Danger Point near Gansbaai in the Western Cape. Just to the south lies a narrow 500 m-long outcrop, Geyser Rock, which is home to a population of over 60 000 Cape fur seals; separating the seals from the island is a 150 m-wide channel named Shark Alley. Long bays and beaches, of which Holbaai is the largest bay, characterize the mainland. At Dyer Island and around much of the Western Cape, there seem to be two distinct white shark seasons.

The white shark's common name comes from its distinctive white underbelly, which contrasts sharply with its slaty-gray dorsal side.

FINGERPRINTING GREAT WHITE SHARKS

The great white shark is an elusive creature that does not give up its secrets easily, so answering questions about its population biology is difficult. University of Cape Town marine biologist and founder of the Great White Shark Trust, Michael Scholl, aims not only to discover how large the population is but how it is structured in terms of age and sex. He has developed a noninvasive method to identify and keep track of individual great whites over long periods. Just as every human being has unique fingerprints, the shape, pigmentation and serration patterns of the first dorsal fin's posterior margins are unique to each shark. Using this methodology, sharks can be identified with minimal disturbance, and the fact that identification can be carried out from a distance makes this a very effective process. In addition to keeping a photographic record of each shark's dorsal fin, Michael Scholl also records scars, pigmentation patterns and any other distinguishing features. Over the last five years Michael has spent more than 713 days at sea observing and photographing white sharks, managing to compile a collection of over 40 000 images. He has resighted individual sharks over 1 500 times and some have had their picture taken over 40 times. As a result of his dedicated efforts the database, which now holds 700 positively identified individuals, is the largest of its kind in the world.

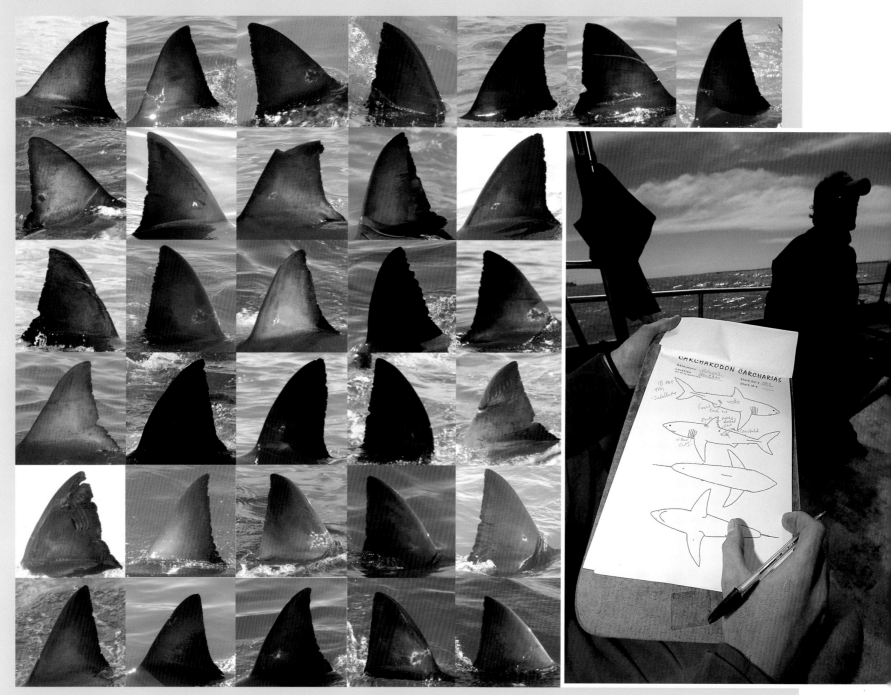

In pursuit of Cape fur seals white sharks will often breach, the entire body clearing the water surface for a fraction of a second. While this behaviour is most well known from False Bay, it also occurs frequently at Dyer Island and probably also around other seal colonies.

WINTER

During the southern winter, white sharks appear in great numbers at Dyer Island. Researchers have sighted up to 28 individuals in a single day. Males and females measuring between 1.5 m and 5.5 m, with an average length of 3.25 m, appear in almost equal numbers, reaching their peak between July and September. Very few sharks encountered at Dyer Island at this time of the year appear to be resident, however; most are seen once and never again, whereas others are resighted a couple of times, but only over a period of between one to two weeks.

It seems that Dyer Island is akin to a fuel station along a well-travelled white shark migration route, where many sharks stop off for a short period to hunt. Pregnant fur seals give birth to a single pup during the height of summer, and six months later in winter the pups are fat and ready to make their first solo sorties. While hugging the shallows next to their haul-out rocks they are relatively safe, but sooner or later they have to cross deep water to access their feeding grounds. And that is when the seals are vulnerable. White sharks predominantly take seals that are floundering on the surface, attacking from below and often killing them outright with a fatal first bite.

At southern African seabird islands, white sharks also frequently attack African penguins, cormorants, brown pelicans, gannets, and even gulls. Seabirds are almost never consumed and many struggle back to land only to die later of their injuries. It could be that mainly young, inexperienced sharks tend to carry out this type of behaviour, either using the birds as target practice or mistaking them for more profitable prey in murky water. In clear water, a white shark's eyesight is excellent. As there are more cones in their retinas than in any other species of shark, it is likely that they can see in colour and with great definition. White sharks have the ability to look for potential prey above the water's surface and will often hold their heads out of the water at the edges of seal colonies and near boats brimming with activity.

All sharks have a special organ running from head to tail just below the skin. This can detect changes in water pressure, allowing the shark to sense potential prey from a distance of up to 100 m. Sharks' sense of smell is also highly evolved and they can taste both water and air through receptor cells inside the nostrils. While they do not possess visible ears, two small sensors in the skull are used to zero in on the splashing sounds of a wounded fish or struggling seal. The great white shark also has the largest brain of all predatory sharks. At 45 cm long, it is on a par with that of dogs in terms of brain to body weight ratio. The cerebellum – the part of the brain associated with learning, memory and thought – is particularly well developed.

SUMMER

Towards the end of winter, the number of great white sharks sighted at Dyer Island decreases significantly. Between October and March they are rarely encountered. Similarly, white sharks depart False Bay's Seal Island in September and are not seen again until the following April.

FLYING SHARKS OF FALSE BAY

Line fishermen who worked False Bay in the 1960s and 1970s have told many tales of hair-raising encounters with great white sharks ramming and jumping at — or even into — their boats. Some returned to port with only the fear in their eyes as testimony, while others had damage to their boats as proof. The most convincing evidence was when boats returned to shore with a white shark still firmly lodged inside.

For many years, people believed sharks were attacking boats intentionally. It was not until the 1990s that it became clear that these sharks were indeed breaching clear of the water, especially around Seal Island, but not to attack boats. Rather, it was in the pursuit of seals and game fish.

Seal Island is a 106 m-wide and 378 m-long rocky outcrop at the northwestern end of False Bay. To a white shark the island is a banquet with 64 000 servings of Cape fur seal. Here, as at Dyer Island, white sharks congregate during winter, when juvenile seals enter the water and leave the island to hunt for the first time. At Seal Island, seals gather at the water's edge every morning in preparation for the long swim to their offshore feeding grounds. They depart in small groups from various launching pads dotted around the island and dive immediately, surfacing only when they are more than 100 m from the island. But not all seals are equally vigilant in steering clear from the surface in the so-called ring of death — a narrow band of water around the island in which the sharks hunt.

The sharks patrol just above the dark and rocky bottom, where their countershading makes them almost invisible from above, scanning the surface for the silhouette of a juvenile or sub-adult seal. As soon as a target is spotted, the shark rushes vertically to the surface, constantly accelerating. It hits the seal at such speed that it erupts from the water like a cruise missile. With a loud thump, an almighty explosion of water announces the shark's return to the water, sometimes with a seal in its jaws. If the shark misses on its first attempt, the seal has a fighting chance since the element of surprise has been lost. However, just under half of all observed white shark attacks at Seal Island end in successful kills, a statistic that compares admirably with that of the lion, the apex predator of the African bushveld, who only enjoys a 25% success rate.

Why exactly the sharks stop frequenting these two seal islands is still for the most part a mystery. In December 1999, following up on leads from fishermen, scientists confirmed that high concentrations of great whites were congregating less than 3 km away from Dyer Island along a stretch of the mainland coast known as Holbaai. The white sharks encountered here during the summer months were almost all females, 96% to be exact. The sex ratio at Dyer Island during winter is much more balanced, with 58% female and 42% male sharks. Also, while white sharks at Dyer Island are predominantly transient, some of the larger females that frequent Holbaai are sighted regularly every few days over a period of several months.

The white shark's vision out of water is excellent and to see what is going on above the surface it spy-hops just as whales do.

Despite their size
and perceived
ferocity great white
sharks are
inquisitive creatures.
This 3.5 m female
swam to within an
arm's length of this
box jellyfish, *Carybdea
alata*, and hung
motionless for
seconds, as if fixated
by its presence.

Conclusive proof as to why so many female sharks venture so close inshore during the summer months is still outstanding, but researcher Michael Scholl has put forward three tentative explanations. They could be coming to Holbaai to mate, to give birth, or simply to feed on the abundance of game fish that migrate into that area during summer.

1 Mating ground theory

Many of the female sharks observed at Holbaai show distinct slashes and cuts that resemble mating scars. While no one has ever observed white sharks mating, their ritual probably resembles that of other sharks, with males fiercely biting females to hang on while they insert their claspers. But if this really is a mating area, where are the males that are supposedly inflicting these injuries?

The male sharks could be present among the females, but for some reason do not respond to odour corridors, or scent trails, and bait. In other shark species it is well known that hormonal changes in the females during the pupping season inhibit their normal feeding behaviour so as not to endanger their own young. Could similar hormonal changes be occurring in male white sharks during the summer months to avoid seriously injuring the females during mating? If the males are present and their feeding behaviour is not inhibited, then perhaps they are in a location where the odour corridors cannot reach them.

At Holbaai, scientific research can only be carried out during offshore wind conditions; the moment the winds turn onshore, conditions become too rough to work in. An offshore wind will consistently take the chum slick (finely minced fish mixture released on the water) out to sea, while an onshore wind would bring the scent corridor towards the coast into the surf zone. It could be that male sharks reside in the surf zone, but because the odour corridor can only reach this area during onshore winds (when research is not being carried out), they have remained hidden from the researchers' eyes. The surf zone would also be the ideal mating venue, since during the act the sharks must stop swimming. Normally, this would result in water no longer flowing over the gills, depriving them of oxygen. By mating in these highly oxygenated, turbulent inshore waters, a steady flow of water over their gills could be maintained and any recovery after mating would be much quicker.

2 Pupping ground theory

The size range of great white sharks that frequent Holbaaai is greater than that encountered at Dyer Island. The number of small sharks from 1.5 to 2.5 m, as well as the number of large animals of 4 m or more, in particular, is much higher. This higher number of large mature, potentially pregnant females and many smaller young sharks could indicate that Holbaai is a pupping ground for white sharks. No pregnant white shark has yet been captured anywhere in southern African waters, but specimens from other localities have shown that litter sizes range from 5 to 14 individuals.

Great whites are viviparous, that is, they give birth to live young. The sharks are born without a placenta and the embryos nourish themselves by feeding on unfertilized eggs while still in the womb. Embryonic white sharks are also known to swallow their own sets of teeth, perhaps to remedy an early mineral deficiency. Gestation times are unknown but doubtless long, perhaps close to a year. The total length of the young at birth is 120 to 150 cm, and a baby shark weighs about 22 kg.

3 Following prey theory

During the summer months, large numbers of migratory game fish such as yellowtail and geelbek, as well as large schools of mullet, appear in inshore waters along the Cape coast. It could be their presence that reroutes white sharks from Dyer Island to Holbaai. This abundance of fish also tempts Cape fur seals away from Dyer Island to these waters, which – unlike at Dyer Island – are murky on most summer days. Thus, being close to the coast not only offers a great abundance of game fish, but also the conditions in which even an adult seal should be fairly easy game for an experienced white shark.

The clumsy young seals that were the mainstay of the shark's diet at Dyer Island in the depths of winter have now grown up to be agile and cautious swimmers, no longer an easy meal, especially in clear water. In terms of calorific value a Cape fur seal, especially a recently weaned pup, is a much more attractive proposition to a white shark than a fish, but its agility means the shark must also expend a greater amount of energy to catch this prey.

This is where water temperature potentially comes into play. The water temperature during the winter months is 15–22 °C, while upwelling in the summer months causes it to drop to 9–14 °C. Unlike other fish, the great white shark keeps its body temperature up to 10 °C warmer than the surrounding water, allowing it to swim faster and digest food more quickly and efficiently. In cold water the shark has an even greater advantage over the fish, which will become sluggish. Unfortunately for the shark, there is no advantage to be gained over the warm-blooded seals, regardless of water temperature.

On careful consideration of all three theories, evidence suggests that it is either mating or feeding that draws the sharks to Holbaai. The pupping ground theory is the least likely because many young sharks already have distinct scars on them when they are first seen here. It is more likely that the pupping grounds are located somewhere off the Transkei coast, as the southernmost shark nets regularly catch white sharks less than 2 m in length. White sharks seem to stop frequenting Holbaai from January onwards and only reappear here again in October the following year. Where they are for three months before reappearing at Dyer Island still remains a mystery.

WHALE HUNTERS OR WHALE SCAVENGERS?

Both whale and dolphin remains have been found in the stomachs of white sharks caught in southern African waters, but this evidence alone is not enough to determine whether these cetaceans were scavenged or actively hunted. At present, there is no evidence that white sharks actually attack and kill large whales, but records of scavenging are fairly common. During the whaling heyday at Durban, white sharks would follow ships and feed on sperm whale carcasses being towed back to port. There are also many known instances of white sharks scavenging from southern right and humpback whales in the Cape region.

It appears that white sharks are principally whale scavengers, but young calves may certainly be at risk immediately after birth, especially when there is a lot of blood in the water and their mothers are weakened. White sharks do, however, appear to hunt humpbacked dolphins off the coast of KwaZulu-Natal. Many of these dolphins that wash up on the beaches or are observed by researchers carry scars that look like they have been inflicted by white sharks, perhaps telling a tale of predation yet to be witnessed by scientists.

In a baited situation, white sharks will go out of their way to avoid confrontations and the largest shark will usually dominate in feeding.

When a humpback whale was killed in an offshore shipping lane, winds and currents pushed the carcass close to Dyer Island where the local white shark population got an unexpected windfall. The first shark came across the carcass in late afternoon and began biting off 14 kilogram chunks of blubber. More sharks soon arrived and fed until late into the night, only stopping when the whale beached the next morning.

White sharks communicate with one another through body posturing and jaw gaping. If these non-injurious means of deflecting competition do not result in one shark's withdrawal, the larger shark will attack. Most of these encounters end with the submission and withdrawal of the smaller and weaker shark, but there are at least two documented cases of larger whites killing smaller ones.

Great white sharks do, however, seem to tolerate each other's presence to a much greater extent around whale carcasses. A decomposing humpback whale once attracted 27 white sharks. Along the east coast, an area lacking in seal colonies, white sharks are believed to occur at low densities and here a whale carcass would provide a rare opportunity for them to come into contact with others of their kind. While there is yet no proof of the notion that whale carcasses act as white shark singles bars, it is nonetheless an intriguing concept.

Dr Ramon Bonfil releases a white shark he has just fitted with a satellite tag (clearly visible on the dorsal fin) as part of a research project investigating the species' large-scale movements.

These tags record water depth and temperature on a daily basis, as well as the intensity of light, or luminosity. The measurement of light allows scientists to calculate the times of sunset and sunrise and establish the shark's approximate daily position. It is possible only to deduce, for example, whether the shark is off Cape Town or KwaZulu-Natal, but no more than that.

More detailed information on a shark's specific location requires use of the Smart Position and Temperature (SPOT) tag, which transmits the shark's position every time the antennae come to the surface, giving a detailed GPS reading. One shark fitted with a SPOT tag at Mossel Bay headed out to sea off the Eastern Cape, then tracked north, finally passing into Mozambican waters. It then turned around just north of Maputo and travelled back thousands of kilometres to Mossel Bay. With this new-found information, especially the fact that we now know white sharks travel into areas where they are not protected, it is high time for the great white shark to be listed on CITES, the convention governing international trade in wild animals and wild animal products.

LOCAL AND INTERNATIONAL TRAVEL

White sharks tagged at Seal Island in False Bay were resighted a year later at Dyer Island, and sharks tagged at Dyer Island were seen afterwards at Mossel Bay and Struisbaai. A white shark tagged on KwaZulu-Natal's north coast was recaptured 27 days later at White Sands near Port Elizabeth, 770 km away. An 800 kg individual caught in the anti-shark nets off the KwaZulu-Natal coast had in its stomach the remains of a seal pup that was tagged 1 400 km away at Gansbaai.

Such data collection not only satisfies scientific curiosity; knowledge of migration is crucial to determine whether white sharks cross from South Africa into areas where they are not protected, such as Mozambique and Madagascar. It is of little use to ensure that white sharks are strictly protected in South Africa and Namibia only to find that they spend much time in areas where they are not protected.

In 2002, to gather this crucial migration data, South African white sharks were fitted for the first time with satellite tags. Dr Ramon Bonfil of the Wildlife Conservation Society, in collaboration with scientists from Marine and Coastal Management, attached two types of tags to the dorsal fins of white sharks. Pop-up Archival Tags (PATs) are programmed to detach automatically from the shark's dorsal fin after either 6 or 12 months. Once detached and floating on the surface, the tag sends all data collected during its ride with the shark to a satellite, which transmits it to the researchers.

One of the most exciting discoveries about the movements and migration of the white sharks of southern Africa was made in 2002. Instead of using tags and satellites, a team of scientists from Scotland and South Africa compared portions of maternally inherited DNA from the white shark populations of South Africa, New Zealand and Australia. The maternal DNA from the white sharks of Australia and New Zealand was not significantly different, but it did differ significantly from that of sharks in South Africa. This suggests that white sharks regularly move between New Zealand and Australia but not between those destinations and South Africa.

Further studies on non-maternal DNA confirmed these results, with one exception. This section of DNA from a 3.5 m male white shark captured in Tasmania was not significantly different to males of the South African white shark population. This suggests that females may be philopatric (non-roving), while males occasionally make long distance transoceanic migrations between Australia and South Africa.

MAN-EATERS OR MAN-BITERS?

In a single year in the United States, 43 687 people injure themselves on the toilets in their own homes. This is 600 times more people than have been attacked by great white sharks in South Africa over 77 years. Statistics also show you are more likely to be killed by a falling

coconut while driving to the beach than to be devoured by a great white shark while swimming in the ocean. The fact is that humans do not constitute part of the white shark's catholic diet. The fat content of even the most obese individuals of our species is far too low to be worth the energy the shark would expend in consumption. Due to their size, strength and occasional ferocity, however, the great white shark is capable of inflicting serious injuries on humans, even killing them.

Between 1922 and 2003, there were 77 unprovoked white shark attacks off the coast of South Africa. Of these, 37 occurred in the Western Cape, 26 in the Eastern Cape and the remaining 14 in KwaZulu-Natal. A single attack has been reported in Namibia but there are no reports from Mozambique. Of the 77 attacks, only 19 were fatal. The question is: if we are not part of the white shark's prey base, why do these attacks occur?

There are three competing but potentially complementary theories. Firstly, an attack may be a simple case of mistaken identity, in which the shark mistakes a person for its natural prey. Another theory is that shark attacks are motivated by aggressive territoriality. Finally, a shark may bite simply out of curiosity or play. In murky water a surfer, a body boarder or even a diver can uncannily resemble a seal or other as yet unidentified food source. Some scientists believe that white sharks have the ability to assess the energy value of their prey within milliseconds of their first bite. In more than half of all known great white attacks on swimmers, sharks have taken only a single bite before swimming away. The victim is unlikely to be repeatedly attacked and eaten by the shark, so if death does occur it is usually due to loss of blood. This evidence suggests that the white shark's experimental first bite informs it of its mistake, preventing a fully fledged attack that would easily snap any human in half.

Since it has been shown, however, that in clear water white sharks can readily distinguish between humans and prey animals such as seals, attacks under these conditions must have another cause. Sharks are by nature territorial, and displays of aggression have been noted between individuals of the same species. It could be that sharks attack in self-defence, trying to defend their personal space from human intruders. In most incidences, the victim was not aware of the shark's presence before the initial bite. Those who see an approaching shark and react accordingly are rarely attacked, which is why there are many more in-water encounters with great whites than attacks.

Sharks use their mouths to investigate things out of curiosity, playfulness or aggression. They also communicate with each other by low-intensity biting, which is an important part of any shark's social behavioural repertoire. Human skin is nowhere near as tough as that of a shark, and were a white shark to give us the same treatment it would cause serious injury.

With all this in mind, it is of little consequence which of the shark attack theories is most plausible when it comes to describing the great white as a man-eater. Occasional 'man-biter' it may be, but to label it a man-eater is inaccurate and undeserved.

WHITE SHARK KILLERS

Situated at the top of the marine food chain, the great white shark does not have many predators. In fact, only three species are known to have killed white sharks, and only one does so with any regularity. It is possible that regular killers of white sharks could be other white sharks; there have been incidences when they have killed or seriously injured their own kind in territorial bouts over food.

Killer whales (orcas), up to twice as long as the average white shark, also occur in its range, but there is only one confirmed record of a killer whale fatally injuring a white shark. The extraordinary incident occurred in 1997, when two female killer whales had killed a sea lion off the Farallon Islands of California. A great white shark passed the whales at close range to investigate the sea lion kill and one of the orcas attacked, tearing open the shark's body cavity, killing it outright. The killer whales investigated the shark's liver but neither of them was seen to feed.

Despite having been protected in South Africa for over 10 years, white sharks are still occasionally poached for their jaws, teeth and fins.

The most important predators of great white sharks are of terrestrial, not aquatic origin. A great white is one million times more likely to be killed by a human than a human is by a great white. The white shark survived the dawn and dusk of the dinosaur era; having been at the top of the food chain for millions of years, it is poorly equipped to deal with predators of its own. This shark is a textbook example of a species with a K-selected life history, meaning it is characterized by a reproductive strategy that includes late maturity, slow growth, few offspring and a high offspring survival rate, which makes it highly vulnerable to overexploitation.

No ethnographic records exist of the hunting of white sharks by southern Africa's native people during prehistoric times. White shark remains have never been found in their archaeological deposits and there are no rock paintings depicting sharks. But even if native people did not hunt sharks, their paths must surely have crossed, whether while diving shallow reefs for abalone, rafting on logs to seabird islands to collect eggs, or while scavenging blubber and oil from beached whales.

The earliest record of humans killing white sharks in southern Africa dates back to shortly before the start of World War I. Hungry great whites would hang around the waters off Stony Point where the Cape Hangklip whaling station was located. They would tear off large pieces of valuable blubber before the whales were hauled up onto the slipway for processing. One day, the captain of a Norwegian whaling vessel decided not to tolerate this any longer and baited a float with strychnine-poisoned whale meat. The sharks consumed the bait

No two white sharks are the same. Some are wild and fierce, others curious and even playful. This one enjoyed having the spot in front of its gills tickled so much that it kept coming back to the boat again and again for over an hour.

hundredfold. Trophy hunting had an especially significant impact since it specifically targeted only the biggest individuals. These are primarily female sharks, which only mature at an age of 15 years and a length of 4.5 m. As a result, a high proportion of the breeding population was wiped out during this period, lowering the number of pups in the following years. One renowned shark catcher from False Bay single-handedly hooked and landed 18 large great white sharks between 1974 and 1977.

Another major cause of white shark mortality is the incidental catch by commercial fisheries. An estimated 100 million sharks are killed by fishermen every year, but nobody knows how large the bycatch of great whites is, or the magnitude of its impact in southern African waters. In the North Atlantic, long-lining boats targeting tuna and swordfish killed large numbers of great white sharks in the 1970s and 1980s, decreasing the number of white sharks by approximately 80%.

WHITE SHARK CONSERVATION

A newspaper once described the white shark as a 4 000-pound ocean predator with a mouthful of dagger-like teeth and a nasty habit of occasionally snacking on humans. A tagline such as this does not help the great white shark compete on a level footing for conservation sympathies and funding against more popular endangered species. But against all odds, on 11 April 1991, South Africa became the first country to give protection to the great white shark; under fisheries legislation it became illegal to catch or kill a white shark, or trade in any white shark products.

The Namibian government adopted similar protective measures in 1993 and today Mozambique is the only southern African country without such legislation. In South Africa, however, one fishery was allowed to continue, and white sharks are still targeted along the east coast by nets set out to protect bathers by the Natal Sharks Board. Some 20–50 white sharks are caught annually, and between 1978 and 1993 the grand total was 616 individuals. During that period any white shark found alive in the nets was automatically killed, but since 1993 they have been released alive.

Research is currently under way to determine the viability of replacing some of the nets with baited drum lines to reduce the bycatch of dolphins, turtles, stingrays and other smaller shark species. Unfortunately, drum lines are believed to target and kill the great white and other large sharks more effectively, as demonstrated by the 4.8 m 1 150 kg white shark hooked on one of the experimental drum lines in February 2002.

without any ill effect. It was only when he tried again, this time using copious amounts of arsenic that he managed to kill most of them.

Recreational fishing for white sharks began in the 1920s and soon grew in popularity, becoming a favourite pastime of farmers holidaying in the seaside town of Hermanus. From the mid 1900s, the death toll was already rising, but white shark hunting and fishing really took off in the aftermath of the *Jaws* phenomenon. The film and book increased the demand for shark fishing or 'killing' trips a

On a more sinister note, there are credible reports of poachers illegally targeting white sharks in southern African waters. The shark's jaw and fins are specifically desired and it is thought that both are removed out at sea. The carcass is then dumped in deep water and because (unlike whales) dead sharks do not float, evidence of these cruel acts does not get washed up on the beaches.

The large dorsal fin of white sharks is in great demand for shark-fin soup. The majority are smuggled to the Far East by Asian crime syndicates, often the same groups that trade in illegal abalone. A large white shark jaw in prime condition can fetch over US$10 000, and most are sold to overseas collectors in countries where the great white is not yet protected. At least one South African curio shop is illegally selling white shark tooth necklaces and loose teeth. There are also those who continue to offer illegal white shark sport-fishing trips

'I think we're going to need a bigger boat.'

Marine biologist Matt Hooper in the film *Jaws*.

under the guise of tagging research. For the record, there are no sport-fishing operations that hold permits of any kind, either to catch or to tag and release great white sharks anywhere in South Africa.

The current white shark population is likely still to be small due to the many decades of persecution. This shark is, in fact, currently listed on the World Conservation Union Red Data list of endangered species as being vulnerable to extinction. Its position as apex predator on top of the food chain means that unnatural mortality of any kind could threaten the survival of the species. The white shark is an important participant in a complicated food web and its removal will interfere with the functioning and healthy equilibrium of the oceans.

WHITE SHARK WATCHING

Great white sharks are superstars, there is no doubt about it. A fish that grosses over US$260 million in movie revenues alone is on a par with the likes of Sylvester Stallone and Arnold Schwarzenegger. In the past, *Jaws*-related notoriety was to the shark's detriment, but today that same notoriety ensures that people are willing to pay large sums of money to observe the great white in the wild.

White shark eco-tourism was first pioneered in southern Australia in the 1980s, with South Africa following suit almost a decade later. It all began with a single operation at Seal Island in False Bay in 1991, and today there are 11 commercial white shark

cage-diving companies operating around the coast. On some days tourists outnumber sharks 200 to 1. Sharks are attracted by creating a scent corridor through chumming – releasing a finely minced mixture of sardines and shark livers into the water. Any white shark patrolling the area that comes across this odour corridor will use its highly developed sense of smell to investigate the source. The shark is lured closer to the boat by a piece of bait, often shark meat or a tuna head attached to a rope. The feeding of great whites is strictly forbidden, but even the most careful operator will lose the occasional piece of bait to a swift shark, so allowances are made. Some operators, however, purposefully allow a shark to get hold of the bait to give tourists a bit of a show.

The key difference between viewing white sharks and more conventional terrestrial game viewing is the necessity to use chum and bait to lure the shark closer to the boat. The act of feeding or attracting land animals like baboons and spotted hyenas with food has eroded their instinctive fear of humans, whom they have now learned to associate with free handouts. Based on such experiences with terrestrial animals, some people fear the possibility that white sharks will become conditioned to associate humans with food and lose their innate fear of people.

Research conducted on other shark species has shown that only under optimal and controlled conditions is it possible to condition a shark to respond to a stimulus in as little as three to five days, provided it receives rewards whenever it shows the desired response. Chumming alone, as carried out by responsible eco-tourism operators, is unlikely to condition white sharks, since there is no food reward associated with this practice. Only if the same sharks are repeatedly fed on a permanent basis is conditioning technically possible. Most white sharks, however, appear not to stay in one place long enough for this to occur – even under ideal conditions.

Several magnitudes more worrisome than the potential habituation of white sharks is the extent of injuries that some shark operators inflict. To give tourists an adrenaline-filled experience, white sharks are pulled so close to the boat that they end up with deep gashes and cuts from thrashing against the boat's propellers and hull. White sharks are particularly drawn to a boat's engine, either due to electrical currents discharged into the water or through visual cues, and many receive nasty cuts from banging into the propellers. One simple and effective solution is the use of sturdy engine covers. While to date only one operator has implemented them, others have started showing interest in this simple yet ingenious solution.

Almost all eco-tourism activities have some negative impact on the wildlife or their environment. How benign are 25 cars at a waterhole when elephants in a herd try to quench their thirst? In today's world, it is not economically viable to protect our natural heritage by totally excluding all human interference. Despite some of the negative connotations of white shark eco-tourism, this is the least destructive way of utilising this species. Without white shark tourism it is likely that this species would have been fished to near extinction long ago. Today, the great white shark is worth far more alive than dead. Seeing this magnificent animal in its natural habitat, guided by a responsible and knowledgeable operator, allows people to reconsider their opinion of the white shark as a ruthless killer and forever disregard such unwarranted misconceptions.

White sharks are attracted to a boat's outboard motors by the electromagnetic fields they discharge into the water. The sharks often mouth the engines and injure themselves in the process.

ABOVE: Sturdy engine covers are a simple and effective solution to stop sharks injuring themselves. The covers have to be replaced on a regular basis.

KELP

the golden forest

eep inside the forest, the light is dim. Even at noon, with the African sun blazing overhead, the rocky reef is enveloped in a mysterious green glow. Only where isolated shafts of sunlight penetrate the canopy are the true colours of the fauna and flora revealed. Animals with eight arms, six legs or no legs at all scramble, slither and glide across spiky orange sponges, purple seaweeds and pink coralline crusts. Abalone, sea urchins and rock lobsters cluster together in the maze of root-like holdfasts, while Cape fur seals hide from great whites in the tangle of trunk-like stems.

These are Africa's only kelp forests and they thrive where the cold Atlantic Ocean washes over rocky reefs, and where upwelling from the deep provides a bountiful supply of nutrients.

KELP FOREST EVOLUTION AND DISTRIBUTION

Few specimens of fossilised kelp plants have ever been found. Any clues to their early origins have been inferred from records of past climates, the fossils of species closely associated with kelps, and present-day gradients of kelp diversity.

The cradle of kelp forest evolution is believed to be the North Pacific, which is today still the undisputed kelp hotspot, harbouring 64 species in 26 genera. The oceans around southern Africa pale by comparison as they provide a haven for only five species in three genera. This points to the North Pacific as the birthplace of kelp, followed by dispersal during periods of cooling in the Pleistocene, a time when tropical marine habitats were greatly reduced. Kelps probably arrived in southern Africa by spreading through the clear waters of the western Atlantic, surviving in cold, deep water below the thermocline, which is the boundary layer between waters of different temperatures. A relic population of kelp found in deep water off the coast of Brazil supports such a dispersal theory.

Southern Africa's kelp forests stretch in an almost continuous band from northern Namibia to just west of Cape Agulhas, the southernmost tip of Africa. They are only interrupted locally by stretches of sandy beaches and soft substrate. The bamboo kelp, *Ecklonia maxima*, is the tallest of the five species that occur in southern Africa and can grow to a height of 15 m. Like all kelp, it is attached to the rocky reef by means of a holdfast, from which a long hollow stipe, or stem, stretches towards the surface. This culminates in a club-shaped, gas-filled float that enables the plant to maintain an upright position and ensures that the strap-like fronds always stay near the surface where light is at its most plentiful. Bamboo kelp occurs from Lüderitz to just west of Cape Agulhas and is the dominant species in shallow water between Yzerfontein and Danger Point.

In deeper water of 10–20 m, split-fan kelp, *Laminaria pallida*, becomes more dominant. While it is also present below 20 m, it tends to be sparsely scattered. It is smaller than bamboo kelp, growing to just over 10 m in length. It lacks a gas-filled float and its hand-shaped blade is dissected into regular longitudinal splits.

As the sun sets, kelp beds are transformed into shimmering forests of gold.

Undersea jungles are not unlike terrestrial woodlands. Kelp plants grow large like trees, fish flit through the canopy like songbirds and starfish crawl in between the holdfasts like hedgehogs among the leaf litter of a forest floor.

From Port Nolloth northwards, split-fan kelp is replaced by *Laminaria schinzii*, which looks almost identical. East of Cape Agulhas, bamboo kelp is replaced by spined kelp, *Ecklonia radiata*, a warm-water-tolerant species that can endure the abruptly increased temperature of this region. Along the south coast, this much smaller species occurs almost exclusively in shallow water, but further north, as the water temperature rises, the mainstay of its population is found in deeper water. Along the subtropical coast of KwaZulu-Natal, it can grow up to 2 m long and occurs in water 30–40 m deep. The fifth species of kelp in southern Africa is bladder kelp, *Macrocystis angustifolia*, a plant from the same genus as the giant kelps of California. Up to 10 m long, it occurs only in very sheltered shallow water, often inshore of bamboo kelp beds and especially around offshore islands.

KELP FOREST BASICS

Like coral reefs, kelp forests do not grow just anywhere. They can only flourish under particular environmental and physical conditions. For instance, their occurrence is limited by the availability of hard substrate, as only rarely, and in very sheltered conditions, do the plants grow on sand. Kelp can also grow only where it can absorb sufficient sunlight for photosynthesis. The exact depth limit, i.e. the seaward extent of the kelp forest, depends on the clarity of the water. The availability of light is so important that its seasonal fluctuation causes changes in growth rates that can differ tenfold between summer and winter.

Kelps also need an ample supply of nutrients, especially nitrates and phosphates. Unlike terrestrial plants, however, they do not absorb nutrients through their root-like holdfast but directly through their fronds. They thrive best in fully saline seawater, whereas freshwater influxes seem to have adverse effects.

An alternation of generations takes place within the life cycle of all kelps. This consists of two distinct phases. The kelp looms large and tall in its first, familiar phase as an asexual spore-forming organism, or sporophyte. During this stage, it produces microscopic zoospores, not unlike pollen, on special tissues of the fronds. Each kelp plant releases billions of these spores into the water column.

Very few spores survive and even fewer settle and develop into microscopic male and female gamete-forming organisms, or gametophytes. Gametophytes represent the second life stage of kelp, the sexually active generation that can only be glimpsed under a

The bladder kelp, *Macrocystis angustifolia*, is the most delicate, but also the rarest, of all the southern African species.

microscope. Male gametophytes release sperm and females release eggs. If fertilised, the female gametophyte grows into a sporophyte, i.e. the macroscopic kelp plant familiar to us all. It is amazing to think that during one phase kelp can only be gazed at with the aid of a powerful microscope, but during another the same plant dwarfs humans, growing to more than seven times our height.

The microscopic gametophyte and early sporophyte stages are very vulnerable to grazers, as well as inundation by sediment. In areas where grazers are abundant, young sporophytes are often found growing on the holdfasts of adults of their own species. Along the southwest transition zone between Cape Hangklip and Cape Agulhas, a region with much higher grazer densities than the west coast, significantly more young kelps occur on the holdfasts of adults.

STRUCTURE AND SHELTER

The large size of individual kelp plants and the expansive nature of the ecosystem allow them to influence environmental and oceanographic conditions significantly. Kelp forests are known to decrease the energy of waves and buffer longshore currents to such an extent that 100 m into a dense kelp bed, current speed is reduced

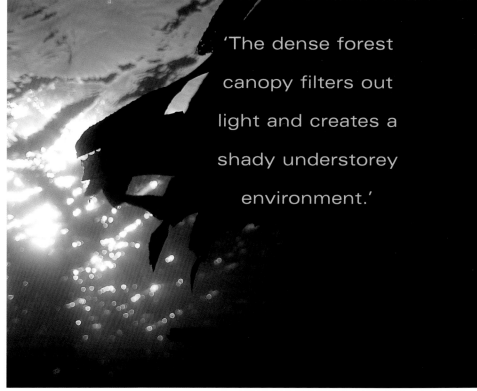

'The dense forest canopy filters out light and creates a shady understorey environment.'

to almost zero. The dense forest canopy also filters out light and creates a shady understorey environment. Most importantly, kelp forests increase manyfold the heterogeneity of temperate reef habitat, extending its structural complexity and increasing the range of micro-habitats available. The kelp forest canopy is one of those microhabitats.

The crowns of kelp plants are home to an epiphytic algae community – one that grows on the kelp but does not feed on it – that can weigh as much as 10% of the kelp plant itself. The total epiphytic biomass will often even exceed the standing stock of all the understorey algae combined. In addition, 27 species of animals reside in the canopy, including various species of crustaceans, such as amphipods and isopods, and a vast population of pea-sized marine snails *Eatoniella nigra*, of which there can be up to 50 000 per square metre of forest.

Polychaetes, or bristle worms, are also well represented by several species, as is one species of suckerfish that occurs only in this microhabitat. The kelp limpet, *Cymbula compressa*, lives exclusively on the stipes of bamboo kelp, while the kelp curler, *Ampithoe humeralis*, builds a nest in the kelp forest canopy much as a bird would do in a terrestrial forest. By folding the secondary blades of the kelp longit-udinally and sealing the adjoining surfaces together, it forms a tubular chamber in which to seek shelter and lay eggs.

The biomass of the canopy fauna in shallow, algae-dominated regions can exceed that of the benthos, or seabed. There are numer-ous species of fish that rely on canopy flora and fauna for food since many of the invertebrates found on the rocky reef itself are not available to them.

THE FOOD WEB

It is the kelp forest's ability to take sunlight and nutrients and transform them into organic matter for animals to eat that makes them indispensable. Without them, temperate reefs would not only be far less productive, they would yield a much lower species diversity, as the bulk of the forest fauna relies directly or indirectly on kelp for food.

Kelp plants themselves are not very nutritious. They have high levels of phenols in their tissues – secondary metabolites that in high doses inhibit feeding in a wide range of marine animals. However, what kelp lacks in taste and nutrition, it makes up for in its prolific nature; growth rates can exceed 1 cm per day.

A school of strepies, *Sarpa salpa,* the most mobile and wide-ranging grazers in southern Africa's kelp forests.

Cape sea urchins, *Parechinus angulosus*, carpet a boulder encrusted in coralline algae and crowned by bamboo kelp.

HERBIVORES

Southern Africa's kelp forests harbour very few herbivores. In fact, under 4% of the total animal biomass consists of grazers and they consume no more than 12% of the total annual primary production. The invertebrate grazers here are also vastly different from those in other parts of the world. While in California sea urchins can lay waste to entire kelp beds, in southern Africa grazers tend to be rather non-aggressive feeders that lack much of the habitat-structuring capabilities of their American counterparts.

The two most abundant herbivores are the Cape sea urchin, *Parechinus angulosus*, and the South African abalone, *Haliotis midae*. Both are true grazers only as recruits and juveniles, when they scrape microalgae and seaweed sporelings from the rocky reef. As they reach adulthood, their foraging strategies change – instead of wandering the reef looking for food, they sit and wait for the food to come to them.

The southern African coastline is very exposed and the constant battering by waves regularly breaks off pieces of fronds, which are distributed along the reef by the currents. Urchins catch this drift kelp and other algae with their tube feet, while abalone assume a so-called trap-feeding position, in which the front section of the body is raised and the muscular foot is extended forwards. When a piece of kelp washes against the foot, the abalone grasps it and clamps down, trapping the seaweed between rock and foot. Trap-feeding is an economical way of feeding, as no energy has to be expended searching for food.

Other herbivores include the alikreukel, a marine snail *Turbo sarmarcticus*, as well as various species of limpet, and two species of fish, the hottentot, *Pachymetopon blochii*, and the strepie, *Sarpa salpa*.

Off California, severe storms frequently obliterate entire kelp forests because giant kelp plants easily become entangled with their neighbours. In southern Africa, the morphology of both bamboo and split-fan kelp is very different – there is virtually no entanglement and they are more adept at surviving the relentless pounding of stormy seas. When the seas get too turbulent, only individual plants are uprooted and less than 6% of the total kelp production is lost in this way. However, considering a standing stock of 554 330 tons between Cape Columbine and Cape Point alone, this translates into 200–300 kg of kelp stranded on a single metre of beach every year.

It is no wonder that a whole suit of sandy beach and rocky shore organisms evolved to take advantage of the subtidal food subsidies provided by the kelp forest. On rocky shores, it is principally isopods and various species of limpet that depend almost entirely on kelp. Sandy beaches are a habitat virtually devoid of attached plants and the vast quantities of kelp that wash up are an energy windfall for no fewer than 27 species. The bulk of the stranded material is consumed by amphipods and kelp fly larvae within 14 days. In the process, they deposit nutrients into the sandy beach system via their faeces, potentially nourishing dense populations of nematode worms and perhaps even feeding nutrients back into the adjacent subtidal soft-sediment benthos.

FILTER FEEDERS

Unlike open-water food chains that are built on a base of phytoplankton, or microscopic floating plants, in kelp forests phytoplankton densities are reduced by up to 95% due to the shading effect of the canopy. However, filter feeders, normally the main consumers of plankton, still make up 70–95% of the animal biomass. They must consume vast quantities of food: a dense population of ribbed mussels can filter a 10 m column of water in less than seven and a half hours. This suggests that instead of phytoplankton there must be another superabundant food source available to these filter feeders.

In fact, mussels *Aulacomya* and *Choromytilus*, the sea cucumbers *Pentacta doliolum* and *Thyone aurea*, sponges (Tethya) and one sea squirt *Pyura stolonifera* have the bulk of their energy requirements

A spotted gully shark, *Triakis megalopterus*, patrols the kelp forest maze in search of rock lobsters and crabs.

met by the kelps themselves. Kelp fronds behave like moving conveyor belts, growing at the base while waves continually erode the tips, breaking off small particles that form detritus. Particulate kelp matter floats to the bottom during calm conditions and only becomes available to filter feeders in more turbulent sea conditions. Generally, suspended particles are most abundant in the water column during heavy seas, which is why the highest filter feeder biomass is almost always found in wave-exposed regions.

Some of the kelp forests' primary productivity is also released in the form of dissolved organic matter (DOM) and mucus. Particulate organic matter (POM) and DOM play an important role in the ecology of kelp forest bacteria, POM as a settlement surface and DOM as their main source of nutrition. Bacteria are surprisingly abundant in kelp forests, and the number of bacteria in the water column and on kelp fronds follows a seasonal pattern, with maximum counts occurring during summer.

CARNIVORES

Several species of carnivore occur in southern Africa's kelp forests. They include reef fish, several species of cat and hound sharks, yearling seals and bank cormorants, as well as the west coast rock lobster and the Cape clawless otter.

In terms of overall biomass, the west coast rock lobster, *Jasus lalandii*, is the most abundant carnivore on the west and southwest coasts. It reproduces by internal fertilization and makes use of large-scale ocean currents and gyres to disperse its larvae away from the parent population. Passive drifting lobster larvae, called phyllosomata, leave on an open-ocean voyage that can last for many months, during which they will go through at least 11 metamorphic stages before they come full circle and are deposited close to the continental shelf. Here each larva undergoes a final metamorphosis, transforming into a swimming puerulus. They then head inshore and settle out of the plankton into either dense beds of seaweed or into the kelp canopy.

THE GREAT SEA URCHIN MYSTERY

Cape sea urchins, *Parechinus angulosus*, are among the most abundant grazers and debris feeders in the kelp forest, covering vast tracts of shallow reef in spiky, colourful carpets. Along the southwest coast of South Africa, urchin densities were once so great that a walk to the water's edge at low tide was almost impossible without the sensation of a pincushion underfoot. Then, in 1994, a major change occurred when most of the urchins vanished in a fairly short space of time. By 1996 they were almost locally extinct and populations have still not recovered to the present day.

Scientists scrambled to pinpoint the cause of this phenomenon. A similar urchin mass mortality affecting the long-spined sea urchin *Diadema antillarum* occurred over much of the Caribbean in 1983 and 1984, resulting in dramatic increases in algae. In that case, the culprit was identified as a bacterial pathogen, which the currents spread all across the region. No such pathogens were ever implicated in South Africa and the major breakthrough came when the data from the previous two years' rock lobster surveys in the same region were examined.

It became apparent that, before the disappearance of the urchins, the number of particularly large rock lobsters had increased markedly. A repeated survey in 1996 revealed that the west coast rock lobster population had increased to plague proportions — a 600-fold increase in biomass was recorded. Subsequent laboratory experiments revealed that large lobsters are capable of consuming sea urchins of all sizes and that the lobsters were responsible for the loss of the urchins.

Although not valuable itself, the humble sea urchin does play a very important role in the life cycle of the South African abalone, which is a commercially valuable species. Urchins are a key nursery habitat for juvenile abalone along the southwest coast, where the spiny canopy protects the abalone from the attentions of predators such as klipfish, octopus and rock lobsters. This relationship is most closely knit if the urchins in question feed primarily on drift algae, because in addition to shelter, the juvenile abalone also gain nourishment. The urchin hosts are messy eaters and pieces of drift kelp regularly find their way beneath the urchins. However, if drift kelp is not available, the abalone will undertake short foraging excursions under the cover of darkness, leaving their urchin shelters to graze on microalgae, but returning within several hours.

To compound matters, the loss of sea urchins has also led to the collapse of all abalone recruitment — a term referring to new, young individuals entering a population by reproduction. It appears that urchins, even if they are feeding mainly on drift algae, somehow have the ability to keep the rocky reef free of sediment. This prevents any abalone larvae from settling and recruiting onto the reef. For now, there are no signs of the population explosion abating and even though there seems to be very little energy-rich food left, the lobsters — having also dramatically decreased the population of gastropods, or marine snails — seem to be surviving well on a diet of sponge and algae.

Rock lobster population explosions are a well-documented phenomenon around the world, and in many cases seem to be linked to years of good lobster larvae survival or to large-scale population migrations. In response, urchin populations suffer dramatic declines until the increase in lobster numbers triggers a population increase in their predators.

In South Africa, major lobster predators in the kelp forests of the southwest coast are carnivorous benthic reef fish such as red roman and red stumpnose. These fish were an important component of the linefishing industry that was already thriving in the 1800s. Comparisons of modern data with catch records collated between 1889 and 1907 show a great decline in many species. The populations of red roman and red stumpnose have been reduced by 83% and 95% respectively.

To protect the South African abalone population, which has already been severely depleted by poaching (*see* 'Abalone wars' on page 60), as well as other inhabitants of the kelp forest, we have to ensure that this marine ecosystem remains balanced and healthy. We must at all costs prevent these kelp beds from becoming like the 'empty forests' of central and west Africa, where the trees in many places are still magnificent and majestic, giving us a false sense of health, but the forest fauna has been hunted to extinction.

A juvenile abalone, *Haliotis midae*, sheltering beneath a sea urchin.

Only when they attain sexual maturity at the age of five do they begin to inhabit the deeper regions of the reef, alongside other adults.

In adult form, lobsters are keystone predators and their presence, or indeed absence, has been shown to shape the structure of the rocky reef. Saldanha Bay on the west coast of South Africa is home to two nearshore islands, Malgas and Marcus. In terms of shape, size and oceanographic conditions of the surrounding waters they seem fairly similar, but all it takes is a look at the rocky reef beneath the surface for similarities to disappear.

The benthos surrounding Malgas Island is profusely covered in foliose algae, home to dense aggregations of west coast rock lobsters and two species of carnivorous whelks, *Argobuccinum pustulosum* and *Burnupena papyracea*. If it is surprising that these molluscs have not been devoured – like everything else – by the hordes of lobsters,

a closer look reveals their secrets. The shells of *B. papyracea* are covered in a layer of stinging bryozoans, or moss animals, which deters all rock lobsters from feeding on them. As for *A. pustulosum*, its shell is much too thick and heavy for any lobster, regardless of its size, to crack.

At first glance there seems little here for the lobsters to eat – their usual prey of mussels or sea urchins has long since been consumed. Stomach contents analysis has revealed that during the winter months the lobsters survive by scraping recently settled small barnacle recruits from the rocks, while in summer they feed on planktonic mysid shrimp. While these two rather unorthodox food sources might at first seem insignificant in terms of biomass, their rapid turnover and constant renewal allows the rock lobsters to fulfil their energy requirements year round.

'If playfulness is a measure of intelligence, then otters must be among the smartest of all wild animals.'

At Marcus Island, however, there are no rock lobsters to speak of and the rocky reef is covered by a dense matrix of black mussels *Choromytilus meridionalis*, large numbers of *Burnupena* whelks, sea cucumbers, brittlestars and masses of sea urchins, preventing almost any algal growth from occurring. To determine the cause of the differences in community structure between these two islands, scientists released 1 000 rock lobsters at Marcus. The results were dramatic and unexpected. Within one hour of release, all lobsters had been attacked and killed by hordes of *Burnupena*.

The tale of these two islands is an unusual one, for it appears that they represent two stable states of the same ecosystem. Once a high-density community like the one at Marcus has established itself, the usual predator experiences a reversal of fortune and becomes the prey, just as the lobster has fallen prey to *Burnupena* whelks. On Malgas, however, lobsters occur in such high numbers that only seaweed and a small number of well-defended whelks can coexist with them. What eliminated the rock lobster from Marcus in the first place remains a mystery.

The Cape clawless otter, *Aonyx capensis*, is the larger of two otter species that occur in southern Africa. Reaching a length of up to 1.8 m, it is also the only species with two distinct populations – an inland freshwater one and a coastal marine one. The marine population is widely distributed and, with the exception of the tropical east coast, occurs wherever fresh water is present year-long at the coast.

While coastal Cape clawless otters get all their food from the marine realm, they depend on fresh water for drinking and for rinsing the salt from their fur after foraging at sea. This is a crepuscular species, which spends the day resting or sleeping in holts – a network of hollows tunnelled into thick undergrowth close to both the sea and a freshwater source. The otters leave their holts to forage twice a day, around sunset and sunrise. Exact departure times vary with the degree of human disturbance. In areas with high dog and human densities, otters will often only emerge in total darkness, while at remote locations they have been known to emerge hours before sunset.

The Cape clawless otter is one of the kelp forests' top predators. While it generally prefers to hunt in shallow water close to shore, one individual has been sighted several kilometres out to sea on Dyer Island. The otter's tactile senses are particularly well developed, with numerous long, stiff hairs called vibrissae around the snout that act as tactile organs. It also has dextrous, sensitive paws for locating prey in murky water, and hunts predominantly by feeling along the reef and under rocks. Prey is captured with the forefeet and either eaten at the water's surface while the otter lies on its back, or hauled onto rocks to be eaten there.

The Cape clawless otter, *Aonyx capensis*, is one of Africa's most secretive and difficult mammals to observe. This one emerged at dusk along a remote section of the False Bay coast and quickly entered the sea to feed.

Detailed dietary studies have shown that marine otters consume at least 25 species of reef invertebrates and reef fish, but the bulk of their diet consists of benthic fish such as klipfish, rock crabs, octopus and rock lobsters. In the 1980s, well before the Hangklip-Hermanus crayfish invasion (*see* 'The great sea urchin mystery' on page 55), the west coast rock lobster made up only 10.3% of the Cape clawless otter's diet at Betty's Bay. Its diet was dominated by fish (59%), octopus (15%) and Cape rock crabs (13%.) By 2002, rock lobsters made up almost 70% of the otter's diet. At Danger Point, just to the east of the boundary of the lobster population explosion, the otter's diet was still dominated by fish, resembling that recorded at Betty's Bay before the rock lobster population explosion.

This otter seems to be a supreme opportunist, making it an ideal bioindicator – an animal that can provide important information about the composition and abundance of certain species within an ecosystem. Currently, gentoo penguins are used to study the abundance of certain plankton species, and emperor penguins are used to establish what marine life occurs under the sea ice.

In the face of burgeoning coastal development, the Cape clawless otter population appears to have remained fairly stable since the 1980s and has proven surprisingly tolerant of human disturbances. Instead of leaving urbanised areas, these creatures seem to have adapted by becoming nocturnal. It has recently been shown that Cape clawless otters live on Gordon's Bay's Bikini Beach, as well as in the heart of Cape Town, in and around the V&A Waterfront.

HARVESTING THE KELP FOREST

Humans harvest a wide array of marine organisms from southern Africa's kelp forest including west coast rock lobsters, abalone and even the kelp itself.

KELP

Kelp has been used in southern Africa since the late Stone Age, when the dried, hollow floats of sea bamboo were used to carry water and store whale oil. More recently, it was used medicinally by the Topnar people who used to live near the Kuiseb River on Namibia's desert coast. They called kelp *hurihab* and dried, roasted and ground it into a powder that was mixed with fats before being rubbed into wounds to prevent infection and accelerate healing. Farmers along the coast, where the soil is sandy and nutrient poor, have been using kelp to fertilize their fields for a long time.

The local modern-day kelp industry began in 1942, when kelp plants – mainly sea bamboo but also split-fan kelp whose holdfasts were uprooted in storms and cast ashore – were collected from the beaches. Even the political prisoners on Robben Island in Table Bay were made to harvest kelp, gathering the long stipes of sea bamboo from the rocks. This drift kelp was dried, milled into small pieces and exported to produce alginic acid, which is used in everything from toothpaste and ice cream to ink, paint and explosives.

This beach-cast industry continues to the present day, when some 3 000 tons of dried *Ecklonia maxima* is collected annually from around the shores of the Western Cape. But the kelp industry does not rely only on beach cast. In 1979 kelp harvesters began cutting kelp directly from the kelp beds themselves. Used in the manufacture of plant growth stimulants, the kelp is macerated, liquidized and packaged. Today, the bulk of fresh-cut kelp has a different purpose; it is used as feed for the booming abalone farming industry.

WEST COAST ROCK LOBSTER

West coast rock lobsters have been exploited in southern Africa since the 1920s and today the fishery stretches from northern Namibia to a little beyond Cape Hangklip. A recreational fishery also operates, offering snorkelling gear and hoop nets, which are deployed from the shore or from small boats.

Both the Namibian and South African rock lobster fisheries have declined dramatically since their inception. Namibia's took a nosedive from the 1960s' high of 9 000 tons to a low of 130 tons in 1993. The cause of this decline is believed to have been the sudden regular

ABOVE AND RIGHT: Commercial fishing for rock lobster began in the Cape in the 1920s and continues to the present day.

appearances of bands of oxygen-depleted water off the coast between Namaqualand in South Africa and central Namibia. These bands restricted the lobster to shallow water less than 15 m deep for most of the year. Where the density of rock lobsters is too high, growth rates are reduced and the reproductive rate drops. Another factor in declining catches is that on the exposed coast it is much more difficult to catch lobster owing to the wave-beaten shallow-water environment.

The South African fishery remained stable until late in the 1980s, when the growth rates of lobster slowed by more than 50% and recruitment decreased significantly, the exact cause of which is still not fully understood. The catches dropped from 4 000 tons to 1 900 tons and *in situ* diving surveys combined with mathematical modelling show that the harvestable biomass of lobster has been reduced to about 5% of its estimated pre-exploitation level.

In addition, recent years have brought an increase in the number and magnitude of mass rock lobster strandings along the west coast. These have been especially prominent and frequent at Elands Bay. These 'rock lobster walkouts' are caused by the decay of intense phytoplankton blooms, which use all the oxygen in the water. Like a sheepdog herding its flock, this band of foul-smelling oxygen-starved water pushes all rock lobsters into the shallows until they are finally forced to walk out onto the beach to breathe, where they die in the hot sunlight. The biggest-ever rock lobster mass stranding took place in the autumn of 1997, when more than 2 000 tons were stranded, an amount equivalent to the entire year's nation-wide commercial landings.

ABALONE

In 1949 modern commercial fishing for abalone started in the coastal village of Gansbaai and soon expanded to cover nearly 580 km of coast between Cape Columbine and Cape Agulhas. In the early days of the fishery, divers used traditional helmet diving gear, but in the dense kelp forests this equipment soon became cumbersome and they changed to the hookah system, which delivers air via a hose from a compressor on the boat. Divers prise abalone from the rock with a collecting tool, usually a large screwdriver or a flat, blunt iron blade.

The catches in the 1950s and 1960s were high, peaking at 2 800 tons in 1965. Catches began to decrease in the 1970s, however, as once-dense beds of abalone were depleted by over-harvesting. Concern over the decline of catches led to the introduction of a host of measures to limit fishing efforts over the next 20 years. Finally, in the early 1990s, the abalone fishery appeared to show the first signs of improvement in 40 years.

The species was also recreationally fished, though divers were only permitted to harvest by free diving, which limited them to shallow depths and inshore areas. Due to intense illegal exploitation of abalone since 1994, however (*see* 'Abalone wars' on page 60), recreational fishing was closed in 2003. Unless a miracle occurs commercial fishing for abalone will soon follow.

When intense blooms of toxic phytoplankton rob the water of all its oxygen, armies of crayfish are forced to walk out of the sea to 'breathe'.

ABALONE WARS

The South African abalone, *Haliotis midae*, is one of the largest molluscs on the planet, attaining a weight of nearly 2 kg and a ripe old age of more than 20 years. It inhabits the kelp forests off the temperate west and south coasts and reaches densities of up to 50 individuals per square metre.

It has been exploited in South Africa for over 125 000 years, first by the prehistoric inhabitants of the region — the San and the Khoi-Khoi — then from the 1940s by modern commercial fishermen. Rampant over-exploitation thrust the fishery into steep decline in the 1960s. Only after the introduction of stringent regulations did the stocks show signs of recovery in the early 1990s, but any hopes of a sustainable harvest were short-lived. By 2000, abalone were once again well on their way to being fished to extinction as South Africa's temperate coast degenerated into a poacher's paradise.

Today this giant marine snail is under threat from international smuggling syndicates. Poaching has devastated abalone populations, which consist of slow-growing animals that mature at a late age, move at a snail's pace and live in a habitat easily accessible to exploiters.

Abalone are broadcast spawners, which involves the release of clouds of sperm into the water by males, triggering the release of eggs in females. For fertilization to take place, sperm and eggs have to meet in the water column. This is only possible if male and female abalone live close enough to one another. Today, with many reefs harbouring far lower densities than ever before, there is uncertainty as to whether their eggs and sperm still meet. The larval stage is also fairly short-lived; larvae are estimated to be on the move for fewer than five days. With dense kelp beds to buffer current velocities, larval movement might be curtailed to less than 50 m.

At the root of South Africa's current poaching epidemic lies the insatiable demand for abalone in the Far East, where gourmets prize its flesh as a culinary delicacy and aphrodisiac. Chinese Mafia syndicates, Triads, set up operations in post-apartheid South Africa and soon began supplying abalone to black markets in the Far East. Using historic and economic circumstances to their favour, they recruited divers from previously disadvantaged communities to poach for them. Poverty is still rampant along this stretch of coastline and few refused an offer to make in a single night's diving what they would normally struggle to scrape together over a period of months.

To combat poaching and smuggling, army helicopters skirt the coast at low level on the look-out for divers, and fishery patrol vessels plough up and down the coast, attempting to intercept boats laden to the gunnels with their illegal harvest. Sniffer dogs have been trained to work at airports, harbours, border posts and container terminals, smelling out contraband abalone. Despite what seems a Herculean effort on the government's part to put an end to poaching, the illegal trade is still rampant. The prosecution of offenders is difficult, the proverbial loophole haunts legislation, and high prices paid for black-market abalone have led to high levels of corruption. Illegal abalone has been transported in police vehicles, ambulances and even smuggled in military aircraft. The profits from selling the abalone in the Far East often return to South Africa in the form of drugs and guns, thus perpetuating a vicious cycle of organised crime.

Unabated poaching at present levels will not only result in the extinction of the species in the wild, it will exact a heavy toll on the functioning of the kelp forest ecosystem. Following the dramatic reduction of abalone, some rocky reefs have begun to disappear beneath a blanket of sediment while others have been smothered by algae. Clean substrates covered by encrusting red algae are the key settling surfaces for many larvae. While the loss of this habitat has already led to a recruitment collapse in the abalone, it could potentially affect many other important marine invertebrates. These and other changes will impair the ecological functioning of the kelp forests and have an impact on all levels of the temperate reef ecosystem.

OPPOSITE PAGE: When this bed of abalone was photographed in 2001 it was one of the last remaining pristine reefs left in the country. Today it too has gone, strip-mined by a poaching syndicate in 2004.

ABOVE: Senior Nature Conservation Officer Craig Spencer empties a bag of shucked abalone stolen from the Betty's Bay Marine Reserve. Between 1997 and 2003 over 700 poaching incidents occurred along this 5.5 km stretch of coast.

LEFT: Abalone has become so valuable that hauls confiscated from smuggling syndicates are examined and transferred under the watchful eyes of guards carrying automatic weapons.

JACKALS, LIONS AND HYENAS

CHAPTER THREE

fishing for a living

'It is a desolate place, an

uninhabited wilderness of

undulating sand dunes

and gravel plains

kept in eternal movement by

ferocious desert winds.'

Southern Africa's desert coast consists of a thin sliver of arid land stretching 2 000 km – from South Africa, north-wards across Namibia, and into southern Angola. It is a desolate place, an uninhabited wilderness of undulating sand dunes kept in eternal movement by ferocious desert winds. A world of gravel plains, endless vistas of rock and pebbles sculpted by the elements. Here, daytime highs can reach 40 °C and even a desert specialist like the shovel-snouted lizard needs to keep two feet off the scalding sand at all times to avoid being baked to death by the heat. Rain seldom falls and many places have not seen a drop in over 100 years.

Surprisingly, however, the desert coast is home to several large mammals, species familiar to most as common residents of the savanna and bushveld, where rich antelope herds provide ample prey. In this desert, such a bountiful prey base is scarce or completely absent in most areas, yet lions, jackals and hyenas roam this arid wilderness and somehow eke out an existence.

The key to their survival is the Atlantic Ocean, which borders the desert's western flank and is several million times more productive than its terrestrial neighbour. Mammals along the desert coast have evolved new sets of behaviours different from those of their inland cousins. The sea now meets the bulk of their food requirements.

Lions bed down in the cold Atlantic surf and tear chunks of blub-ber from stranded whales. Black-backed jackals forage along the drift line, dining on jellyfish and anything else that strong onshore winds and waves throw up onto the beach. Brown hyenas enter seal colonies and, oblivious to the frantic bleating of the mothers, kill young seal pups with swift bites to the head. As night falls, porcupines emerge from their daytime shelters and, under cover of darkness, compete with limpets as they graze algae from the rocky shores at low tide.

LEFT: Conventional prey is scarce or largely absent along the Skeleton Coast, yet somehow a suite of terrestrial carnivores, like these jackals, survive and even thrive here.

RIGHT: South of Lüderitz steep cliffs plunge straight into a violent and unpredictable sea.

JACKALS, LIONS AND HYENAS
fishing for a living

OCEAN RICHES

The Atlantic Ocean adjacent to the desert coast is one of the richest marine ecosystems on the planet. Driven by the Benguela current, upwelling lifts cold, nutrient-rich bottom water to the surface. Deprived of sunlight for many years, this water holds no plant or animal life, only very high concentrations of nutrients. When it is exposed to sunlight, microscopic free-floating plants called phytoplankton rapidly bloom into a nutrient-rich soup.

Zooplankton feeds on the phytoplankton and is in turn eaten by baleen whales and vast schools of sardines and pilchards, which in their turn lure game fish, sharks and other marine predators. This cornucopia of marine life is also attacked from the sky. Seabirds such as Cape gannets and Cape cormorants, which breed in their hundreds of thousands on offshore islands, also come to claim their share of these marine riches.

But the species that best illustrates the ocean's richness here are the hundreds of thousands of Cape fur seals that thrive along this coast. Dotted along the shore are 22 seal colonies, nine of which are breeding colonies. Of the world's southern African fur seal population, 66% lives along this Desert Coast and the colonies at Kleinsee, Wolf and Atlas bays are perhaps the largest mainland seal colonies in the world. In late October and early November, big male bulls are the first to haul out at the colonies after almost a year at sea, staking out territories and awaiting the arrival of the females.

Dusk at Wolf Bay, one of the world's largest mainland seal colonies.

INSET: Around seal colonies, the desert's silence is broken by a cacophony of grunts, barks and squeals.

Returning from a feeding trip out to sea, a mother and her pup reunite in the surf.

Many females are heavily pregnant and pupping occurs within one or two days of their arrival at the colony. They usually give birth to a single pup, but twins are born on rare occasions. To produce enough milk, the female has to return to the sea to feed at regular intervals. Every morning, when the sun is still below the horizon and the seal colony is just a puzzle of shifting shapes, a steady stream of seals moves down well-worn gullies towards the sea. The pups cannot swim until they are about six weeks old, so their mothers drop them off at the water's edge in a crèche guarded by one or two females. This is a vulnerable time for the pups; if their mothers should fail to return, they will die of starvation or overheating.

High mortalities also occur when the pups are first learning to swim. Many drown or suffer fatal injuries from being smashed onto rocks. The females are ready to mate again just a few days after giving birth, beginning the cycle of birth and death anew.

It is these vast colonies of seals, the schools of fish, the flocks of seabirds and pods of whales and dolphins that form the prey base ensuring the survival of the many terrestrial mammals that miraculously occur here.

THE SURVIVORS

Along the desert coast lions, hyenas, jackals and even porcupines have embraced the sea as a source of food.

LIONS

The revelation that lions roam seaside beaches and feed on marine life came only in the early 1980s, when a male lion was photographed ripping open a beached pilot whale carcass in the Skeleton Coast Park. He fed mainly on the blubber, his head almost disappearing into the whale's body cavity and then reappearing stained dark red and brown. Even when the tide came in, he was reluctant to abandon his prize and continued feeding until he was knee-deep in the surf.

Subsequently, lions were also observed feeding on Cape fur seals, which they dragged several kilometres inland, but it is not known whether they hunted or scavanged them. These desert prides also fed on seabirds. One lioness was observed charging into a group of roosting white-breasted cormorants, and succeeded in catching at least one individual. Subsequent examinations of lion droppings revealed that cormorants made up a substantial part of their diet.

ABOVE: A male lion feeding on a pilot whale. Namibia's Skeleton Coast National Park is the only place in Africa where this behaviour has been observed.

LEFT: An unfitting end for the king of beasts. Bottled and preserved in alcohol, this fully formed foetus came from the womb of a lioness shot and killed by herdsmen in 1984.

While life was tough along this desert coast, the lions survived and were even able to produce offspring. Unlike bushveld lions, however, these desert dwellers had vast home ranges that at times took them outside the protection of the park. One old male crossed the park's southern boundary, wandered past the fur seal colony at Cape Cross and loitered around a popular campsite. After complaints from fishermen, the lion was shot. Several years later, another male lion left the Skeleton Coast Park. He was darted 300 km south of Swakopmund in the dry Kuiseb River bed and returned to the park, but soon afterwards his tracks were again found near the Kuiseb delta.

The female lions did not fare much better. One after the other they were shot by herders as they crossed the park's eastern boundaries. The last Skeleton Coast lion was shot in 1984. She was a pregnant female with four almost fully developed cubs inside her. Many thought this was the end for these unique seafood-eating felines, but others were more optimistic as a small population – some say as many as 50 – continued to inhabit the hinterland near Palmwag and Purros to the east of the park.

However, it took 18 long years before lions again settled along the coast, the first a female who gave birth in the dry bed of the Hourasib, only a tantalizing 2 km away from the coast. Then, towards the end of 2003, a small pride of five lions was seen on the beach. While these individuals have yet to learn the ways of the coast's previous inhabitants, it will probably only be a matter of time before they, too, are chasing down white-breasted cormorants or tearing into the blubber of a stranded whale.

BROWN HYENA

The brown hyena, or strandwolf, is one of two hyena species that inhabit southern Africa. The size of a large dog, it is smaller than the spotted hyena. Its distinctive sloping back, dark shaggy brown coat, the white around its neck and shoulders, and the white stripes on the lower parts of its legs make it instantly recognisable. While both species are distributed widely across the southern continent, the spotted hyena dominates in most places. But along the Desert Coast, where the spotted hyena does not occur, the brown hyena is king.

This coastal population lives along the arid reaches of Namibia's west coast, where it relies heavily on marine resources for food. In fact, the sea provides 80% of the brown hyena's diet. The secrets of this species' success are its powerful jaws and formidable teeth, and its ability to digest and obtain energy from almost anything. During the heat of the summer, the strandwolf usually reaches the coast only when darkness has descended over the desert. Most travel to the coast from inland resting places or den sites, often covering distances of more than 30 km in the search for food. Some individuals also spend the day at the coast, lying up in the coastal hummock dunes or roaming the labyrinthine foundations of an old diamond-processing plant.

The particular marine food that makes up the bulk of any brown hyena's diet depends largely on the location of an individual's territory. The owners of territories that include seal colonies subsist almost exclusively on Cape fur seals. Brown hyenas will readily scavenge dead seal pups, as well as adult seals that have washed up on beaches that are down current from the colonies. However, the image of the brown hyena as a beachcombing scavenger is not entirely accurate, since recent evidence shows that it also frequently hunts live juvenile seals. This solitary predator infiltrates the seal colonies on a nightly basis and, with a single crushing bite to the skull, quickly dispatches seal pups. During times of plenty it often eats only the brain and the intestines, leaving the rest to the jackals and seagulls.

Away from fur seal colonies, brown hyenas will feed primarily on marine birds, such as African penguins, various species of cormorants and kelp gulls. While it is believed that most birds are scavenged, it is possible that hunting does occur but has yet to be observed.

Within the boundaries of this forbidden wilderness, the number of brown hyenas is probably higher than anywhere else in its range. Outside this protected realm, persecution for allegedly attacking livestock and pets has resulted in a steep decline in their numbers over the last few decades. In addition, brown hyena parts are also considered valuable *muthi* in traditional African medicines.

The elusive brown hyena is normally only active at night, but may sometimes be seen on cool winter days.

'Brown hyena parts are considered valuable *muthi* in traditional African medicines.'

'Jackals whose territories include Cape fur seal colonies feed on little else.'

CURRENTS of
CONTRAST

THE BLACK-BACKED JACKAL

The black-backed jackal is probably southern Africa's most abundant medium-sized carnivore. It is also the most adaptable and opportunistic predator on the continent.

Characterized by its dark saddle, rufous-tan back and bushy black-tipped tail, this small canine becomes active in the late afternoon, just as the baking desert sun threatens to sink below the horizon. Packs of jackals descend from the coastal hills via paths that have been trodden by countless generations. They roam the coast, mostly keeping to well-defined paths in the lee of low, vegetated hummocks, sheltered from the cold sea breeze. Once at the water's edge, they weave in and out of the drift line searching for edible morsels relinquished by the sea, occasionally venturing deep into the surf to scavenge dead birds and fish.

When the human inhabitants abandoned the mining towns, animals soon took their place. Today jackals and brown hyenas call a casino, a diamond-processing plant and many stately mansions home.

MOISTURE FROM THE SEA

The cold waters of the Benguela current have a profound influence on the terrestrial climate. Moisture-laden air that passes from the cold sea to the hot land does not relinquish any rain. Life-giving water is only available in a different form. On most nights, as the land cools, moisture in the air above the sea condenses and a band of fog

forms. As the night progresses and the earth cools further, the fog bank drifts inland, becoming densest during the early hours of the morning. As the fog condenses, it leaves a blanket of moisture droplets on the sand dunes, gravel plains, plants and animals.

Of the few plants that eke out a living along the Skeleton Coast most rely almost exclusively on fog for their water requirements. While the majority of plants take up the moisture through their roots, some are believed to be able to absorb this moisture directly through their leaves. Animals also rely heavily on fog for water. Jackals will 'drink from the sea' — on early-morning forays, they can be seen licking dew from rocks.

Reptiles such as the palmato gecko, horned adder and sidewinder all drink condensed fog moisture by licking it from their bodies. Insects also drink moisture that condenses on their own bodies. Of all of them, it is the tenebrionid beetle *Onymacris unguicularis* that has by far the most

refined technique. It will climb to the top of high dune crests and adopt a head-down stance while facing the incoming fog. Water condenses on its body's highest point, then trickles down into the beetle's mouth. These beetles can increase body water by over 30% in a single fog-basking session.

A smaller, flying-saucer-shaped relative, *Lepidochora discoidalis*, constructs trenches on the seaward side of sand dunes as soon as fog is imminent. The trenches trap more fog than the surrounding flat sand and the beetles drink the extra water that is trapped on and between the grains of sand.

At night and in the early morning fog condenses on the bodies of both the palmato gecko (TOP RIGHT) and the sidewinder (TOP LEFT). The former licks the moisture from its eyes, the latter from its armour of reptilian scales.

AFRICA'S FORBIDDEN WILDERNESS

The Sperrgebiet, also known as Diamond Area 1, is a vast stretch of coastal desert that lies in the southwestern corner of Namibia, bound by the Orange River to the south and the cold Atlantic Ocean to the west. Here, ferocious winds pick up peppercorn grains of sand, transform them into projectiles, and spray the surroundings with shotgun-like pellets — smoothing stones, hollowing out the bricks of buildings, and stripping cars of paint in a matter of hours.

Diamonds were first discovered here in 1908. Almost immediately, the then German government declared the area a 'prohibited zone' and restricted access to all but mining personnel. Today, almost 100 years later, security in Diamond Area 1 is stricter than ever and penalties for unauthorized entry or the handling of diamonds are high: 200 000 Namibian dollars or imprisonment for up to 15 years, or both. The mining company NAMBED has what is probably the world's most sophisticated privately owned security department. Radar and listening stations are positioned on high peaks and a commando strike force, ready at a moment's notice, makes this the most ferociously guarded stretch of desert in the world.

For over 90 years, strict security and access control have kept the Sperrgebiet a vast wilderness area in an almost perfect state of preservation, home to brown hyenas, oryx, jackals, ostriches, Cape fur seal colonies, rocky shores rich in limpets and mussels, and a rare succulent flora. Immersed in the rugged splendours of this wilderness, it is easy to forget that its preservation has not come without a price. In those regions where mining has occurred, the impact on the environment has been devastating, but such damage is fortunately largely restricted to an area that makes up less than 5% of the Sperrgebiet's vast 26 000 km².

In the mining process, vast quantities of sand are stripped from fossil beaches to expose diamond-bearing gravel, then dumped in heaps at a different location. This creates an undulating, lunar-like landscape vastly different from the original coastal relief. Removal of the topsoil leaves the land barren of all vegetation. In some southern areas, plant growth on these dumps begins to show signs of recovery after 5 to 10 years, while in the north some areas might never recover. Abandoned mining settlements and equipment, some dating back as far as 1910, litter the landscape, but here the desert is carrying out its own cleanup operation. Ghost mining

LEFT AND BELOW: After a laborious sieving and sorting process a small diamond finally comes to light, picked from the gravel by hand.

OPPOSITE: Where bustling diamond-mining towns once thrived, today only ruined buildings remain, carved to near skeletons by the ferocious elements.

Like brown hyenas, jackals whose territories incorporate Cape fur seal colonies feed on little else. During the summer a lone jackal makes short work of a recently born, defenceless seal pup. Then, as the pups grow bigger and stronger, the jackals have to hunt in packs to subdue them. A large pack can even take on an injured adult seal. As supreme opportunists, jackals readily scavenge on the dead pups that wash up in their hundreds during the summer months. Not surprisingly, the density of jackals tends to be much higher around fur seal colonies than elsewhere.

Away from the seal colonies jackals survive mainly on seabirds such as Cape and white-breasted cormorants, terns and African penguins, to name just a few. It is presumed that the majority of these are scavenged from the shoreline, but it is likely that some sick or young individuals are hunted while roosting on beaches. Another black-backed jackal hunting technique is to charge into large flocks of birds in the hope of grabbing a confused individual in the panic. At Sandwich Harbour, some jackals have used this technique to become expert flamingo killers, ambushing at night. In the morning all that remains is a trail of headless torsos and discarded beaks to tell the grizzly tale of the jackals' nocturnal hunting successes.

Jackals will also readily scavenge on beached cetaceans such as heavysides, dusky and bottlenose dolphins, as well as sperm and southern right whales. Seven species of bony fish (including kob, steenbras and barbel) and several species of shark (such as hound and spotted gully shark) are scavenged at the drift line. In some places, jackals have become frequent fish hunters and have been known to enter river mouths and lagoons to catch live mullet trapped in the shallows. At Sandwich Harbour jackals dig up sand eels from the mud during low tide. Marine invertebrates such as rock crabs and brown and white mussels are also part of their diet. These are hunted from intertidal rocks or stolen from kelp gulls. The strangest prey, however, must surely be jellyfish, which the jackals pick up on the drift line in the vicinity of Walvis Bay.

PORCUPINES AND OTHER CREATURES

Not all survivors of the burning shore are as impressive as lions or brown hyenas. There are quite a few smaller, less visible creatures that have also turned to the oceans for food. Porcupines, for instance, are surprisingly common along this coast. On the Lüderitz peninsula they have been observed venturing onto the rocky shores at night, during low tide. There they graze on intertidal seaweeds, effectively becoming – together with limpets – the dominant herbivores of these intertidal rocky shores. To date, however, no one knows how frequent and geographically widespread this behaviour really is.

The yellow mongoose also comes down to the shore on moonless nights and forages among the drift kelp. But it is a skilled hunter, not a vegetarian, and is on the lookout for *Tylos granulatus*, a giant southern African isopod. This 5 cm long burrowing species emerges from the sand on only the darkest of nights.

Finally, the smallest of all the survivors, the tiny golden mole, burrows from the dunes down towards the high-tide mark. From there, it follows the drift-kelp mass, feeding on the larvae of kelp flies that lay their eggs on the rotting kelp.

towns, as they are called, are eroding rapidly from the incessant wind and fog. Every year, more and more buildings crumble and disappear beneath the desert sands. Far from being devoid of life, the ruins provide shelter for wildlife — jackals wander the casino while hyenas roam the processing plant.

Contrary to popular belief, diamonds are not forever. When the deposits eventually run out in the not-so-distant future, a new use will have to be found for Diamond Area 1. The Sperrgebiet could be perfectly integrated into the recently created Ai-Ais and Richtersveld National Park Transfrontier Conservation Area. The Sperrgebiet would become a corridor linking it and the Namib-Naukluft Park, creating one of Africa's largest conservation areas.

SEABIRDS

dwellers of
the ocean sky

CURRENTS of
CONTRAST

f the more than 900 bird species that call southern Africa home, 14 are distinctly different from the rest. Their hunting and foraging grounds are not the deserts, forests or savannas, but the oceans.

Although seabirds spend the majority of their lives soaring above, resting on, or diving beneath the oceans, once a year, when it comes time to breed, they are forced to seek out a prolonged terrestrial existence. At first glance, with thousands of kilometres of coastline to choose from, they seem spoilt for choice, but reality tells a different story. With the exception of a handful of inaccessible cliffs and caves, the mainland coast is entirely unsuitable for nesting. In the past, marauding lions, leopards and scavenging hyenas prevented the birds from successfully raising their young. Today, the culprits are smaller predators such as mongooses and caracals, as well as domestic animals and humans.

Instead, the bulk of southern Africa's seabirds have found their ideal breeding grounds off the west coast, where the Benguela current streams past 26 offshore islands. Some of these are just barren rocks barely projecting above the ocean's surface, while others measure several square kilometres. Ten lie between Cape Agulhas and Lambert's Bay and a further 11 off the coast of Namibia. Four additional islands lie along the warm south coast bathed by the Agulhas current, but situated in an area where localised upwelling of cold, nutrient-rich water frequently occurs.

CAPE GANNETS

Once a year the majority of the world's population of Cape gannets, *Morus capensis*, congregates on six islands to breed and, in late spring, Mercury, Ichaboe, Possession, Bird (Lambert's Bay), Malgas and Bird (Algoa Bay) islands turn a ghostly white as carpets of birds cover them. Malgas Island is the world's largest Cape gannetry, playing host to over 40 000 adult birds, which are packed sardine-like at densities of up to six birds per square metre.

In November, most adults are either in the final stages of incubating eggs or have recently hatched young. A clutch consists of a single egg, which is incubated in a raised turret-shaped nest, tens of thousands of which are densely packed together in the colony. The egg must be incubated for 40 days, and male and female gannets take it in turns to keep it warm by cupping their feet over it.

When the young chick has hatched, its parents alternate the task of going to sea and collecting food for the ravenous youngster. Depending on their age, gannet chicks receive three to five feedings per day, and up to 500 g of fish are needed per feeding to appease the new arrival's appetite.

Weighing up to 3.5 kg, the Cape gannet is a heavy bird and it needs a long runway to become airborne, especially on windless days. As these runways must be wide and free of obstacles, they always lie at the edges of the colony. Hesitant at first, the gannet will walk onto the runway, turn into the prevailing wind and begin running, flapping its wings hard and heaving itself slowly into the air. Soon it soars high above the colony and its in-built navigational compass guides it out to the open sea. Its 2 m wingspan allows it to travel great distances to seek out schools of fish. By attaching a small satellite transmitter to a female Cape gannet, scientists gained insight into where these birds go when foraging at sea. The transmitter revealed that on a single foraging trip this female travelled well in excess of 400 km, crisscrossing the waters of the continental shelf.

On windy days boulders at the ocean's edge become launching pads as Cape gannets, *Morus capensis*, take to the sky and soar effortlessly above the colony. (LEFT) Once a year Malgas is covered in a snowy blanket as Cape gannets gather here to breed.

Cape gannets catch fish in a manner so spectacular that it is scarcely rivalled by any other species. Having spotted their prey from a height of up to 30 m, they dip steeply into a gravity-driven plunge. A split second before entering the water, they stretch their wings backwards, allowing the bill to penetrate the water like an arrowhead at a speed of more than 100 km per hour. They can dive to depths of up to 5 m, leaving a metre-high spout of water in their wake. The chosen fish is seized during the dive and, by the time the bird surfaces 5–10 seconds later, has already been swallowed. The feeding frenzy only ends when the school of fish has suffered heavy losses and dispersed, making it harder for the gannets to catch them. In the past, pilchards were

ABOVE: After much begging from the chick, the parent regurgitates freshly caught fish directly into the youngster's throat.

the Cape gannets' primary target, but when this stock collapsed due to over-fishing, the birds switched to hunting anchovies and scavenging offal from trawlers.

Returning to the colony after a feeding trip, their stomachs full of fish, gannets circle at a low altitude, flying in a holding pattern not unlike that of an airplane awaiting permission to touch down. A special landing call is emitted, known only to the gannet's mate, who responds with its own unique vocal call. The returnee then homes in on this target. Most birds land clumsily, dropping out of the sky with an almighty thump right next to their partners. After an initial violent reaction, an intricate and fascinating greeting display follows. The birds begin fencing. Pairs stand abreast of one

When there is little or no wind, takeoffs are anything but graceful. Gannets hurtle down long runways at the edges of the colony until their wings provide enough lift for them to take flight.

another, wings outspread, clashing their bills against each other and intermittently sweeping their heads down over the necks of their partners. They call loudly throughout this performance, which can last anything from one to twenty minutes.

The young chicks, covered in downy white feathers, are hungry and will often interrupt these performances with incessant begging for food. Whining in a high-pitched squeak, they will batter their parents' bills with their own. Feeding takes place in a mouth-to-mouth fashion: the chick inserts its bill deep into the adult's gape and fish is regurgitated directly into its throat.

By February, the colony has been transformed from a sea of pure white to one speckled like a Dalmatian, since most of the youngsters have developed their sleek silver-mottled plumage. By this time, their parents have had enough of their offspring's insatiable appetite and all feeding has stopped. The young gannets now have 10 days to learn to fly and capture food before their energy reserves run dry. The youngsters gather at the fringes of the colony, where they exercise their wings, flapping hard while simultaneously hopping into

the air, briefly experiencing what it is like to defy gravity and become airborne. Driven by hunger, the young gannets venture into the water, where they congregate in small groups, rafting together, flapping their wings, taking off, and ending their short flights in shallow practice plunge dives. Their flying abilities improve and finally they take off and leave for the rich fishing grounds of West Africa's Gulf of Guinea. Only after three years do they return to their original colony to breed for the first time.

LEFT: About to face the toughest test of its young life, this juvenile gannet will need to strengthen its wings as much as possible before attempting its first flight.

TOP: Cape gannet chicks hatch during the hot summer months and are vulnerable to heat stress. To prevent them from baking to death the parents rise from the nest to fan cool air onto their young.

ABOVE: Juvenile gannets sport a downy feather coat for several months, a time during which they can weigh more than their parents. Once they lose their down, they also lose enough weight to start flying.

SEABIRDS
dwellers of the ocean sky

THE KILLING SEALS

The annual Cape gannet breeding spectacular on Malgas Island attracts the attention of a motley band of Cape fur seals. Their appearance in these waters in February coincides with the young gannets' early attempts at flight. The seals linger in the background, patrolling the open water about 100 m away from the bay in which the juveniles gather to practise their takeoff and flying skills. Many of their initial flights are short, covering only several metres and lasting just a few seconds. As their skills increase, however, they fly further and further out to sea until either their energy reserves are sapped, or the winds fail them. These birds then have to raft in deep water, waiting for the wind to pick up again or their strength to return.

This is just the sort of situation for which the seals are waiting. They dive quickly, disappear from sight and approach the unsuspecting victim from below. Without warning, a seal will surface just inches from a young gannet. Striking it hard like a torpedo, its jaws grip the bird's backside, shaking it vigorously and slapping it repeatedly onto the water's surface. The seal then turns away, presumably to escape the bird's sharp bill, then attacks again and again as the wounded bird desperately tries to flee. It takes several attacks for the seal to eat away all the nutritious fat. The mortally wounded bird is then left to die and drift at the mercy of the current. Many dead or dying birds are washed into the shallows or rock pools, where armies of crayfish and whelks descend upon the carcasses. A few days later, only a skeleton remains to tell the grisly tale of the young bird's demise.

During February 1990, Cape fur seals killed a minimum of 21 juvenile gannets per day, taking out at least 2.5% of the fledglings from that breeding season. Certain seals are more proficient bird killers than others, and one very adept bull seal made 61 gannet kills in under five days. There have even been reports of very bold individuals landing on the island and taking gannets directly from within the colony.

It is not only Cape gannets that fall victim to predatory seals. At Dyer Island, for example, seals regularly feed on Cape cormorants and African penguins using a technique called 'degloving'. This entails stripping the bird's pelt, leaving the flesh and bones exposed. Seals killed more than 842 African penguins in a 12-month period at Dyer Island, while at Lambert's Bay 4% of adult penguins are lost to seals annually.

Predation is not the only negative impact seals have on seabird populations. There is also intense competition for breeding space on some islands. Seals have already displaced all or most seabirds from at least six islands, and a recent dramatic decrease in the number of bank cormorants on Mercury Island can be attributed partly to the presence of seals. Cape fur seal populations were depleted by decades of extensive harvesting and are now beginning to recover, and the competition between birds and seals is expected to increase.

CORMORANTS

The Cape cormorant, *Phalacrocorax capensis*, a small blackish bird with bright yellow facial skin and a green iris, is southern Africa's most abundant seabird. A count carried out in the late 1990s yielded around 72 000 breeding pairs distributed across more than 70 colonies between northern Namibia and Algoa Bay in South Africa. Dyer Island off the southwest Cape coast is South Africa's most important breeding site, with more than 35 000 Cape cormorants congregating here annually.

Their breeding peak is between October and February, when clutches of one to five eggs are laid and incubated for almost a month. Young Cape cormorants leave the nest after about five weeks and fledglings are able to swim before they can fly some three months after hatching.

The Cape cormorant is one of the few seabirds that also frequently breed on cliffs and one such colony can be found at Cape Point. It has recently been discovered that chacma baboons scale these cliffs and feed on their eggs, perhaps even hatchlings. Another unusual predator of Cape cormorants is the great white pelican, which has been known to gobble up quite a few chicks on the guano platforms at Walvis Bay and on Dassen Island.

Adult Cape cormorants generally feed in large flocks, targeting surface-shoaling fish less than 70 km from the shore. In the past, the mainstay of their diet were pilchards but after those stocks collapsed due to over-fishing, anchovies and bearded gobies became the most important food items.

The bank cormorant, *Phalacrocorax neglectus*, is distributed from Hollams Bird Island (halfway between Lüderitz and Walvis Bay) to Quoin Point just west of Cape Agulhas. Its range broadly coincides with the distribution of the bamboo kelp, *Ecklonia maxima*, as the South African population of bank cormorants hunts almost exclusively in these kelp beds. They can dive to a depth of 28 m, with an average foraging dive lasting about 45 seconds. They feed mainly on rock lobsters. After the legs and antennae are detached and discarded at the surface, the lobsters are swallowed headfirst. Klipfish, blennies and rock suckers are also important prey items.

The foraging ecology along the species' northern range is very different, as these bank cormorants feed in offshore waters and primarily hunt pelagic gobies. The species' breeding behaviour also differs significantly between South Africa and Namibia. In the south they nest in small colonies of fewer than 50 pairs, while in the north more than 6 000 pairs nest together on Mercury and Ichaboe islands

In late afternoon and early evening Cape cormorants return to their colonies and congregate in large numbers to roost together for the night.

TOP: Bank cormorants have experienced significant population declines in recent years and are now among southern Africa's rarest and most threatened seabirds.

TOP RIGHT: Cape cormorant on nest with chick. On hot summer days, cormorants regurgitate water onto their chicks to cool them down.

ABOVE: A crowned cormorant chick begs for food.

alone, making up 75% of the total population. Bank cormorants nesting on Namibia's offshore islands also have to contend with a predator that is largely absent in the south. Killer whales (Orcas) have been known to hunt bank cormorants and, during 1986, two killer whales killed over 250 juveniles at Mercury Island.

The crowned cormorant, *Phalacrocorax coronatus*, is the smallest of the marine cormorants. It also has the smallest population, consisting of under 8 000 individuals. This species, with its distinctive black crest on the forehead and its piercing red iris, breeds throughout the year but displays a distinct peak over the summer months. There are 37 breeding colonies between Walvis Bay and Cape Agulhas. A clutch most commonly consists of three eggs that hatch after an incubation period of no less than 23 days. After hatching, the chicks are fed for at least 30 days, becoming independent at between 45 and 60 days of age. Crowned cormorants feed mainly by pursuit diving, swimming underwater as they hunt bottom-dwelling fishes such as klipfish in the shallow waters of kelp beds and rocky shores.

The white-breasted cormorant, *Phalacrocorax carbo*, is southern Africa's largest cormorant. A black bird with a distinctive white patch stretching from chin to breast, it inhabits both marine and fresh waters. The coastal population breeds from the Kunene River mouth in northern Namibia to Morgan Bay in the Eastern Cape and consists of around 8 000 individuals. In the Western Cape, breeding occurs mainly between April and December, while on islands in Algoa Bay it peaks between October and July. The clutch commonly consists of three to four eggs that are incubated by both parents for around 28 days. Both parents feed the chick, regurgitating food directly into its open mouth. On hot days they will also regurgitate water onto the chick's back to prevent it from overheating. Young white-breasted cormorants fledge when they are between 49 and 56 days old. Feeding is by pursuit diving and hunts are either carried out alone or in groups and fish such as horse mackerel, klipfish and mullet fall prey. Fish is swallowed headfirst, and the species has been known to swallow small stones, possibly to facilitate diving.

OCEAN FERTILIZERS

Seabirds are well known for being important structuring agents of the marine environment, as they are major predators of fish and other marine resources. They also influence their surroundings in other, often unexpected, ways.

Bird droppings, collectively termed guano, are very rich in nutrients, particularly in nitrogen and phosphorus. On an almost daily basis rain, wind, sea spray and waves wash guano from the bird colonies into the sea, fertilizing a narrow band of ocean around each of the islands. Microscopic floating plants called phytoplankton thrive in this nutrient-rich environment. This, in turn, attracts high numbers of equally tiny floating animals called zooplankton. When sea conditions are right, swarms of red-banded jellyfish gather in the shallows to feed on this plentiful microscopic life.

The rocky reefs that slope away from the islands, the intertidal zones in particular, are also heavily affected by the presence of guano. The rate at which seaweeds grow is often determined by the availability of nutrients; as a result of this guano-enhanced nutrient status, seaweeds from the shores of bird islands grow at much faster rates than those from the mainland. Often, seaweeds will grow more quickly than an army of grazers can eat them, and algae mats often dominate bird islands' rocky shores. These support large populations of small crab-like creatures called amphipods, an important food source for many smaller wading birds, such as turnstones and sandpipers. Limpets, a type of mollusc, are the 'antelopes' of the rocky shore algae 'savannas' and they, too, benefit from the birds' presence, attaining much larger sizes because of the copious quantities of algae available.

ABOVE: A white-breasted cormorant makes a 'nutrient' contribution to the sea.

RIGHT: Ponds of guano accumulate in depressions until heavy rains or stormy seas wash them into the ocean.

AFRICAN PENGUINS

The African penguin, *Spheniscus demersus*, the continent's only flightless seabird, is known to breed at 27 localities from Hollams Bird Island in central Namibia to Bird Island in Algoa Bay. The four largest penguin colonies – Dassen, St Croix, Robben and Bird islands – are situated in South African waters and collectively they are home to 90% of the African penguin population.

In South Africa the breeding peak occurs between February and June. African penguins nest predominantly in burrows dug in guano or sand, or in crevices between rocks. A clutch of up to two eggs is laid and the parents take turns to incubate them for about 40 days. Once the young penguin chicks have hatched, their parents ply them with fish for about 50 days.

Unlike the other 13 species of seabird, all of which travel to and from their feeding grounds on the wing, African penguins have to make these journeys by swimming. Most penguins leave their respect-ive colonies early in the morning and head out to sea to locate patchily distributed schools of Cape anchovy, horse mackerel and round herring. Foraging trips can last anything from 10 hours (after which the penguins return to their colonies in the evening) to 170-hour feeding marathons covering distances of nearly 300 km.

Penguins dive to capture their food and adult birds in prime condition find it relatively easily to outpace all their prey species. Less experienced juvenile birds generally swim significantly more slowly than adults and cannot outpace faster species such as round herring, so it is believed they target primarily larval and juvenile fishes.

High swimming speeds can only be achieved by maintaining a sleek coat of feathers, which must be renewed once a year. Before moulting, the penguins will spend up to 35 days at sea fattening up in preparation for their ordeal on land, which can last about 21 days. Once the moult is complete, the birds spend up to 42 days at sea feeding to replace their fat reserves.

An African penguin, *Spheniscus demersus*, engulfed in sea spray. It is the most aquatic of all seabirds, and the only one that cannot take to the skies.

CURRENTS of
CONTRAST

GULLS

Of the three species of gull that occur in southern Africa only the kelp gull and Hartlaub's gull feed predominantly on marine organisms. The third species, the grey-headed gull, breeds inland and only rarely hunts in the sea.

The kelp gull, *Larus dominicanus*, is a large species with a distinctive black back and yellow bill. It is distributed between Luanda in Angola and Ilha Inhaca in Mozambique, though breeding only occurs between Cape Cross in Namibia and the Riet River in the Eastern Cape. In the late 1970s and 1980s, the breeding population consisted of around 22 398 birds, of which just under 50% made their homes on Dassen and Schaapen islands. Kelp gulls are known to nest at 52 locations, over half of which are on the mainland.

Kelp gulls have perfected the art of cracking mollusc shells. This gastropod, *Oxysteles,* is being dropped onto a rocky area from great heights.

White pelicans and flamingos in evening light.

Kelp gulls feed prolifically on rocky shore molluscs, but as their bills are not strong enough to break mussel shells, these gulls have developed a unique way of cracking them. Kelp gulls will fly as far as 0.5 km to find a suitable rocky spot, where they drop the mussels from a height of several metres to break the shells. Through trial and error, kelp gulls have learned to drop mussels onto rocks and not onto sand or over water. While 63% of mussels dropped onto rocks crack sufficiently for the gulls to feed on them, only around 25% are cracked on sand and all mussels dropped into water are lost. Kelp gulls will also use rock substitutes as drop sites, such as roads, jetties, breakwaters and even the roofs of houses and cars. The velocity of a mussel on impact depends on the height from which it is dropped, so the higher a gull flies before dropping it, the more likely it is the mussel will crack. But the gull also runs a far greater risk of losing its meal – the higher the gull flies the longer it will take for it to reach the ground, giving other gulls the chance to swoop in and steal its prey. Kelp gulls have also been observed using the same technique on various species of gastropod molluscs (marine snails).

Hartlaub's gull, *Larus hartlaubii*, is smaller than the kelp gull and can easily be identified in its breeding plumage by its distinctive pale grey hood. Breeding occurs between January and October and has been reported from 48 localities between Swakopmund and Dyer Island. There are an estimated 12 000 breeding pairs, 28% of which nest at Robben Island. Near human habitation, Hartlaub's gulls are attracted to rubbish dumps, while out at sea they scavenge on discards from fishing vessels. It is believed that before the arrival of humans they fed on small crustaceans and fish that came to the surface at night.

TERNS

The roseate tern, *Sterna dougallii*, is southern Africa's rarest breeding seabird. It is only known to nest at two locations, namely Bird Island in Algoa Bay (240–250 pairs) and Dyer Island (10–20 pairs). Outside southern Africa, the roseate tern is widely distributed, and the 90 000-strong world population is therefore not globally threatened.

The species is essentially monogamous. Pair bonds are formed just prior to arrival at the colonies in May and often last for several seasons. Breeding occurs in densely packed colonies and both sexes incubate and care for the young. Roseate terns feed in flocks up to 100 strong, and catch small shoaling fish by plunge diving in shallow water.

The swift tern, *Sterna bergii*, is a common resident of the southern African coastline and its distribution extends well north, east and west of the subcontinent's biogeographic boundaries. Some 6 000 breeding pairs are restricted to 27 locations between Swakopmund in Namibia and Stag Island in Algoa Bay, South Africa. The species' non-breeding distribution extends from Luanda in Angola to Kosi Bay in KwaZulu-Natal. During any given year, breeding tends to occur only at six or seven sites out of 27. Sites between Saldhana Bay and Cape Town are usually more frequently occupied. Nesting occurs predominantly on offshore islands, with breeding activity tending to peak in late summer. By early autumn most youngsters have fledged. Most fledglings leave the colony with at least one parent and the majority of them will travel up along the east coast. The diet of the swift tern consists primarily of pelagic shoaling fish.

The Damara tern, *Sterna balaenarum*, is the only southern African seabird that breeds exclusively on the mainland. The total population hovers around 13 500 birds and 98% of them breed along the coast of northern Namibia, in the dune fields adjacent to the Namib Desert. Smaller breeding colonies and pockets of isolated breeders also occur in South Africa, where 125 breeding pairs are distributed over nest sites in the Alexander Dunefields, Port Nolloth, DeMond and Struisbaai.

Damara terns nest between October and February and monogamous pairs return to the same nest sites year after year. One to two eggs are laid in a shallow scrape and the chicks hatch after about 25 days. In Namibia, black-backed jackal and gull predation are major causes of egg and chick mortality. Damara terns fledge after 23–28 days and often form nurseries in the intertidal zone, where they are fed small fish by their parents.

Adult terns will typically dive and spear small fish swimming just below the surface. There is little in the way of detailed information on this species' diet, but needle fish, small mullet and larval blennies have been identified from stomach contents.

At the end of March the surviving fledglings depart for the west coast of Africa, where strong upwelling conditions off the Ghanaian coast create good feeding conditions as fish move inshore to spawn.

GREAT WHITE PELICANS

Great white pelicans, *Pelecanus onocrotalus*, breed at only two marine locations along the southern African coast, namely at Dassen Island and on the bird rock guano platform near Walvis Bay in Namibia. Some 650 pairs presently nest on Dassen Island, with another 200 or so pairs occurring at Walvis Bay. The species breeds during spring and summer.

Traditionally, great white pelicans are fish eaters who often form co-operative groups to herd fish into dense shoals to facilitate foraging. In Namibia, they also turned to shadowing fishermen and staking out fish cleaning areas in the hope of scavenging a meal. Pelicans on Dassen Island and Bird Rock Guano Platform added an even more unorthodox food source to their diet when, in the 1990s, they were observed feeding on kelp gull and cormorant chicks. They were seen to spread out in a line and walk through the breeding areas, catching large numbers of chicks in their oversized bills.

THREATS TO SEABIRDS

As we move into the first decade of the 21st century, four species of southern African seabirds are listed as near threatened, one as endangered and three as vulnerable. The populations of most species are in serious decline and there is little doubt that seabirds are in trouble.

The African penguin perhaps best illustrates the precarious situation of seabirds. At the start of the 20th century, southern Africa was home to over two million individuals, but by the mid-1950s only some 300 000 remained. Today, only about 179 000 adult birds are left, and 10 out of 37 breeding colonies have been abandoned. On some Namibian islands the penguin population has declined by up to 75% and if this trend continues there will be no wild African penguins left by 2070. On one occasion even Mother Nature seemed to have it in for the species. When lightning struck an old railway line used to move heavily laden carts of guano to the jetty on Dyer Island, thousands of penguins are said to have been electrocuted.

A group of great white pelicans squabbles over scraps scavenged from a fish-cleaning station along the Namibian coast.

Workers mining seabird guano on an island off the Namibian coast during the early 20th century.

A pitchfork left behind during the guano rush serves as a reminder that Malgas Island's seabirds, today part of the West Coast National Park, were not always protected.

Bank cormorants, too, have experienced a dramatic decline in recent years, and surveys have revealed that the number of nests has decreased by more than 25% in 25 out of 44 colonies. Similarly, there were about one million Cape cormorants in the early 1970s, but that number fell dramatically to just over 120 000 pairs by the mid-1980s. The total population of Cape gannets has shrunk by 54% since 1956.

The list of possible causes for these and other dramatic seabird population declines is lengthy, and includes the direct exploitation of bird products, such as eggs and guano, and the loss of their prey base through over-fishing, to name just two. In the case of the African penguin, the cause of the initial decrease was almost certainly the harvesting of eggs and scraping of guano, while further declines in the 1980s were due to a collapse of fish stocks. As if this besieged flightless seabird is not already staring down the barrel of a gun, major oil spills are at present threatening to bring the African penguin's proposed date with extinction forward by several decades.

EXPLOITATION

The bones of seabirds are regularly found in prehistoric coastal middens, suggesting that during the late Stone Age southern Africa's indigenous people ate Cape gannets, Cape cormorants and African penguins. It is likely that the bulk of seabird remains found in midden deposits were the result of beachcombing activities, though there is some evidence of a more proactive exploitation strategy. The Topnar people of the Kuiseb delta on the Namibian coast were said to have used logs to raft out to seabird islands and sandbanks where they harvested eggs and hunted seabirds. In prehistory, seabirds were valued not only as food but also in the manufacture of clothes. Capes made from penguin skins have been recovered from archaeological excavations in the vicinity of Lüderitz.

In more modern times, the exploitation of seabirds has been limited to their eggs and guano. The exploitation of seabird eggs, especially those of penguins, was big business. Between 1900 and 1930 alone, 13 million eggs were collected and even as recently as 1956 the egg harvest totalled more than 125 000. Egg harvesting was finally ended in 1969, but only after the penguin population had experienced dramatic declines.

The quest for penguin eggs also negatively affected another species of seabird – the kelp gull also became a victim of persecution. In colonies with little or no human disturbance, there is little egg or hatchling predation by kelp gulls, but in seabird breeding colonies with high levels of disturbance, the eggs and chicks of penguins and other birds often fall prey to opportunistic kelp gulls. So, to keep penguin egg numbers high for a profitable harvest, kelp gulls were shot or poisoned and their eggs destroyed – a practice that was still carried out by some island keepers as recently as 1978.

Sealers were the first people to visit the Benguela bird islands. It was one of them, a man named Benjamin Morrell, who put these islands on the map. In his adventure travelogue published in 1842, he commented on the island of Ichaboe off the coast of Namibia, and in passing described guano deposits up to 23 m thick. Just a year later, 400 ships lay at anchor at Ichaboe and a shantytown had sprung up along the island's desolate shore to house guano scrapers. Chaos ensued as people killed each other over bird droppings and the rights to harvest them. To quell the great guano war, two British warships were dispatched to bring order and control the harvest, but by then guano that had taken tens of thousands of years to accumulate had been removed, leaving nothing but bare rock.

A layer of guano is important primarily as a substance in which penguins can construct their nesting burrows, but other seabirds were also affected by the constant disturbance. In subsequent years, the harvest was more controlled, but only later did conservationists succeed in ending it. For just over 150 years humans reaped the benefits of the so-called 'white gold' until finally the last bag of fertilizer was filled in 1996 on Lambert's Bay's Bird Island.

OIL POLLUTION

Just a stone's throw from Malgas Island lies the port of Saldanha, home to one of Africa's largest oil terminals. Every year, 25 supertankers dock here, transferring 15 million barrels of oil – 375 barrels for every Cape gannet on the island. In addition, several hundred cargo and bulk carriers, which also hold vast quantities of bunker fuel oil, enter the port every year, passing through a narrow shipping channel within 100 m of Malgas Island.

At the current rate of shipping traffic, the statistical probability of an oil spill exceeding seven tons is one every 21 years. A proposed increase in traffic will increase this figure to one every 14 years. On 23 June 2001, the first major oil spill of the new millennium occurred when the bulk ore carrier MV *Treasure* sank 8 km off the coast of Cape Town, spilling over 1 100 tons of fuel oil close to the seabird havens of Robben and Dassen islands.

Together, these islands are home to 40% of the world's population of African penguins. The African penguin has been classified as vulnerable to extinction and its flightless nature makes it the species most commonly affected by oil pollution. In response to this environmental catastrophe, the biggest ever coastal wildlife evacuation and cleanup was initiated. Almost 20 000 oiled birds were cleaned and rehabilitated; of these, only about 2 000 died. Oil continued to escape from the stricken vessel so 19 000 unoiled penguins were captured, airlifted off the two islands and transported almost 1 000 km east to Port Elizabeth.

Penguins seem to possess a similar instinct to homing pigeons and they immediately began their long swim westwards. Scientists predicted the birds would arrive back at their island homes within two weeks, thereby giving cleanup crews enough time to pump the remainder of the oil from the vessel and clean up the island's soiled shores. The cleanup operation saved the lives of thousands of birds.

Some 120 million tons of crude oil pass along the Benguela coast every year, a region with some of the most severe weather in the world. It is simply a matter of time before we once again see African penguins' lives threatened by the sticky blackness of crude oil.

Another dawn greets Malgas Island. These buildings are all that remain of the guano-mining infrastructure. Some were recently renovated and are today used by scientists and field rangers.

Shortly after the *Treasure* oil spill, the *Ikan Tanda* ran aground off Scarborough in 2001, nearly becoming South Africa's next big seabird disaster.

COMMERCIAL FISHERIES

For decades the South African fishing industry has been claiming that seabirds cost them vast quantities of commercially valuable fish every year. This accusation went so far that in 1953 some politicians were pushing to end the protection of all seabirds and begin the systematic destruction of their eggs in important breeding colonies.

In southern African waters as a whole, Cape gannets consume less than 1% of the adult anchovy biomass. So, while some species of seabirds are indeed important predators of commercially valuable fish in southern Africa, they are not a threat to commercial fishing interests. Until the 1960s, pilchards were the fish of choice for humans and birds, but following the collapse of this stock due to over-fishing, purse seine fishers – who use a net to encircle schools of fish – began instead to harvest the smaller but more abundant anchovies – and many seabirds made the same dietary switch.

In fact, it is the commercial fishing industry that is a major threat to the continued existence of seabirds. Seabird numbers are known to fluctuate in accordance with the abundance of their prey, so the fate of the fish is closely linked to their health. Many of the dramatic declines in seabird populations in the past can be attributed to fishing vessels netting fish right out of their bills, so to speak. What few commercial fishermen realise is that seabirds can actually bring them benefits. Dietary data on African penguins and Cape cormorants, for instance, has revealed important information about the rate of recruitment in anchovies and other fish stocks. Seabirds can even indicate the health of fish stocks and thus serve as effective biological warning systems, with the ability to predict the fishermen's fortunes for the upcoming fishing season.

But it is not all doom and gloom for southern African seabirds. Penguin surveys conducted as recently as 2001 indicate that the population could actually be increasing for the first time from an all-time low of about 26 000 breeding pairs in 1998 to between 46 000 and 56 000 breeding pairs in 2002. These recent increases are believed to be the result of population increases of the penguin's two most important prey items, the pilchard and the anchovy. There may yet be hope for this tuxedo-clad inhabitant of the Benguela and its relatives.

BLUE WATER ... HOOKS OF DEATH

Pelagic seabirds are creatures of the open ocean that are only seen near the coast when strong winter storms blow them off course. They also do not breed in southern Africa, having instead chosen the lonely sub-Antarctic, like South Africa's Prince Edward Island, for their nesting grounds. Large colonies of wandering, grey-headed albatrosses, northern and southern giant petrels, and white-chinned petrels occur here.

These high-value seafoods are targeted by long-line fishing fleets that operate in the waters of the southern Indian Ocean and the sub-Antarctic islands. It is estimated that they set over 100 million hooks annually. Many albatrosses and petrels drown when they get hooked while attempting to scavenge the bait.

Fortunately, such mortalities are easy to reduce. It is possible to eliminate bird bycatch by implementing measures such as only setting lines at night, putting up bird-scaring lines, using weighted thawed baits that sink faster, and by not dumping offal while fishing, which attracts more birds. Today most legal operations follow these guidelines, but there are still many pirate fishing vessels that carry a heavy seabird bycatch burden.

Long-lining is not only taking a toll on pelagic seabirds, but also results in the bycatch of large numbers of sharks. Due to the high prices paid for shark fins in Asian countries, this bycatch is almost as lucrative as the target species. Despite widespread outcry and worldwide protests many crews still slice the fins off live sharks and wastefully dump the carcass at sea. This is done to optimize space in the freezer holds of such vessels. While shark finning is illegal in South African waters, it is perfectly within the limits of the law to land shark fins taken from sharks outside South Africa's territorial waters at South African ports. Every day thousands of shark fins can be seen drying in the Cape Town docks.

This petrel drowned when it became hooked while scavenging the bait from a longline.

SOUTHERN RIGHT WHALE

the journey

W hen early seafarers rounded the Cape of Storms more than 500 years ago, southern right whales were very abundant. Thousands, if not tens of thousands, visited the many sheltered bays during the winter months. The population was so large that enough whales died of natural causes to allow the indigenous people of the Cape to meet a large proportion of their food requirements by scavenging their meat and blubber.

Today perhaps one or two carcasses wash up on our beaches annually – a fraction of what must have sustained the Khoisan. On a calm winter's day, perhaps a dozen or so of the V-shaped blows so characteristic of this species may be spotted out at sea, but nothing like the hundreds that must have misted up the air when Vasco da Gama sailed these waters. Yet there are more southern right whales in southern African waters than at any other point in the last 150 years. Targeted by major whaling campaigns in the early 1800s, the species had been decimated by 1835 and was on the verge of extinction towards the end of the 19th century.

This chapter tells the story of two journeys – one the great migratory voyage that takes the southern right whale from Antarctic waters to the seas off southern Africa and back again; the other is a journey back in time, through the whaling era, to the end of the 19th century when the species stood on the brink of extinction and from then on to the beginnings of a stable population.

Callosities, raised growths of roughened skin, are a distinguishing feature of southern right whales.

LEFT: Southern right whales were first hunted in the shadow of Table Mountain just over 300 years ago.

CLASSIFICATION AND CHARACTERISTICS

All whales are classed as cetaceans, and belong to one of two distinct suborders, the toothed whales (Odontoceti) and the baleen whales (Mysticeti). Toothed whales are active hunters who find their prey using echo-location and feed with their teeth, whereas baleen whales lack teeth. Instead, their mouths are giant living strainers that comb plankton from the water.

The southern right whale, *Eubalaena australis*, is among the largest of the baleen whales. It is dark blue to black in colour, with an irregular white patch on the ventral side. Some calves are born all white but normally darken over time. Southern right whales can reach a ripe old age of more than 50 years and when fully grown can weigh 58 tons and reach a length of 17 m. The species lacks a dorsal fin and the flippers are stubby and spade-like in shape. The blow of the southern right is very distinctive: the spout forms a V-shaped fan up to 6 m high, with the left blow usually somewhat higher than the right.

ABOVE: The southern right whale is inquisitive, often coming up to boats and eyeballing its occupants at close range.

BELOW: The southern right whale's blow is instantly recognisable by its distinctive V-shape.

Southern right whales have unusual growths of raised, roughened skin on their heads and around the eyes and jaw – the same places where humans have hair. These growths are called callosities and the biggest one around the head is called the bonnet. The fact that male whales have more scratch marks and more abundant callosities than females has caused some scientists to speculate that the bonnet could be used as a small horn during male fighting bouts. Each individual southern right whale has a pattern of callosities that is unique, much like fingerprints in humans. Cetacean biologist Dr Peter Best of the University of Pretoria's Marine Mammal Research Institute has been using these markings to identify and keep track of individual animals for more than 30 years. Almost everything we know about the southern African population of right whales comes from this meticulous study.

EVOLUTION: WALKING WITH WHALES

Ironically, life on planet Earth evolved in the oceans. Animals and plants only colonized land 350 million years ago. Among the early mammals that thrived on land were mesonychids, a family of primitive four-legged ungulates believed to have lived near estuaries and lagoons. While the mesonychids were by no means whales, the oldest known cetacean is a direct descendant of this group. *Pakicetus*, whose 50-million-year-old fossilised skull was discovered in the foothills of the Himalayas, was a small, furry-hoofed carnivore that resembled a cross between a sea lion and a jackal rather than a whale. Only its narrow cetacean-like skull, displaying a long muzzle and teeth designed to hunt fish, reveals its true position on the evolutionary cetacean ladder.

Still largely terrestrial, *Pakicetus* hunted along river courses and in shallow seas, leading a rather amphibious existence not unlike that of a modern-day Cape clawless otter. Over millions of years, *Pakicetus* evolved via many transitional forms into the whales we encounter today. With every form, the nostril migrated further away from the

tip of the snout until it reached the top of the head, eventually forming a blowhole that allowed the animal to breathe without having to lift its snout above water. The front limbs transformed into flippers, while the hind legs became greatly reduced until they disappeared from sight. The hind leg remnants in modern whales are tiny and internal, serving as an anchor for the muscles of the genitalia.

All fur was lost and a thick layer of insulating blubber acquired. The outer ears gradually disappeared; instead, sound was transmitted to the inner ears via a specialised fat pad in the jawbone. Crucial metabolic changes also occurred, the most monumental of which was the loss of dependence on fresh drinking water. The only evidence of this transformation from hoofed, jackal-like, terrestrial carnivore to whale lies in the whale's DNA, which has retained the genes that code for visible hind legs. During the whaling era, ships would occasionally land whales with leg-like appendages protruding from the flank, an occurrence known as a genetic throwback, or atavism.

The early whales of prehistory were all toothed – baleen whales only made their debut about 35 million years ago, but in addition to rudimentary baleen plates they also had teeth. As a token from that prehistoric time, modern baleen whales still grow teeth while in the womb, but these are reabsorbed before birth.

The right whales first appeared on the cetacean family tree 22 million years ago, and the bulk of fossils found date back to 10 million years ago. Fossil finds point to the fact that all species of right whale evolved in the southern hemisphere. It appears that during the last Ice Age some individuals migrated northwards, later splitting up and separating into two new species, the North Atlantic and Pacific right whale. The right whale population that remained in the southern hemisphere became the southern right whale, but unlike its northern cousins, it is also found in populations off South America and Australia/New Zealand that did not evolve into separate species. Movement between southern hemisphere populations is not well understood and is believed to be uncommon, but individuals from South America have been sighted in the mid-Atlantic, and mid-Atlantic individuals have been sighted off the South African coast.

THE JOURNEY

The journey of the southern right whale begins in the untamed wilderness of the Southern Ocean and ends along the southern African coast..

DECEMBER — MAY

In the southern summer, the waters between 40 and 50 degrees South are 10 to 20 times richer than those around southern Africa. A combination of high nutrient concentrations and 24-hour sunlight stimulates rapid phytoplankton growth. This, in turn, attracts vast amounts of krill, small semi-transparent shrimps and various species of small pelagic crustaceans called copepods.

Southern right whales plough slowly through these dense swarms, their mouths arched wide open, letting as many as 540 baleen plates

filter out vast quantities of zooplankton. These narrow plates hang on the sides of the upper jaw; each is more than 2 m long and densely packed with very fine sieve-like hairs that allow only water to pass through. Southern right whales usually feed on or just below the surface, but have been known occasionally to follow concentrations of copepods to the seabed. They need to consume around 1.5 tons of food daily and can swallow up to two tons during a good day's foraging.

In March, when summer draws to a close, the water cools and severe storms become more frequent. The days grow shorter, phytoplankton productivity decreases drastically, and as the sea ice forms the zooplankton retreat beneath it. These environmental changes are believed to be cues that signal the beginning of the southern right whale's journey from the Antarctic to the southwest coast of South Africa, across more than 2 000 km of vast featureless ocean, devoid of any landmarks.

Scientists are still unsure how whales find their breeding and mating grounds, but magnetite has been found in the tissues that surround the brain. It has been suggested that they are able to use the Earth's geomagnetic field to navigate along magnetic gradients.

Seabed features and the smell and taste of fresh water discharged from rivers on the continent might also play a role in route finding. Predominantly pregnant females, mature females and males wanting to mate make the trip. Immature males and females only rarely visit the South African coast and when they do, their appearances are of a short duration. They either remain in the Southern Ocean or migrate to other destinations, where they have yet to be detected by scientists.

JUNE — NOVEMBER

The first southern right whales arrive along our coast between May and June and their numbers peak during late August and September. The whale's distribution around the coast is by no means random. Large sheltered bays between Cape Hangklip and Plettenberg Bay, often those with river mouths, are consistently favoured. Locations with high concentrations of whales fall into two categories. There are assemblages with high numbers of cows accompanied by newborn calves, and others with large concentrations of so-called unaccompanied whales, which seems to indicate distinct calving and mating areas.

A mating group such as this one usually consists of one female and several males.

Despite their bulky build, southern right whales are fast and powerful swimmers.

Calving

Since scientific observations began in the 1960s, the highest concentrations of whales accompanied by calves have always been in the Cape Infanta area, near the De Hoop Nature Reserve. Almost 50% of all calves are born there, making it the most important southern right whale breeding ground in southern Africa. Cow and calf pairs do also occur elsewhere, albeit at lower densities.

Female whales appear to migrate in three-year cycles, the first two years of which are characterized by two successive visits to the coast, first to mate and then to calve. The third year is a rest year, where their absence from southern Africa presumably allows them to recover from the tremendous strain that pregnancy and weaning have placed on their bodies. Female whales that arrive at the calving grounds in their birthing year are already heavily pregnant, having carried the single calf in their womb for almost 12 months. Had they given birth in Antarctic waters, their newborn calves would have frozen to death very quickly. While neonatal whales are almost 6 m long and weigh about a ton, they have virtually no insulating layer of

blubber beneath their skin compared to the stately 36 cm layer in adult whales. A blubber layer this thick is a necessity in the polar regions, but in the warm southern African waters it can cause a whale to overheat. The tail fluke and flipper are the only parts of the whale without the blubber layer, so to cool itself the whale hangs vertically upside-down in the water, 'standing' on its head with its tail fluke in the air. This allows the blood just beneath the surface to be cooled by air and wind.

From the day it is born the calf consumes well over 100 litres of milk per day and grows at an astonishing daily rate of 2.8 cm. It also gains up to 100 kg every day. After a few months a calf can weigh eight or nine tons and measure 8 m. The bond between newborn calf and mother is very strong and close contact is maintained at most times. At the age of three and a half months the calf is ready to make the journey back to the Southern Ocean feeding grounds, but continues to suckle for at least another three – perhaps even nine – more months.

Juvenile whales do not appear frequently along the South African coast and where they spend their time is as yet unknown, but

WHALE TALK

Southern right whales are not as vocal and melodic as humpback whales, whose hauntingly beautiful underwater arias have caught the imagination of the public, but they do have a wide repertoire of low-frequency tones. These include clicks, grunts and moans, as well as unique upswept vocalisations that rise in frequency.

Acoustic communication is useful when sea conditions are calm and the level of ambient noise is low, but when the sea is rough and the winds are howling, communicating acoustically can become less effective. At these times, a more extreme form of communication is called for, and it is believed that behaviours such as breaching and lobtailing fulfil the need to communicate in such conditions and over great distances.

Breaching is without doubt the most spectacular form of whale behaviour. When a whale re-enters the water after leaping clear of the ocean, the displacement of vast quantities of water produces an explosive thump that can be heard almost a kilometre away through the air and even further underwater. To execute this aerial display, the whale swims horizontally at great speed, then tilts its head upwards and raises its flukes, or tail. This converts its horizontal momentum into vertical motion and the whale emerges from the water like a cruise missile fired from a submarine. Southern rights will frequently breach three or more times in succession and this often triggers breaching behaviour in other whales in the vicinity.

Lobtailing is the repeated slapping of the tail fluke onto the water. This also produces loud splashes, but of a lesser magnitude. Lobtailing and breaching seem to occur more frequently when a stiff wind is blowing, making the sea quite choppy, which supports the notion that they are indeed part of the southern right whales' communication repertoire. However, not all scientists agree with the communication theory, some believing that breaching and lobtailing are primarily ways of dislodging parasites, or are purely signs of playfulness.

Southern right whales are thought to breach either to communicate or to rid themselves of parasites.

SOUTHERN RIGHT WHALE
the journey

whalers active around Tristan da Cunha in the past reported large catches of juvenile and subadult whales. On reaching sexual maturity at around six years of age and conceiving for the first time, at least 93.4% of female calves born on the South African coast return here to have their first calf. Strong site fidelity to the exact location of the whale's birth is not apparent and only 50% of female cows give birth in the area where they were born themselves.

Mating

Mating areas tend to be located well away from breeding grounds. Such spatial segregation of mating and breeding areas is believed to prevent unnecessary mortality of calves, which may occur when eager males separate them from their mothers during mating attempts. Walker Bay and Plettenberg Bay seem to be the most important mating locations.

In these areas, it is not uncommon for a receptive female to have up to seven males in hot pursuit of her, all jostling for position to mate. She may demonstrate her unwillingness to mate by rolling onto her back, keeping her genital region out of reach, which makes copulation impossible. This type of behaviour can go on for days, with the female circling and diving shallowly in a kind of courtship dance until eventually she gives in. The final act of mating is relatively non-aggressive and females will mate in almost orderly fashion with the several males that are present.

Successful reproduction in southern right whales does not seem to be governed by social circumstances, but purely by sperm competition, so the father of the calf will generally be the animal that can provide the highest volume of sperm. It is no coincidence that right whales have the largest testes in the animal kingdom, together weighing over a ton. However, it is also believed that the gallons of sperm received by the female during copulation can flush out the previous suitor's sperm, perhaps indicating that the last to mate has the best chance of being the father of next season's calf. There are no long-term pair bonds between males and females and when the mating season ends around September, the males begin their journey back to the summer feeding grounds in Antarctica. As with most cetaceans, they take no further interest in rearing their young.

Around October, the rest of the whales also begin their migration south. A loss in body weight is believed to trigger physiological changes that are translated by the whales as their cue to move. An increase in air temperature could also play a pivotal role. However, research results from the last five years have shown that not all southern right whales migrate south at the beginning of the summer. The pattern of seasonal migration established through painstaking research over the past 30 years occurred during a period in which right whale populations were low and clustered around the south coast. With the recent increase in population size, the right whale seems to be recolonising former whaling grounds along the west coast, such as around Cape Columbine, where whales can now be observed year-round, feeding on strong upwelling cells rich in zooplankton.

HUNTING THE RIGHT WHALE

Yielding vast quantities of fat, oil, meat and bones, it comes as no surprise that southern right whales were hunted during stone age, colonial and modern times.

PREHISTORIC EXPLOITATION

Southern Africa's indigenous hunter-gatherers, the San and the Khoi-Khoi, exploited southern right whales and other cetaceans during the Middle and Late Stone Ages. However, since they did not have boats or other means to hunt whales at sea, they had to scavenge meat, blubber and oil from stranded individuals. Successful exploitation of such windfalls required a method of storing and preserving vast quantities of meat and blubber, otherwise the bulk of the carcass would become rotten in a matter of days.

Evidence of prehistoric preservation methods is found in the records kept by early travellers to the Cape and describes indigenous people burying whale meat and blubber beneath the damp sand at the water's edge, presumably to keep the meat fresh for longer. A novel experiment by University of Cape Town archaeologists, using seal meat (as whale meat was not readily available at the time), set out to test this. Their results showed that this prehistoric 'refrigeration' method could actually extend the life of the meat by up to two weeks.

Historical observations also tell us that indigenous people burned the whale fat to provide light, and smeared it on their bodies to keep warm. Until very recently, though, the only evidence of the pre-colonial use of whale meat and oil were accounts from the pens of 17th century chroniclers; archaeological evidence was practically nonexistent. While the bones of dolphins are often found during excavations of archaeological sites, there was little direct evidence that the prehistoric inhabitants of this region also ate the meat of larger cetaceans such as the southern right whale. Whale bones are only rarely found in prehistoric food dumps, or kitchen middens, probably because they were too heavy to be carried back to camp. Direct evidence only came to light during recent excavations of shell middens along the west coast of South Africa, when archaeologists spotted peculiar looking barnacles amid the shell debris. These barnacles were identified as belonging to the genus *Coronula* and occur exclusively on the skin of whales. The only plausible explanation for their appearance in the midden is that they arrived with the whale skin to which they were attached.

Whale bones were used in prehistoric construction – the ribs and jawbones were used to build the foundations of shelters that were later covered by skins. The remains of such structures can still be found to this day at the Ugab River mouth, along the southern reaches of Namibia's Skeleton Coast National Park.

COLONIAL WHALING

Early colonial records show that southern right whales were common in Table Bay and Saldanha Bay around 1652. At this time exploitation focused mainly on seals, and the whales spent the winters

WHALES OF THE KALAHARI

Prehistoric rock paintings and engravings of marine animals are very rare in southern Africa, though they do occur with much greater frequency elsewhere. For example, whale engravings and paintings are fairly common in coastal Norway and on the Pacific coast of the United States. One of a handful of marine life paintings discovered in southern Africa occurs in a remote northwestern corner of Botswana, where four lonely chunks of rock rise abruptly from the ocean-like expanse of the Kalahari Desert. The quartzitic rock walls of the Tsodilo Hills harbour over 3 000 rock paintings dating back to between 800 and 1 300 years ago. Among the paintings of rhinos, elephants and elands are drawings of whales.

So how did these ancient artists who lived at the foot of the Tsodilo Hills — with over 500 km of inhospitable desert between them and the present-day Namibian coast — know what whales were and what they looked like? Were they seasonally mobile? Did they spend part of the year inland and the other part on the coast, scavenging whales and other marine life?

There is evidence from the west coast of South Africa that inland people visited the coast seasonally and perhaps the same case can be made for the past people of the Kalahari. Another painting depicting early humankind's relationship with cetaceans can be seen on a small stone found during the excavations of the Klassies River mouth caves in the Eastern Cape. The painting depicts a person swimming with two dolphins and is the earliest reference of this type of interaction in the world. Sceptics believe both paintings actually depict freshwater fish, but unless one of these prehistoric artists comes back and explains his or her own work we will probably never know which interpretation is correct.

unharassed at the Cape. It was only at the end of the 18th century that American whalers discovered the abundance of southern right whales and began actively hunting them. French and British ships soon joined the Americans in their exploitation of southern rights in the whaling grounds off Lüderitz, Walvis and St Helena bays. At that time southern right whales were so abundant that boats took on full loads of oil in just a few weeks and sometimes so many whales were taken that only the head with baleen was recovered and the rest of the body discarded. It is estimated that in just two years 1 200 southern right whales were taken from St Helena Bay alone.

In 1792 a local shore-based whaling industry using small open boats began in Table Bay and this trend soon spread to other bays along the coast. The species' common name 'right whale' originates from these early days of whaling when it was considered the 'right' whale to catch. Their normal swimming speed was a leisurely 7 km per hour, slow enough for a whaleboat to outrun and harpoon them. Most importantly, they floated when dead. These whales also hold vast quantities of oil, an average of about 7.3 tons, but a large whale could yield up to 25 tons. In those days whale oil was used in household lamps, soaps and ointments, and for cooking. The whale baleen's pliability made it useful for brooms, brushes, umbrellas, skirt hoops, men's stiff shirt collars and corsets. A large southern right whale yielded over two tons of baleen, which must have made a lot of corsets. Together, the large quantities of oil and blubber made it a very valuable catch — so much so that a single right whale could cover the expenses of an entire whaling expedition.

Around 1835, less than 40 years since its inception, the catches of open-boat whalers declined dramatically, first in St Helena Bay, then in Table Bay, and finally in Algoa and Plettenberg bays. Despite the declines, southern rights continued to be taken both locally and by foreign vessels until well into the early 20th century. Over a period of 120 years, open-boat whalers landed more than 1 894 animals, the last one in 1912. When compared with the catches of the foreign fleets, the number of southern right whales taken by the open-boat fishery was almost insignificant, but its impact was equally devastating, since it seemed to have targeted reproductively mature females with calves. While the initial depletion of the southern right population can without doubt be attributed to the activities of foreign pelagic whalers, continued hunting carried out by open-boat whalers during the latter half of the 19th and beginning of the 20th centuries may have been instrumental in preventing an earlier population recovery.

MODERN WHALING

Modern whaling, using Norwegian-type steam catchers with mounted harpoon guns, started in Durban in 1909. The fishery expanded rapidly and by 1913 there were 17 land stations and 11 floating factories between Mozambique and Gabon. At this time whale blubber was melted down to produce lubricants for various types of machinery. The expansion of the fishery was, however, almost as rapid as its collapse — by 1918 there were only four land stations left.

THE SANGOMA AND THE WHALE

The fat, bones, baleen and other parts of cetaceans are an integral part of the traditional medicines of the Zulu and Xhosa peoples. While cetacean products, whale fat in particular, were much more readily available in herbalist shops in Durban during whaling days, surveys of traditional medicine markets in South Africa, Swaziland and Mozambique in 2002 have shown cetacean products to be widely available. Today, when a whale does wash up along the coast, word spreads quickly and sangomas and nyangas from as far as 100 km inland flock to harvest whale parts. This often occurs in great secrecy since the possession of, and trade in, cetacean products is illegal in South Africa.

Cetacean parts are used to cure a wide range of physical and mental illnesses. Dolphin jaws are crushed and pulverised, mixed with water and drunk to cure illnesses that involve possession by evil spirits. The bones of large whales are used to ensure that livestock, especially young cows, grow big and strong. The whale's vertebral discs are crushed and mixed into the cow's drinking water. Whale fat is used in rainmaking ceremonies. Whales are used because it is said, 'When the sky sees the fat of the whale, it will say, surely the drought is very great when even this sea animal is dead, and it will allow the rain to fall.'

'When the sky sees the fat of the whale, it will say,
surely the drought is very great when even this sea
animal is dead, and it will allow the rain to fall.'

WHALE WATCHING

Whale eco-tourism is a US$1 billion industry and, with over nine million people participating annually in almost 90 countries, it provides an income for 492 communities around the world. The southern right whale-watching industry in Argentina is worth US$27 million. Just as it was the right whale to catch during the whaling era, it is today the right whale to watch. It is a relatively active species that frequently breaches and sometimes displays great curiosity around boats, often raising its head clear of the water – a behaviour called spyhopping – to get a better look at a boat and its occupants.

In South Africa, tourists have been watching southern right whales from the shore ever since the species started making a comeback in the 1970s. Since then the town of Hermanus in the Western Cape has become a world-class land-based whale-watching destination. Boat-based whale watching was only introduced in 1998 and while binoculars and cameras are less threatening than harpoons, *ad hoc* approaches by boats can force whales to initiate energy-costly escape dives.

To ensure that the new industry does not impact negatively on the whales or on the flourishing land-based industry, whale-watching operators must abide by a strict code of conduct. Southern right whale calving grounds and some mating grounds are closed to the boat-based whale-watching industry and operators are not allowed to approach mother-calf pairs, even in non-sanctuary areas. Unaccompanied whales can be approached to a distance of 50 m and boats are allowed to remain with any whale or group of whales for a maximum of 20 minutes. Boats without whale-watching permits are obliged to remain at a distance of over 300 m from any whale.

During this time southern right whale populations were already on the brink of extinction and the fishery concentrated instead on other species. Over 30 000 humpback whales were killed, followed by 14 222 blue whales, and almost the same number of fin whales. Southern right whales could fetch up to six times the price of a humpback. So, despite their rarity they were still occasionally caught. Between 1918 and 1930, modern whaling fleets in the Cape province took 16 right whales, while in Natal whalers took 28 between 1912 and 1935. During almost 200 years of whaling, an estimated 200 000 of these gentle animals met their deaths at human hands.

A REMARKABLE RECOVERY

On 16 January 1935, the League of Nations Convention for the Regulation of Whaling gave protection to the southern right whale. Due to an administrative error, however, the ban was not incorporated into South African legislation until 1940. In those five years, as a result of this technicality, nine southern right whales were killed and legally landed.

Since 1940 there are only four known cases of right whales taken in African waters, all from the east coast near Durban. One was a serious error of judgement, when a right whale was mistakenly killed while swimming among a pod of sperm whales. The other cases were deliberate violations of the ban. In the Southern Ocean, Soviet whalers were still hunting southern right whales and between 1951 and 1970 they are estimated to have killed over 3 000 animals.

Before the advent of whaling, the world population of southern right whales was estimated at around 300 000 individuals. Scientists reckon that over the course of the whaling era approximately 99% of southern right whales were killed and for a long time some were convinced that the species was indeed extinct. In the early 1960s

South African newspapers began carrying reports of sightings of large black whales close to shore during the winter months, which surely must have been southern right whales. Scientists confirmed this seasonal reappearance of southern right whales in the 1970s, and since then the population has been recovering – increasing in size at a rate of 7% per year. Cow-calf pairs, in particular, have shown an increase over the past 30 years. While the population still stands at only 10–15% of its original size, today there are more southern right whales off the coast than at any other time in the last 150 years.

Whaling records show, however, that in the past southern right whales frequented a much wider stretch of southern African coastline during the winter than they do at present. Whalers took large numbers of southern right whales as far northwest as Angola's Baia dos Tigres and as far northeast as southern Mozambique's Delagoa Bay. In the early days of the species' recovery its principal range was much reduced, with reasonable numbers occurring only from Lambert's Bay on the west coast to Port Elizabeth on the east coast, and the bulk of individuals found between Cape Point and Plettenberg Bay. At present southern right whales are still scarce along the east coast, are only rarely seen as far north as Durban, and are never sighted in Mozambique.

In Namibia, Elizabeth Bay, Lüderitz and Walvis Bay were once important whaling grounds, but between 1960 and 1980 only three southern right whales were sighted along the coast. Since then southern right whale sightings along this stretch of coast have been on the increase. Between 1971 and 1998 there were 36 sightings, including 12 calves. New evidence has also emerged that whales are returning to a summer feeding ground on the west coast, around St Helena Bay and Cape Columbine, where their presence seems to be associated with an upwelling zone, rich in nutritious zooplankton. Over time, it seems that the species is slowly recolonising some of its former haunts.

While the recovery of the southern right whale is indeed one of the world's great conservation success stories, the species' recovery has been, and will continue to be, slow. A worldwide population of fewer than 15 000 means that the species is still extremely vulnerable. Modern threats, such as collisions with ships, entanglement in fishing gear and the depletion of Antarctic food resources through over-fishing, could prove destabilising to the population. Ship strikes and entanglement with fishing gear are believed to be major factors suppressing the recovery of the two northern right whale species, but in the case of the southern right whale only 15% of the known mortalities can be attributed to these two factors. To date only seven individuals are known to have died from collisions with ships. Many whales show scars of entanglement by fishing gear, but scarring does not seem to increase in mature females observed over many years. This suggests that at certain times southern right whales are more prone to entanglement, probably when they are young, more curious, and likely to be attracted to drifting or anchored objects.

Previous generations encountered the natural world in a far more intact and healthy state than we are experiencing at present. The southern right whale scenario presents a unique situation in which the opposite is true. Those who inhabited the coast between 1883 and 1960 did not have the pleasure of welcoming large numbers of southern right whales to the coast every winter. In fact, even to see a whale would have been a rare event. Today, we are among the first generations to bear witness to a marine ecosystem in which the southern right whale is starting once again to become a functional component.

Previous generations encountered the natural world in a far more intact and healthy state than we are experiencing at present. The conservation success story of the southern right whale makes for a welcome change from that norm.

LIMPETS

a life between the tides

CURRENTS of
CONTRAST

magine life submerged in freezing cold water for two six-hour periods every day, assaulted by pounding waves and exposed to washing-machine-like turbulence. A life spent dodging marine predators – from camouflaged fanged fish to dextrous eight-armed octopuses on the prowl. Imagine being high and dry when not submerged, exposed to air and left to bake in the African sun while trying to evade terrestrial predators – gulls, oystercatchers and even baboons that peck, pull and tug at you in their attempts to win a meal. This is the life of a limpet.

Rocky intertidal shores are the interface between land and sea and they are among the world's harshest ecosystems, where only the hardiest organisms can survive. The most prolific and well-adapted survivors are, without doubt, the limpets, a group of gastropods, or marine snails, that have adopted a cone-shaped shell instead of the familiar spiral, snail-like shell, and evolved a powerful foot.

When it comes to limpets, southern Africa is the world's foremost biodiversity hotspot. Here, up to 16 different species of all shapes, guises and sizes can be found on a single west coast rocky shore. Some limpets are among the most abundant inter-tidal organisms, in places exceeding 2 600 individuals per square metre; others are rare and seriously endangered.

In the eyes of many people, limpets are static, even boring creatures. Some visitors to rocky shores think that they are just part of the rock. It may surprise you to learn that some limpets are expert parachutists; others wield their shells like sword-carrying samurai; some are expert gardeners that cultivate and tend their own algae food, while others brew noxious chemical cocktails to deter even the most ferocious predator.

LIMPET BIOLOGY

It is very important to distinguish between the so-called true limpets, Patellacea, and two other groups: the false limpets, Siphonariidae, and the keyhole limpets, Fissurellidae. This chapter deals primarily with the true limpets, which are not only more abundant, but also of greater ecological importance. The true limpets consist of five families, with only two, the Patellidae and Nacellidae, occurring in southern Africa. The family Patellidae includes the most common and abundant species and is made up of four genera, of which three, *Helcion*, *Cymbula* and *Scutellastra*, occur here. More than half of the world's Patellidae limpet species occur in southern Africa – 18 endemics alone are found between Angola and KwaZulu-Natal.

Limpets distinguish themselves from most other gastropods by not having the typically coiled shell with the aperture at the base of its growing edge. Instead, a limpet's shell is a more or less symmetrical cone that covers the entire soft anatomy, apart from the base of the foot, which clings to the rock. Escaping the constraints of a coiled shell has allowed them to become dominant

Granite limpets, *Cymbula granatina*, await the return of the sea during a spring low tide.

At low tide granular limpets, *Scutellastra granularis*, cluster together in a crack that retains higher moisture levels than the adjacent bare rock walls.

on rocky shores exposed to heavy wave action. The flat shell creates little drag and, combined with the larger aperture, has allowed for the development of a foot nearly as large as the surface of the shell. This gives limpets great sticking power in the face of mountainous seas.

The foot stays attached to the rock through adhesion, which involves the secretion of a thin layer of mucus between rock and foot. The more rigid a limpet's foot, the stronger the adhesion, because it is less prone to flex away from the rock. Nonetheless, this type of shell also brings some disadvantages. The large foot and the shell's extensive flat surface area mean that a great deal of heat is absorbed from the sun, as well as from the rock. In addition, water easily escapes via the wide aperture. Limpets are therefore more prone to desiccation and over-heating than other gastropods, which is perhaps why they are most prevalent on temperate shores and decrease significantly in number in tropical regions.

Hidden beneath a hard shell, the limpet is an entirely soft-bodied creature. Sandwiched between the shell and the foot sits a mass of twisted organs – the kidneys, gut, blood vessels and gonads. The distinct head is adorned with sensory tentacles and stalked eyes. The mouth is equipped with a formidable radula, or rasping 'tongue', containing many rows of teeth that are capped with iron oxide so hard that they can erode rock. The back edge of each tooth is softer and erodes more easily. This serves to keep the harder front edge constantly sharpened. While all southern African limpets are herbivores, their radulas are designed to scrape microalgae and sporelings from the rock, and most species wouldl quickly starve to death among dense beds of macroalgae.

Most limpets occupy a well-defined home scar formed by first softening the rock with secretions from their mucous glands and then by excavation with the radula. The shell of each limpet fits its scar perfectly. In addition to reducing desiccation, this also increases the limpet's hold on the rock and reduces predation. Most will leave their home scars to forage for food at a species-specific point in the day/night and tidal cycle. They probably return to their home scars after each foraging bout by following the mucous trail laid down on their outward journey.

The number of limpets that return to their home scars can be reduced by experimentally scrubbing the rocky shore with corrosive chemicals, though some nonetheless manage to return. This suggests that while mucous trails are important, limpets must also know and be able to recognize rock topography. Perhaps they even have a kinaesthetic memory and the ability to remember direc-tions, distances and angles and to retrace their movements.

LIMPETS IN PREHISTORY

The origin of the Patellacea limpets is currently under debate, with two competing theories. One suggests that southern Africa was the evolutionary epicentre where all four genera evolved and from where they dispersed and radiated to other parts of the world. The other theory proposes that *Scutellastra* is the most ancient group of all present-day Patellacea limpets and that the genus was widely distributed across the prehistoric rocky shores that fringed the Tethys Sea at a time when all continental landmasses were still fused together. This theory argues that, through continental drift, the subsequent formation of ocean basins and the birth of new currents, the many populations of *Scutellastra* became isolated from one another and evolved into the three other modern genera. Unfortunately, limpets are poorly represented in the fossil record because they inhabit a high-energy environment, so there is not enough evidence to prove or disprove either of these theories at present.

In southern Africa, the paths of humans and limpets have crossed for over 125 000 years. In fact, limpets were among the organisms targeted in the world's earliest known marine fishery at the Klassies River mouth in the Eastern Cape, where the ancestors of the San hunter-gatherers collected small quantities of limpets during low tide. In the Late Stone Age, marine foods were utilized more frequently, and along the west coast limpets sometimes dominated the catches of the prehistoric fishery, with the granite and granular limpets making up over 95% of the entire marine invertebrate harvest.

In prehistoric times, hunter-gatherers and pastoralists collected limpets primarily for food, but the shells were used as ornaments and tools to decorate pottery.

It is believed that limpets were prised off the rocks with special levers made from bone or hippo ivory. Limpets were not only collected for food – the shells were used as ornaments and tools for decorating ancient pottery with patterns. Some middens have even yielded limpet shells with traces of paint pigments, perhaps suggesting that the artists who created southern Africa's world-renowned rock art used them as paint containers. Prehistoric burial mounds appear to have been decorated with limpet shells and today, along remote stretches of the west coast, some modern graves are still covered in this way.

The limpet shells discarded by prehistoric peoples not only reveal snippets of their activities and lives, they provide information about the climate and environment during that time. The shell of the granular limpet has been used successfully as a so-called palaeothermometer. Prehistoric changes in sea surface temperature are preserved in the crystal structure and mineral composition of the limpet's shell. By measuring the outer aragonite and inner calcite layers of each limpet shell, the sea temperature at the time the limpets were harvested can be established, allowing for a detailed understanding of past marine climates.

THE ROCKY SHORE

Rocky shores are tidal systems where twice a day the combined gravitational pull of the moon and sun drags the ocean away from the land, laying bare the rocky reefs that were previously submerged beneath a tumble of waves. Only hours later is the ocean dragged back again. A characteristic feature of rocky shore flora and fauna all around the world is its division into visible levels of zonation.

This is a result of their different tolerances for physical stressors such as desiccation, large temperature fluctuations, changes in salinity, pounding waves and torrential turbulence, and the role of the flora and fauna in biological interactions such as competition, predation and recruitment.

Rocky shore organisms have to be able to contend with life in the sea as well as on land, but since most of them have a marine origin, it is life out of water that is most stressful. These stressors vary depending on the location on the shore, but desiccation stressors decrease as one moves down the shore. Low on the shore, exposure to air will be brief and intermittent, while high up it will be prolonged and regular. It is believed that physical stressors generally limit and shape species composition on the high shore, while bio-

Late Stone Age burial mounds were covered with limpet shells and along remote stretches of coast this practice appears to continue to the present day.

CURRENTS of
CONTRAST

Pear limpets, *Scutellastra cochlear*, tend highly productive seaweed gardens that they prune, fertilize and protect from intruders.

logical interaction is a more important structuring agent on the mid and low shore. Rocky shores are the principal habitat for all but two southern African limpet species.

Much of what we know of southern Africa's rich limpet fauna comes from the research of Professor George Branch, who began working on limpets for his PhD in the 1970s. Together with many students, he continues the study of these gastropods and their rocky shore home to the present day.

GARDENERS, SAMURAI AND SKYDIVERS

To those in the know, limpets are among the most exciting marine invertebrates, though it is unlikely that the uninitiated have ever seen a limpet do anything that can be described as even remotely interesting. Most limpet activity occurs at too slow a pace for us to notice – either in short, unexpected bursts, or when observation is most difficult. Southern African limpets employ a variety of strategies to find food, seek shelter, or escape from, and defend themselves against, predators. What follows is a selection of the most ingenious, even outlandish behaviours.

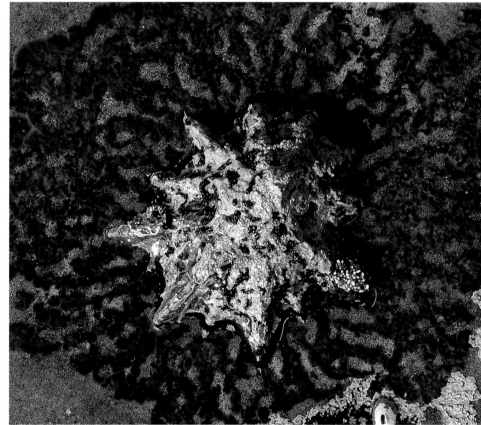

The *Ralfsia* garden of a long spined-limpet, *Scutellastra longicosta*.

GARDENING LIMPETS

Just as humans cultivate vegetable gardens by pruning, providing nutrients and removing competitors and predators, several species of limpet do much the same thing. By selectively grazing on often competitively superior species, the limpets allow competitively inferior, but more nutritious and less well-defended algal communities to thrive in their immediate vicinity. They also increase the productivity and nutritional value of their algae by maintaining them in a young and fast-growing state. They even fertilize the algae in their gardens with their own waste products, which are rich in ammonia.

The pear limpet, *Scutellastra cochlear*, inhabits the lower reaches of exposed rocky shores and reaches the highest densities of any limpet, with up to 2 600 individuals crammed into every square metre of rock. Densities are so high that juveniles only find living space on the shells of adults, where up to 35 can be stacked on top of one another. The zone where pear limpets are most abundant, the cochlear zone, appears to have been grazed to near-annihilation, in stark contrast with the seaweed-rich zones immediately above and below it.

A closer look reveals, however, that each limpet is surrounded by a narrow fringing garden of delicate filamentous algae. The gardens are created by intermediate levels of grazing. If grazing intensity is too low, dense beds of macroalgae become established, whereas if grazing intensity is too high then only heavily defended encrusting algae survive. While algal biomass is significantly lower in the cochlear zone compared with adjacent zones, algal productivity is significantly higher due to the limpets' gardening efforts.

The long-spined limpet, *S. longicosta*, also gardens, but by cultivating a single species – the encrusting *Ralfsia* – it manages to increase garden productivity to an even higher degree than the pear limpet. Instead of randomly grazing, it cuts regular paths across *Ralfsia*, creating many new growing edges and thus enhancing productivity. These limpets are very territorial and will protect their gardens from limpets and other herbivores foolish enough to intrude; they dig their long spines under the shells of invaders and push them away.

Juveniles are rarely found on rocks. Instead, they live and tend *Ralfsia* gardens on the shell of the winkle *Oxystele*. Only once they have outgrown their hosts do they move onto the rocky substrate, but until they can locate an unoccupied *Ralfsia* patch they have to graze on other, marginally nutritious algae. This diet is so meagre that they cannot accumulate enough energy reserves to reproduce, so long-spined limpets only become mature once they have acquired a *Ralfsia* garden on the rock.

On highly productive west coast rocky shores Argenville's limpets, *Scutellastra argenvillei*, occur in such high densities that they can only grow upwards and not to the sides. As a result they often have very outlandishly elongated and stretched shells.

An Argenville's limpet in the trap-feeding position waiting for a blade of kelp to wash by.

LAZY LIMPETS

While the majority of southern Africa's non-gardening limpets have to travel long distances to find food, some species have evolved a foraging strategy that allows them to sit back and wait for food to come to them. Argenville's limpets, *Scutellastra argenvillei*, and the granite limpets, *Cymbula granatina*, are sit-and-wait grazers, a strategy that must have considerable merit since they are among the largest and most abundant limpets in the world. Along the west coast they can attain shell lengths of up to 10 cm and occur at mean densities of up to 600 individuals per square metre, yielding a mind-blowing 19 kg of limpet every square metre.

While they share a common foraging strategy, each occupies a different habitat. Argenville's limpet lives predominantly on semi-exposed shores and maintains a distinct belt along the low shore, just above the landward edge of the subtidal kelp forests. At low tide, each limpet lifts its shell high above the rock and waits for a kelp frond to be washed against its foot by a passing wave. The shell is then quickly clamped down, trapping the frond between the shell's sharply serrated edge and the rock. Feeding begins immediately, with a single frond often being shared by many individuals.

The granite limpet also occurs in the mid- and low-shore zones, but is restricted to sheltered west coast bays that lack an adjacent kelp forest. Gut contents analysis has nevertheless shown that their diet is also dominated by kelp, but how do they gain access to it? Severe wave action often breaks off kelp fronds, which are kept in suspension and transported by longshore and tidal currents into sheltered boulder bays occupied by the granite limpet. At high tide it lifts its shell high above the rock – as Argenville's limpet does – but also raises the front portion of the foot, splaying the front lobes into two arm-like appendages covered in very sticky mucus. When a piece of drift kelp washes against the limpet's foot, it is not the shell that traps the kelp, but the foot.

Both Argenville's and granite limpets can only survive in such high densities due to the food subsidy provided by the adjacent subtidal kelp forests. If kelp is experimentally withheld for prolonged periods of time, the mortality rates of both species increase dramatically. It appears that neither population is controlled – as is usually the case – by predators (i.e. from the top of the food chain), but rather by the availability of kelp (i.e. from the bottom up).

WARRIOR LIMPETS

The goat's eye limpet, *Cymbula oculus*, has two main predators, the spiny starfish *Marthasterias glacialis*, which can attain a diameter of 30 cm, and the *Thais dubia* whelk. Spiny starfish operate with speed and brute force, while the whelk's strategy of attack involves trying to push its proboscis under the limpet's shell or, if that fails, to attempt to drill a hole through the shell itself.

But the goat's eye limpet is no pushover. Although juveniles have no option but to flee in haste, often reaching breakneck speeds of up to 3.7 mm per second, adults stand their ground. They appear to be able to distinguish between different kinds of predators and vary their responses accordingly. A medium-sized limpet will, almost without exception, fight a whelk, first by mushrooming its shell upwards, then slamming it down onto the predator, the shell's sharp edge often cutting off the whelk's proboscis or part of its foot. Intense and prolonged battery has even been known to chip the predator's thick shell. If, however, the same-size limpet is faced with a starfish, it turns and flees. Only the largest individuals stand their ground against this five-armed foe. Wielding its shell like a samurai sword, the limpet can sever many of the starfish's tube feet and force it to retreat.

PARACHUTE LIMPET

The kelp limpet, *Cymbula compressa*, is not only one of the more unusually shaped limpets, it is one of the few species that does not inhabit rock, instead living exclusively on bamboo kelp, *Ecklonia maxima*. To fit the cylindrical stem of the kelp perfectly, the shell is elongated and compressed at the sides, with a concave opening. The larvae recruit directly into the canopy and juveniles live on the hand of the kelp, well segregated from the adults, which occur only on the stipe.

This limpet does not feed on the kelp itself but on the epiphytes that grow on their host, in the process preventing the plant from becoming heavily fouled. A heavy epiphyte load increases drag and can make the plant more likely to become dislodged during storms. If the plant is torn free from the rocky reef, it floats to the surface and drifts ashore, ending up on the drift line. Although it might be presumed that most limpets follow the fate of their host, kelp limpets have developed an escape response that allows them to cheat death. They are believed to be able to sense the pressure changing as the kelp plant floats to the surface. In response, the limpets release their grip on the stipe and freefall through the water column, landing on the rocky reef below. From there, they must begin a long and arduous journey to find another kelp plant – one that is unoccupied, as this species is fiercely territorial and will not tolerate another adult limpet on the same plant.

CHEMICAL WEAPONS LIMPET

With the exception of the 'warrior limpets', a limpet's defence against predators is usually to escape or to clamp its shell down onto the rock as tightly as possible and hold on. The latter anti-predator strategy works well for species such as the pear limpet, whose tenacity is the greatest of any southern African species measured – it requires a force of more than 5 kg per square centimetre to remove.

Some species have a much lower tenacity. The Cape false limpet, *Siphonaria capensis*, for instance, is so weak that it is the only species to forage exclusively at low tide, presumably to avoid being washed off the rock while on the move. It might be expected to turn tail and flee at even the slightest hint of an octopus, oystercatcher or starfish, but surprisingly it stands its ground and can do so because it has evolved into a living chemical weapons factory.

When confronted by a predator, glands in the limpet's mantle and foot produce streams of milky mucus. This either makes the species unpalatable, or is toxic, because even though the Cape false limpet is one of the most abundant, easily accessible and easily captured species, there are no known predators that willingly prey on and consume it. For example, of 38 000 limpet shells discarded after the limpets were eaten by oystercatchers, none was of a Cape false limpet. Experiments where encounters were staged between these limpets and several species of klipfish, the suckerfish, and three species of whelk, all resulted in the predator being repelled by the mucus. The limpet did not flee once, seemingly having no need for an escape response, thanks to its chemical weapons arsenal.

LIMPET PREDATORS

Many species of fish, marine invertebrates, shore and seabirds and even some species of terrestrial mammals will occasionally snack on a limpet or two, yet only two – a benthic fish and a coastal bird – are true limpet specialists. For the giant clingfish and the African black oystercatcher, the limpet-rich rocky shores of the South African west coast and its offshore islands are their primary hunting grounds, prowled by the fish when the rocks are covered by a watery blanket at high tide, and the bird at low tide.

GIANT CLINGFISH

The giant clingfish, *Chorisochismus dentex*, is endemic to southern Africa and commonly found sheltering in low-shore rock pools during low tide. It can attain a size of over 25 cm and its pectoral fin is modified to form a powerful sucker. This novel adaptation allows it to inhabit wave-battered low-shore regions where its limpet prey is abundant.

Every return of the tide liberates the clingfish from its temporary rock pool captivity to hunt across the rocky intertidal landscape. It seeks out limpets that are either on the move, or have their shells raised off the rock. Adopting a head-down position vertically above the limpet, the fish drives its long incisors under the shell, then straightens like a high-diver coming out of a somersault, giving rise to upward momentum that allows the fish's body to act as a lever to lift the limpet off the rock. The prey is snatched and swallowed – shell and all – in just under three seconds.

Granite limpets are sit-and-wait-grazers that take full advantage of the bounty of seaweeds deposited onto rocky shores with every incoming tide.

The shells accumulate in the stomach, where they are encased in a thick layer of mucus. They are later regurgitated or passed through the gut whole. Prey items are generally less than 9 mm long, but limpets of up to 50% of the fish's own body length can be consumed. This suckerfish is likely to be the most important consumer of limpets along the west coast rocky shores, perhaps only rivalled by the region's other limpet specialist, the African black oystercatcher.

AFRICAN BLACK OYSTERCATCHER

The African black oystercatcher, *Haematopus moquini*, is perhaps southern Africa's most endangered coastal bird because the bulk of the population inhabits only half a dozen or so offshore islands off the west coast. On these islands they occur at incredibly high densities, several magnitudes higher than on the mainland.

The oystercatcher feeds on many intertidal creatures, particularly mussels and limpets. Four species of limpet are regularly consumed: Argenville's, the pear limpet, the granite limpet and the granular limpet – the latter making up almost 90% of the birds' diet at some localities. The oystercatchers are prolific limpet predators, removing a staggering 2.8 million limpets annually from just 2.5 km of rocky shore on Jutten Island.

Limpets are famed for their tenacity, enduring pounding waves without wavering. For a human to prise a limpet from the rock takes an implement, a lever of sorts, and a great deal of brute strength. So how does a medium-sized, dainty coastal bird defeat the limpet's tenacity? Catching small limpets is relatively easy. The bird simply forces its lower mandible between the limpet and the rock while the upper mandible grips the spire of the shell and levers it off. To tackle larger limpets, an element of surprise is necessary, because they can only be sliced off the rocks when caught unawares, before they can clamp down. Hunting limpets is no random affair – the successful oystercatcher cunningly approaches its quarry from behind and delivers a sharp, well-aimed blow to the limpet's shell margin, knocking it off the rock.

There is great variation in the shell shape of granite limpets, some being pear-shaped while others are more round or elliptical. It is important for oystercatchers to identify which is the front and which is the back of the limpet – undeniably easier in pear-shaped limpets. Observations have shown that they prefer to attack pear-shaped limpets over their more rounded counterparts. In areas with high oystercatcher densities, the less pear-shaped a limpet is, the more likely it is to survive to maturity and reproduce, passing on the genes for a more rounded shell. Through this process of localized natural selection, oystercatcher predation has changed the average shell shape of some limpet populations. Granular limpets can also decrease their chances of oystercatcher predation by growing very large, but in practice this is only possible at offshore bird islands where the limpets can grow much faster due to the presence of guano to fertilize the algae on which they feed.

CHACMA BABOONS: LIMPET PICKERS AND SHARK KILLERS

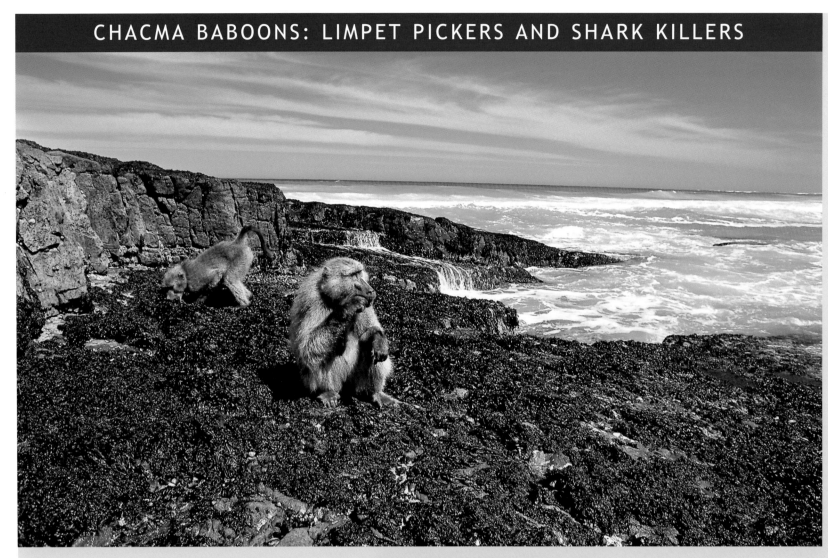

Among the limpets, seaweeds and scuttling crabs of southern Africa's rocky intertidal shores stalks a predator that is more closely related to humans than to any fish or sea slug. At the tip of southern Africa, chacma baboons supplement their plant-based diet with regular servings of seafood. Every few days they meander down to the ocean's edge to do some fishing. Mussels, limpets and lobsters, even baby sharks, are on the menu.

These baboons inhabit the craggy hillsides blanketed by the endemic fynbos shrubs of the Table Mountain National Park, enduring a climate of cool wet winters and hot dry summers. During and immediately after the rains, plant foods are available in great abundance, but as soon as the dry season takes hold pickings become slim. It is during this time that the baboons turn to the sea, for what the land lacks in productivity the Atlantic Ocean makes up in bountiful richness. This stretch of ocean supports some of the highest standing stocks of intertidal organisms in the world. Kilometre-long kelp beds thrive in the nutrient-rich, plankton-choked waters, which are home to armies of lobsters and hordes of small sharks.

OPPOSITE TOP: The chacma baboons of Cape Point, whose home range encompasses the southernmost tip of the Cape Peninsula, feed only on inter-tidal life such as limpets and mussels for short periods, and then only every couple of days.

OPPOSITE BOTTOM: These baboons do not appear to util-ize this bountiful source of protein to its fullest potential. Perhaps this is because con-suming vast quantities of salty seafoods would greatly increase their water requirements, and fresh water is scarce during the summer months.

LEFT: A female baboon with young infant slung underneath her, about to bite the top off a limpet.

The mainstays of the baboon's marine diet are mussels and limpets, which they pry from the rocks with their dextrous fingers and strong teeth. Their buttocks firmly planted on the ground in an almost cross-legged sitting position, the baboons pull vigorously at clumps of mussels until the rock surrenders the desired quarry. Individual mussels are then cracked open between the molar teeth, and the meat is licked or sucked from the shell. When available, the Mediterranean mussel, *Mytilus galloprovincialis*, seems to be the preferred item in terms of quantity. In one sitting, the Cape Point gang of baboons consumed over 500.

Following closely behind in popularity are granular limpets, which occur on the higher, less productive reaches of the shore. Given their tenacity, limpets require a different foraging strategy, as no amount of pulling will dislodge them from their home scars. Bending forward, the baboons grasp the upper two-thirds of the shell with their teeth and easily break off the conical top, eagerly scooping out the gonads and digestive gland with their fingers.

Rock crabs are also taken. They are pounced on after being chased from their shelters as the baboons turn over boulders. When calm seas coincide with spring low tides the baboons venture right to the water's edge, searching the crowns of bamboo kelp plants for the egg cases of various species of small shark. After drinking the egg yolk with relish they will often suck and nibble on the unborn shark.

On an almost daily basis the baboons' paths cross mementos of prehistory, so-called shell middens. These accumulations of shell debris and fish bones are the refuse dumps of southern Africa's Middle and Late Stone Age aboriginals. Archaeological excavations have shown that these prehistoric hunter-gatherers subsisted largely on marine organisms and their diet closely mirrored that of the coastal baboons today. A fascinating question is: which were the first primate fishermen on planet Earth? Did early man observe and imitate the baboons, or did the baboons watch and learn from the humans?

In the past, the Cape Point gang has been touted as the world's only troop of non-human primates to exploit marine resources, but new research has shown otherwise. In fact, there are a further seven marine-foraging baboon troops in the Cape region alone, and anecdotal reports from the not-so-distant past mention baboons feeding on marine resources at another 10 locations along the coast.

Today, this unique marine foraging behaviour appears to be under threat as intense development has pushed many baboon troops off the coastal plain, restricting them to the mountainous hinterland and forcing them to leave behind their legacy as limpet pickers.

Enduring crashing waves, a pair of African black oystercatchers, *Haematopus moquini,* searches the intertidal zone for their limpet prey.

LIMPETS IN DANGER

Today southern Africa's extraordinary array of limpets is faced with numerous threats, including loss of habitat, over-exploitation and alien invasive species.

A SEAGRASS RARITY

The eelgrass limpet, *Siphonaria compressa,* occurs only in Langebaan Lagoon along the west coast of South Africa and feeds exclusively on the living blades of the seagrass *Zostera capensis.* The species has been listed as highly endangered, the only marine invertebrate to have this dubious honour in southern Africa. This is not only the result of its very restricted distribution and specialized habitat, but of its proximity to the busy port of Saldanha Bay, which handles numerous oil tankers and cargo vessels and is home to large-scale industries, including a steel mill, a cement works and oil storage facilities.

Seagrass in the lagoon has decreased in recent years but the exact cause is, as yet, unknown. Without the seagrass beds, this limpet is bound to become extinct – a repeat performance of an event that took place along the eastern seaboard of the United States in the late 1920s. The limpet *Lottia alveus,* which is also restricted to the blades of seagrass, almost became the first marine invertebrate to become extinct in historical times. It was so badly depleted following the loss of its seagrass host plant – due to a widespread case of slime mould – that it was considered extinct for a long time.

In Langebaan Lagoon, eelgrass beds only line the soft sediments of the mid to upper intertidal zone and appear to be excluded from the low shore by the burrowing activities of the sandprawn *Callianassa kraussi.* The main reason for the underlying rarity of the eelgrass limpet appears to be the fact that the high and midshore where eelgrass grows are suboptimal habitats for the species. When sandprawns are experimentally removed, eelgrass begins to thrive on the low shore and becomes home to eelgrass limpets at much higher densities than are ever found in high and mid-shore seagrass beds.

ALIEN INVASION

Along the west coast of South Africa an alien invasion is currently under way. The culprit is a marine invertebrate, the Mediterranean mussel, *Mytilus galloprovincialis.* It is believed to have arrived on west coast rocky shores some time during the 1970s, when this mussel's larvae probably hitched a free ride in the ballast water of tankers from southern Europe and escaped at Saldanha Bay. Today, the Mediterranean mussel occupies a 2 000 km stretch of coast between Port Elizabeth and Swakopmund and is the dominant intertidal mussel species on the west coast, having out-competed the indigenous ribbed mussel, *Aulacomya ater.* This displacement of the native mussel was possible only because the invader has a faster growth rate, is more tolerant of desiccation and has a far higher reproductive rate.

The alien mussel also out-competes limpets for space. At exposed sites, it has practically wiped out Argenville's limpet, reducing its population to small remnant patches cut off from their kelp food supply. In response, the limpets in these zones have abandoned their sedentary lifestyle of sit-and-wait grazing, have become more mobile and have adopted a free-ranging strategy. At semi-exposed sites, the limpets and mussels still coexist, with Argenville's occupying most of the shore. These observed patterns can be explained by the fact that exposed sites have a higher concentration of particulate foods that allow the mussels to grow bigger and more quickly. Juvenile Argenville's limpets do manage to settle into the alien mussel bed initially, but they cannot reach adult sizes there due to a lack of space. In fact, less than 3% of Argenville's limpets living on mussel beds manage to reach sexual maturity.

The invasive mussel has also had a negative impact on the small human population that ekes out an existence along the arid shores of the west coast. The inception of a small-scale fishery of limpets to benefit the impoverished local population has been on the cards for many years. Given the evidence that the alien mussel takes over even more rapidly in patches cleared of limpets, however, its implementation appears out of the question at present.

Only the African black oystercatcher has benefited. In many places its diet has shifted to one dominated by the Mediterranean mussel, and the new superabundant food source has resulted in a much higher reproductive success.

OVER-EXPLOITATION

Due to their sedentary nature and easy accessibility, limpets are very vulnerable to exploitation by humans. This is particularly evident along the east coast, where human population densities are considerably higher than on the west or south coast. Direct fishing impacts include decreases in limpet densities and reductions in their mean size. This leads to a vicious cycle: the smaller the limpets become, the greater the number required by the harvesters to prepare a meal. The result is the eventual decimation of the resource.

In some species the reduction in size has led to skewed gender ratios. The goat's eye limpet, for example, is a protandrous hermaphrodite. This means it begins life as a male, then becomes female as it increases in size. Human harvesters select for the biggest individuals, so almost always take females – unwittingly reducing the reproductive output of the species dramatically.

Limpet over-exploitation also has many indirect effects. For instance, as many species are prolific roaming grazers of seaweed sporelings, areas of rocky shore that are denuded of limpets are usually invaded by dense beds of seaweed. These seaweed beds, which are inedible to most limpets, also shade the rock and thus reduce the amount of microalgae available to the remaining limpets.

Alien mussels crowd out a last remaining patch of limpets along an exposed west coast rocky shore.

PART TWO

THE REALM OF THE AGULHAS

Where the warm Indian Ocean laps against southern Africa's eastern shores, the Agulhas current fuels a great cauldron, boiling over with biodiversity.

SARDINE RUN

the greatest shoal on Earth

CURRENTS of
CONTRAST

iles out to sea, off the wild shores of the Eastern Cape, a pod of more than 4 000 common dolphins ploughs through the waves, leaping and diving, their wakes stirring the ocean into a white froth along a 4 km front. This armada of hunters is on a course that will intercept with a sardine shoal of Herculean proportions – 12 km long, 2 km wide and 30 m deep. The fish are not yet aware of the dolphins' presence and are travelling slowly north. Accompanying them are tens of thousands of Cape gannets. At the moment the sardines are still swimming at too great a depth to be reached, but the birds bide their time and soar patiently above.

When the dolphins intercept the shoal they split into smaller pods and the usually near-silent underwater world is filled with the piercing screams of echolocation. Working together, they carve and slice patches of fish from the shoal and herd them towards the surface. The sardines adopt a defensive formation, bunching together more and more tightly, creating a so-called baitball. While some dolphins continuously circle the ball of swirling fish, others rush in to grab their share. They are joined by schools of bronze whaler sharks, several hundred strong. As the number of predators increases, the baitball becomes penned near the surface. This is the moment the gannets have been waiting for and, in mere seconds, thousands of birds rain from the sky. They penetrate the sea's surface like arrowheads, seizing sardines before exploding from the water like corks popping from champagne bottles.

Very few fish caught up in a baitball escape predation and the feeding frenzy becomes intense. In less than an hour all that is left are showers of fish scales disappearing into the depths and reddish-brown surface slicks of oil and blood. The dolphins, sharks and gannets are long gone, already moving north in pursuit of the main shoal and more opportunities to feed.

SHOALS OF PLENTY

At the centre of this natural history spectacular is the humble sardine, *Sardinops sagax*, which, to confuse matters, is also known as the pilchard. This epipelagic fish of the herring family spends most of its life in dense shoals, almost constantly in the company of others. It prefers cool water of between 14 and 20 °C and is normally associated with areas of intense upwelling, where it feeds on an abundance of phyto- and zooplankton.

For 10 to 11 months sardines inhabit the coastal shelf region between northern Namibia and Port Elizabeth, but for the rest of the year their distribution changes dramatically. When a tongue of cold water licks the eastern flank of South Africa every June/July, replacing the usually warm water with cold, millions of tons of sardines are soon on the move. The sardine run is neither a spawning nor a feeding migration, but a temporary range extension of *Sardinops sagax*, when it follows this inshore cold-water intrusion northwards.

Little is known about the oceanography that drives the phenomenon but an area north of Port St Johns, where the continental shelf narrows, appears to be of great significance. The sardines travel as far as Waterfall Bluff every year, but the final stage of the run, crossing from the Eastern Cape into KwaZulu-Natal, is not a guaranteed passage. Waterfall Bluff appears to be a holding area, and only when the prevailing currents reverse and cool water begins to well up are pulses of sardines able to leak northwards into KwaZulu-Natal. When water temperatures remain too high, as in 2003, the fish do not move any further north, or if they do so it is out of sight – in very deep water, or far offshore. If conditions are favourable, sardine shoals can be seen racing all the way to the North Coast, but once they reach Durban the fish disappear. Some argue that they move offshore and then move back south with the Agulhas current. However, they would have to travel at great depth to find a comfortable temperature regime.

Common dolphins are the most important predators on the sardine run.

Bottlenose dolphins, *Tursiops truncatus*, do not feed as prolifically on sardines as the common dolphin, but a group of 2 500 transient animals joins the local population during the sardine run.

SWIMMING FOR THEIR LIVES

During the sardine run the subtropical east coast receives an injection of life, leading to mass congregations normally only seen in the realm of the Benguela current. Many marine predators take advantage of this annual feast and hunters of all taxonomic affinities spend time in hot pursuit of this unassuming silvery little fish.

Despite the magnitude and spectacular nature of this event, we know very little about how the predators interact with their prey and each other. Prof. Vic Peddemors of the University of KwaZulu-Natal is trying to find out exactly that and will spend four years deciphering the roles played by common dolphins, bronze whaler sharks and Cape gannets. Much of the following section is based on his preliminary observations and insights – for there is practically no published material available to date.

COMMON DOLPHINS

The common dolphin, *Delphinus delphis*, is possibly the sardine run's most important predator. Not only does it consume vast quantities of sardines, its diet changing from one dominated by squid to one consisting of 85% sardines, it is also believed to be important in shaping the sardine run. These are the only hunters that occur in large enough numbers and are fast and intelligent enough to anticipate and control the behaviour of the sardines. It is common dolphins that drive the shoals to the surface, concentrate them into baitballs and make the fish available to the birds and sharks.

The common dolphins that appear off the northern reaches of the Eastern Cape and KwaZulu-Natal coasts are not permanent residents, but are believed to spend most of their time south of East London. During June and July between 15 000 and 20 000 animals move inshore and to the north as their numbers peak during the height of the sardine run. There is some speculation by scientists that the females use the abundance of food to wean their calves, as well as to re-establish their fat reserves before falling pregnant again.

BRONZE WHALER SHARKS

Bronze whaler sharks, *Carcharhinus brachyurus*, also called copper sharks, are the most numerous sharks associated with the sardine run, though others such as duskys, *Carcharhinus obscurus*, blacktips, *Carcharhinus limbatus*, bonnet hammerheads, *Sphyrna zygaena*, and even great whites, *Carcharodon carcharias*, are also spotted frequently. Studies analysing the gut contents of all these species have shown sardines to be present in large numbers.

CURRENTS of
CONTRAST

A collaborative research project between the University of KwaZulu-Natal and the National Geographic Society sees Critter-cam being fitted to the dorsal fin of a bronze whaler shark.

Lacking the speed, intelligence and co-operative abilities that dolphins use to carve off baitballs, sharks are thought to be limited to hunting stragglers at the edges of the shoal. When a shark decides to swim though a dense patch of sardines, the fish instantly part, forming a doughnut of empty water around it. However, once dolphins have sliced off a swirling tornado of fish, the sharks' luck changes and they appear to feed much more successfully.

The role and foraging behaviour of bronze whaler sharks during the sardine run are still, for the most part, a mystery. We also do not know whether it is the same sharks that follow the shoals for the entire sardine run or whether different populations intercept the fish at the edges of their feeding territories. To obtain answers, Vic Peddemors aims to throw an arsenal of high-tech weapons at the problem. In conjunction with the National Geographic Society, he will use an animal-borne video camera system called Critter-cam. This device is attached to the shark's dorsal fin with a soft clamp and will shoot hours of video footage from the shark's perspective. At a predetermined time Critter-cam detaches itself from the shark and floats to the surface, where it sends out a VHF signal that enables it to be found and picked up. The video footage obtained in this manner will hopefully show how the sharks' foraging behaviour differs in the presence of common dolphins.

CAPE GANNETS

Cape gannets, *Morus capensis*, are the most important avian predators of sardines, but there are no colonies along the northern Eastern Cape coast and KwaZulu-Natal. The northeasternmost colonies are situated on the bird island in Algoa Bay off Port Elizabeth. Scientists presume it is predominantly this population that follows the sardines north, but it cannot be ruled out that birds from the west coast could also be involved.

Despite their diving prowess, Cape gannets are limited by being able to attain a maximum depth of around 5 m. They must therefore wait until the fish come close to the surface, driven there by currents and winds, or by the common dolphin. The arrival of the sardines is often heralded by flocks of gannets, and many believe they are the first to spot the shoal from high above, with the dolphins looking to the gannets to tell them where the fish are. There are, however, many situations where common dolphins feed on sardines without gannets being present, and vice versa.

BOTTLENOSE DOLPHINS

Bottlenose dolphins, *Tursiops truncatus*, are larger than common dolphins but less prolific sardine feeders. They do not appear to have the speed or stamina to herd or carve off significant proportions of the shoal. Their normal diet consists of whitefish caught in shallow water and their digestive systems seem to be unable to handle the high oil content of a sardine-rich diet – captive animals fed on a sardine-rich diet exhibit symptoms of diarrhoea. Studies have shown that sardines make up less than 5% of the bottlenoses' annual diet, but scientists have not specifically examined their diet during the sardine run, so it could be substantially higher.

It has recently been discovered that there are two stocks of bottlenose dolphins off South Africa's east coast. One is a resident population off KwaZulu-Natal that numbers around 900, the other appears to be migratory and consists of some 2 500 animals that move from the Eastern Cape into the waters of KwaZulu-Natal during the sardine run.

GAME FISH, BRYDE'S WHALES, FUR SEALS AND PENGUINS

Several species of predatory fish are also associated with the sardine run, the most common being elf, *Pomatomus saltatrix*, yellowtail, *Seriola lalandi*, and geelbek, *Atractoscion aequidens*. Some of these species are believed to have timed their spawning season to take advantage of the abundant food supply.

Cape fur seals, *Arctocephalus pusillus*, important predators of sardines in the Cape region, are also present to the north of their normal range during June and July, though not in great numbers. The African penguin, *Spheniscus demersus*, whose normal distribution mirrors that of the seals, is only occasionally sighted during the sardine run, but an increased rate of juvenile strandings along the KwaZulu-Natal coast may mean it is more prevalent than once thought.

Bryde's whales, *Balaenoptera edeni*, in contrast, appear to be year-round residents in these waters and they are probably the most efficient sardine predators of all. Rushing in quickly from the deep, they can easily engulf a sizeable portion of a baitball in a single lunge.

CURRENTS of
CONTRAST

HUMPBACK WHALE MIGRATION

Coinciding with the sardine run is another great natural history event — the migration of humpback whales from the Antarctic to their breeding and mating grounds off the coasts of KwaZulu-Natal and northern Madagascar. This is the longest migration by any mammal on Earth, with some populations travelling more than 16 000 km.

Between June and August, some 5 000 whales swim north past the east coast of southern Africa. They are often seen side by side with large shoals of sardines, although, amazingly enough, there are no records of them ever feeding on sardines in this region. In Antarctica, the southern hemisphere population appears to feed almost exclusively on krill, this being in great contrast with some humpback populations in the north. Those off the west coast of North America are prolific fish eaters, gorging themselves on herring, a close relative of the sardine. Co-operative feeding behaviour has been reported from that region, including the use of bubble netting, an approach in which a group of whales releases a series of small bubble columns blown in a circle beneath the fish. These enclose the shoal and concentrate it, making it an easier target for the whales.

Whether our humpback whales do not feed on sardines because they are travelling, or because they just do not know how to, or whether in fact they do feed on them, but we have yet to observe them, is at present unknown.

SARDINE FEVER

Attendance during the sardine run is not just limited to birds, sharks and dolphins – it also includes people, some of whom wish to catch and eat sardines, while others come simply to take in the spectacle.

FISHING

Every year seine netting crews from as far south as Port Elizabeth and as far north as Richards Bay await the arrival of the sardines in Port Edward. The teams, armed with Land Cruisers fitted with oversize roof racks stacked with a colourful assortment of crates, speed up and down the coastal roads seeking out the spot where the sardines will make landfall in KwaZulu-Natal. For most of the fishermen along this coast, it is the only time of year when the ocean gives up its riches in such profusion.

When the first shoal is sighted close to shore, the race is on. Even though there are enough sardines in these waters for all the fishermen, the bulk of the money is made in the first couple of days. The novelty value of the season's first sardines is high and the first crates can fetch prices as high as R150 per crate, whereas towards the end of the run the price drops to as low as R10 a crate.

Boats laden with 100 m-long and 8 m-deep seine nets punch through the surf, attempting to encircle a shoal close to the beach. If they are successful, an armada of helpers pulls the net back to shore. With the net only halfway out of the water, sardines are already being scooped into waiting crates, while men with large poles prevent the net from slipping back into the sea with the strong backwash. As each filled crate leaves the net it comes under attack from children trying to steal a few fish.

When the sardines pass into KwaZulu-Natal, people flock to the shore. But not everyone is after sardines — many fishermen also seek the predatory game fish that follow the run.

Compared with the commercial catches made along the west and south coasts, which amount to close to 100 000 tons, the total volume fished during the sardine run is small, the largest ever annual catch amounting to just 700 tons. Nonetheless, the quantity of fish caught in the nets is impressive and often draws thousands of spectators. The frenzy reaches a peak when a shoal of sardines beaches itself. Driven onto the beach by a combination of current, winds and predators, they can now be harvested practically without getting wet. Every man, woman and child frantically begins scooping up sardines in anything from old buckets to hats. People have even been known to fill their clothes with these fish and walk home in various stages of undress. An event like this is a real bonanza for the coast's poorer communities, whose access to protein is usually fairly limited.

CURRENTS of
CONTRAST

The plunge-diving displays of Cape gannets are the sardine run's signature event and often herald the approach of a shoal.

TOURISM

Today the sardine run is no longer just about catching fish to eat; in recent years its value in terms of wildlife tourism has been recognized. Comparable to the famed wildebeest migration of the Serengeti, the sardine run has the potential to become one of the top events of the wildlife-watching calendar. It has already been covered by major natural history film crews and photographers, and the scores of films, articles and books that will be released over the next few years are sure to spur recreational divers, bird and whale watchers to journey to the east coast to witness this phenomenon for themselves.

This large haul taken near Scottburgh was one of the first of the season and it filled hundreds of crates. Each sold at over R150.

Sardine fever
hits both young and old.

The arrival of this type of tourism has shifted the economic value of the event from the sardines to the predators that follow them, for it is the dolphins, sharks, gannets and whales that people pay to see. For sardine-run tourism to reach its full potential, however, the active participation of science will be required. The Holy Grail would be to predict the movements of the shoals and their predators reliably by using indices such as water temperature or plankton densities. At present, the uncertainty about when in June or July the event will occur is preventing the sardine run from drawing a much wider audience.

SHARK NETS

To protect bathers from sharks along KwaZulu-Natal beaches, some 45 km of gill nets — the so-called anti-shark nets — have been set along the coast between Mzamba in the south and Richards Bay in the north. The rationale is that reducing the population of sharks in the vicinity of bathing beaches greatly reduces the probability of swimmers being attacked.

In addition to catching many hundreds of sharks annually, the nets also have a considerable bycatch component consisting of large gamefish, rays, skates and turtles. Small cetaceans are also affected and three species of dolphins are regularly caught. Between 1980 and 1988, 250 bottlenose, 290 common and 53 humbacked dolphins drowned in the shark nets. Rough calculations have shown that this adds up to 3.5% of the bottlenose, 4% of the humpback and 1.9% of the common dolphin populations of KwaZulu-Natal being caught annually. While catches of common dolphins are highest in terms of numbers, their larger population size and limited seasonal occurrence in these waters makes them more resilient to such impacts. More worrisome is the impact on bottlenose and especially humpbacked dolphins. Both species have small and residential populations and such high catch rates are unlikely to be sustainable.

In the past, it was during the sardine run that catches of sharks, especially bronze whalers and duskies, but also of dolphins, were at their highest. Today the nets are lifted every June/July when spotter planes warn of the approaching shoals. The stance of the local authorities concerning tourism has changed dramatically in recent years and for two months of every year the KwaZulu-Natal South Coast markets itself as a wildlife, not a bathing, destination.

WARNING ⬥ GEVAAR

THE SHARK NETS AT THIS BEACH HAVE BEEN REMOVED FOR THE SARDINE RUN. THE RISK OF SHARK ATTACK IS THEREFORE INCREASED. ENTER THE SEA AT YOUR OWN RISK. THE RELEVANT AUTHORITIES ARE NOT LIABLE FOR INJURY OR DEATH, WHETHER DUE TO THEIR NEGLIGENCE, OR HOWSOEVER ARISING, SHOULD YOU DO SO.

DIE HAAINETTE LANGS HIERDIE STRAND IS VERWYDER WEENS DIE SARDYNLOOP. GEVOLGLIK IS DAAR 'n TOENAME IN DIE GEVAAR VAN HAAIAANVALLE. U GAAN DIE SEE OP EIE RISIKO BINNE. DIE TOEPASLIKE OWERHEDE IS NIE AANSPREEKLIK VIR BESERING OF DOOD, AS GEVOLG VAN OF HUL NALATIGHEID OF ENIGE ANDER OORSAAK, INDIEN U SO DOEN NIE.

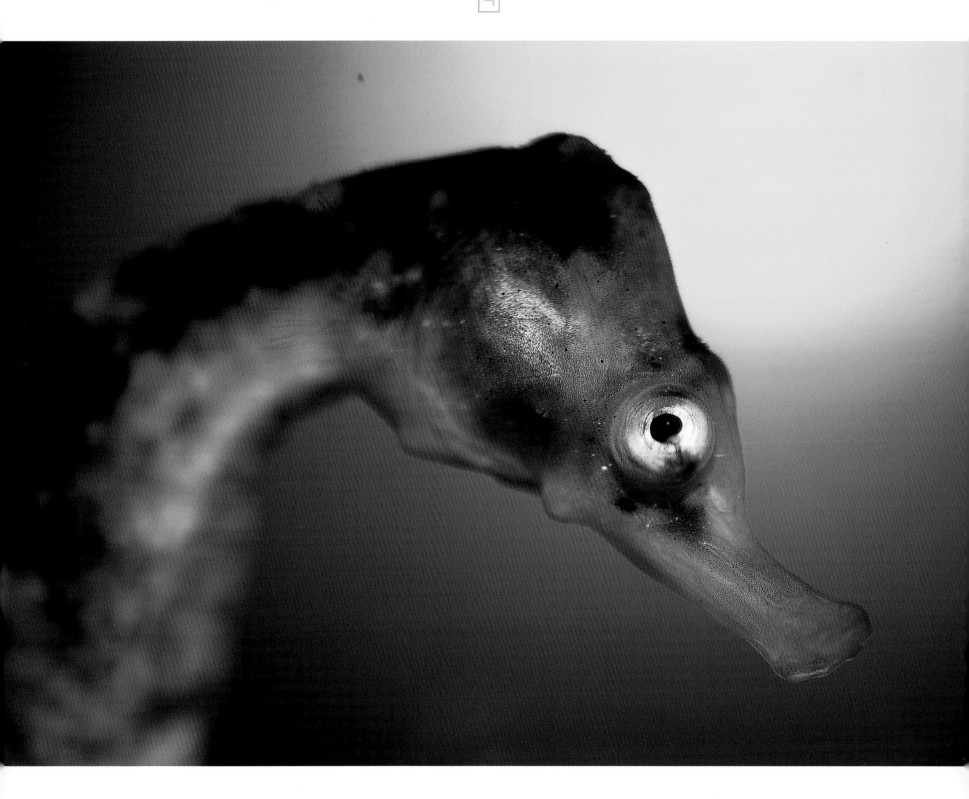

n the murky depths of South Africa's most heavily used estuary, just metres from unaware swimmers, pleasure boaters and seafront diners, lives a creature stranger than anything the imagination of a science-fiction writer has ever produced. With its horse-like head, grasping tail of a monkey, kangaroo-like pouch, independently roving eyes of a chameleon and armour-plating of an Indian rhino, it was pronounced by taxonomists to be everything from a sea monster to a shellfish to an insect to an amphibian.

Finally, it was given the scientific name *Hippocampus capensis*, which in Greek means 'horse-headed sea monster of the Cape', and was classified correctly as a fish. The Knysna seahorse might have all the attributes of a mythical being, but it is a creature of flesh and blood, complete with fins, gills and swim bladder. It is one of 32 currently recognized seahorse species, all belonging to the Sygnathidae family, which includes the pipefish, pipehorses and sea dragons.

Seahorses evolved at least 40 million years ago and have survived with only very minor changes in body structure, indicating that this strange assemblage of body parts must be an evolutionary success.

DISTRIBUTION

The Knysna seahorse is the world's only exclusively estuarine species and is restricted to just four small estuaries along the south coast of South Africa. To date, populations have only been confirmed to occur in the Knysna, Keurbooms, Swartvlei and Klein Brak systems, resulting in another accolade – that of being the seahorse with the smallest range.

Recently, genetic tests have shown that seahorses originally only occurred in the Knysna Estuary and that the Keurbooms and Swartvlei populations came into being much later, probably at the beginning of the last interglacial period. As the sea levels rose, all three estuaries became connected and it is presumed that some seahorses colonized the other systems at this time. When the sea levels dropped again, the new population became separated from those in the Knysna Estuary by terrestrial barriers. There also appears to have been no genetic interchange via the ocean in recent times, as the three seahorse populations are genetically very distinct.

The Knysna seahorse is highly tolerant of changes in salinity and is only absent from the strongly tidal areas at the estuary's mouth. It usually lives in association with the seagrass *Zostera capensis* or the green algae *Codium* and *Caulerpa*. Seagrasses are the world's only flowering marine plants. They are an important habitat, offering the seahorses anchor points to prevent them from being washed out to sea by everyday tidal currents. In addition, the seagrass beds are also important nursery grounds for many species of juvenile fish. Their root-like rhizomes help to stabilize and trap sediments, preventing excessive siltation and erosion, and increasing water clarity. Furthermore, they help to oxygenate the water and can dampen wave action and provide food in the form of detritus.

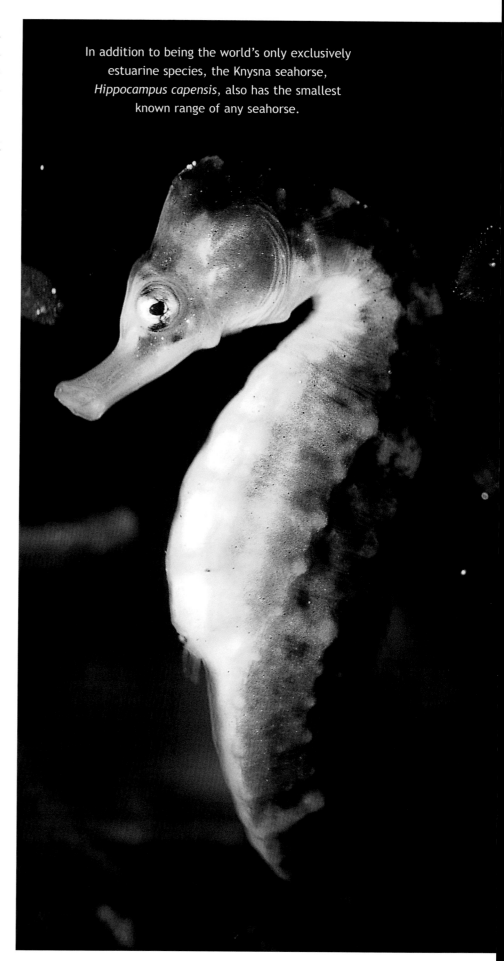

In addition to being the world's only exclusively estuarine species, the Knysna seahorse, *Hippocampus capensis*, also has the smallest known range of any seahorse.

Despite the seahorse's sophisticated reproductive strategy, the young must be able to feed and fend for themselves immediately after birth, because the parents show no further interest in rearing them. Adulthood is reached in about six months and sexual maturity is attained at approximately 5 cm.

DRIFTING INTO DANGER

Due to its very restricted geographical distribution, the Knysna seahorse is without doubt the world's most endangered seahorse. The species' survival is closely linked to the health of its estuarine home, the destruction and degradation of which is a constant threat. Human settlement and associated industrial, domestic and recreational activities are on the increase, especially in its Knysna stronghold.

New housing and marina developments are springing up across the Knysna Estuary and the needs of the seahorses are frequently overlooked when the time for environmental impact assessments comes. To date no extensive study has been carried out to gauge what effects these developments could have on seahorse populations. At present the best guess is that changes in water flow could result in dramatic movements of sediments, resulting in significant losses of seagrass beds – prime seahorse habitat. This notion is highly alarming considering the fact that many seagrass beds are already under threat. Constantly degraded and chopped up by boat propellers, this habitat has become severely fragmented.

Some claim that canals constructed in new developments and marinas will make up for any losses of natural habitat, but this is a contentious issue. Although seahorses are known to occur on man-made structures and will readily use many objects as anchors, repeated surveys of the Leisure Island boat harbour yielded fewer than 23 seahorses, and searches of Thesen's Jetty and the Knysna Quays yielded none at all.

At present, lack of data on the seahorse populations makes managing and monitoring the impact of development on the species difficult. The Knysna seahorse's future hangs in the balance as a tug of war is carried on between the interests of development and conservation.

Lagoon under siege: the beauty of the Knsyna Estuary is proving to be its downfall, attracting more and more development and people to its already crowded shores.

INTERNATIONAL TRADE IN SEAHORSES

Across the globe, seahorse populations are plummeting due to the great demand for them in traditional Asian medicines, and the curio and aquarium trade. In 1995 more than 20 million seahorses were dried, ground into powder and sold in China, Taiwan, Japan and Korea to treat ailments such as asthma, impotence, thyroid disorders, broken bones, skin ailments and heart disease. In addition, several hundred thousand more were sold as curiosities, such as seahorse keyrings, ornaments and paperweights. A further hundred thousand or so were traded live for the aquarium industry.

But it is traditional Asian medicine that consumes the bulk of the seahorses, and demand continually outstrips the supply. In Hong Kong up to $1 250 has been paid for a single kilo of high-quality seahorses. The use of seahorses in traditional Asian medicines only dates back 600 years, but Greek and Roman herbalists used seahorses as early as 324BC. In Europe during medieval times doctors prescribed them as miracle cures for most ailments, including fever, snakebite and rabies. In 1750s England, seahorses were thought to increase milk flow in lactating women.

While the use of seahorses in Western medicine ended during the 18th century, in Asian medicine they are still used today. As China's economy boomed in the 1980s, the demand for seahorses rose dramatically, plunging populations around the world into severely threatened status. Since traditional Asian medicine is recognized by the World Health Organization as a valid form of medicine accepted by more than a quarter of the world's population, a complete trade ban is not sensible. More sustainable fishing practices and aquaculture are potential remedial measures and have already been implemented successfully in the Philippines and Vietnam.

At present there is no evidence that the Knysna seahorse is exploited and traded for traditional Asian medicines, the curio or the aquarium trade, but several other southern African species are. Over 30 countries are involved in the international trade in seahorses, and Mozambique is the main source in southern Africa. Seahorses are a bycatch in seagrass seine-net fisheries in central and northern Mozambique. Seahorses are also sold on the curio markets in Cape Town and elsewhere around the country, with a single seahorse fetching about R20.

THE TEMBE-THONGA

people of the sea and lakes

n a remote corner of South Africa lies a place called Maputaland, bordered in the west by the cloud-drenched peaks of the Lebombo Mountains and in the east by the turquoise blue of the Indian Ocean. In its northern corner, alongside the Mozambican border, sits a sparsely populated coastal wilderness known as Kosi Bay. Here long narrow beaches, highways for armies of ghost crabs, are sandwiched between the ocean and some of the highest coastal dunes in the world. Draped in lush forest vegetation, the dunes are alive with the calls of African fish eagles and the rustling of duikers in the undergrowth. In the lee of the dunes, the lofty crests give way to a sloping mosaic of grassland and thicket, which rapidly descends towards a complex of four interconnected lakes.

Few roads penetrate this wilderness and myriad paths testify that travel is still largely on foot. Some 200 homesteads are central to this web of trails, loosely grouped into villages, each consisting of several reed and thatch huts encircled by a strong wooden fence to keep out the marauding hippos that abound in the waters of the southern lakes.

These dwellings belong to the Tembe-Thonga, a people believed to have migrated here from present-day Zimbabwe more than 500 years ago. Unlike the rich agricultural land they left behind, the soils of their new home were sandy and unproductive. Today the Tembe-Thonga of Maputaland are marine hunter-gatherers, relying on the ocean and lakes for food, healing and magic. In this watery wilderness, the Tembe-Thonga are as much a component of the marine and estuarine ecology as the tiger sharks cruising the shallow reefs of the Indian Ocean.

Rocky shore harvesters Nomathemba and Buyisiwe Mthembu use sharpened vehicle leaf-spring blades to harvest red bait, *Pyura stolonifera*, from rocky ledges at spring low tide.

THE TEMBE-THONGA

people of the sea and lakes

THE ROCKY SHORES

Beaches dominate the Kosi Bay coastline. In this kingdom of shifting sand, rocky outcrops and headlands are rare and interspersed, making up less than 5% of the coast. Despite the scarcity of these rocky areas, the Tembe-Thonga people rely on them considerably for food, as even the smallest sliver of rock provides a habitat for many marine animals that cannot survive on the sandy beaches.

This rich intertidal resource is not always accessible. Only during two bimonthly spring tides does the combined gravitational pull of the moon and the sun draw the sea back far enough to expose the bulk of intertidal animals that inhabit the 14 rocky ledges between Kosi Mouth and Black Rock. In days gone by, the Tembe-Thonga believed that a giant whale, *umkhomo*, created the ebb and flow of the tides by alternatively vomiting and inhaling seawater. Today, they understand the connection between the tides and the moon, pinpointing the days when the rocky shores will be exposed by referring to the moon's shape and position in the sky. If it is full and rises in the east or is just a thin crescent in the western sky right after sunset, they can harvest on the next four mornings. If the moon is only half its size and sits in the middle of the sky, it is the time of neap tides and any attempts to harvest would be futile.

Following the moon, about 200 Tembe-Thonga women and girls from several communities venture onto the exposed rock platforms to collect intertidal marine invertebrates. Armed with reed-woven collecting bags and vehicle leaf-spring blades, one end sharpened and the other wrapped in cloth as a makeshift handle, they walk up to 10 km from their homesteads to reach the nearest rocky shore. Every inch of intertidal rock in Kosi Bay is owned by a particular community. Each headman, or *induna*, makes sure that only his people harvest from that particular rock ledge. The harvesters usually arrive well before the tide has dropped to its lowest level, often while waves are still breaking over the more productive, low-shore hunting grounds.

Waiting for the tide to drop, they comb the high shore for Natal volcano barnacles, *Tetraclitas squamosa rufotincta*, Natal and Cape oysters, *Saccostrea cuccullata* and *Striostrea margaritacea*, and salmon-lipped whelks, *Thais bufo*. They probe the rock pools for octopuses, *Octopus vulgaris*, and sea cucumbers that have been trapped by the outgoing tide. When the sea has retreated far enough, the women venture to the edge of the platform, where the greatest quantities of organisms live. They take great risks to harvest right at the edge of the sea; powerful waves have washed harvesters out to sea, many never to be seen again.

ABOVE: Machete in hand, Phumlile Mthembu easily cuts through the tough outer casing of red bait.

LEFT: Sea cucumbers are harvested from rock pools, dried in the sun and ground up for use in traditional medicine and magic.

ABOVE: The edible portion of red bait is soft, glows a luminescent orange and lies hidden inside the leathery test. It tastes of the ocean and has a texture not unlike that of an oyster.

RIGHT: Women from Enkovukeni process the fruits of a morning's harvest. The bulk of the catch consists of red bait, but some urchins, mussels and limpets have also been gleaned from the rocks.

The women talk of an ancient rule to keep them safe from harm. Even when the tides are right, they do not harvest when a brownish layer of foam, created by surging seas, washes up on the shore. They say, 'It is that time of the month for the sea. Since it is taboo to touch a woman during the time she menstruates, it makes sense that we should not touch the sea either.' The women also know to be cautious during the time the marula tree, *Sclerocarya birrea* (locally named *umganu*), bears its smooth round fruits. This happens during the late summer months when the tide does not go out very far and the roughest seas lash the coastline.

The most desired marine invertebrate harvested in the low shore region is the humble brown mussel, *Perna perna* (*see* 'The return of the mussel', page 151). All the harvesters rejoice when they come across them, but only the women from one community are fortunate enough to have a supply so large that they can target them specifically. Of Kosi Bay's mussel harvest, 80% comes from one of the ledges known as Black Rock, and each collector removes an average of 11 kg of mussels every day of the spring tide.

The bulk of the rocky shore harvest is made up of red bait, *Pyura stolonifera*, a large sessile sea squirt. It prefers to inhabit crevices in the infratidal zone – the interface between the intertidal and the sub-tidal zones. The sharp end of the vehicle spring is brought down onto the base of the exterior shell with great force, and water spurts from the animal's siphon tube as it surrenders its permanent hold on the rock. To the untrained eye, it seems as though the harvesters are randomly hitting and stabbing the shore, as their quarry is well hidden and overgrown with seaweeds.

The bigger and fatter the red bait, the more valued it is. Red bait puts on weight and size when the gonads ripen just before spawning. The Tembe-Thonga look to the Natal plane tree, *Ochna natalitia*, to tell them when the red bait is at its fattest. When the tree's yellow flowers have faded during winter, a black fruit appears, and when the remainder of the flower surrounding the fruit (the calyx) turns red, they know the time has come. They call this tree *umvuthwisa 'masenene'* or the tree that ripens the red bait.

Tools of the trade. Today most harvesters are armed only with sharpened vehicle leaf-spring blades and collecting bags. In the past however they also used hoes, axes, spades and cane knives.

MEDICINAL AND MAGICAL USES OF MARINE ORGANISMS

The Tembe-Thonga call
the bleached bones of cuttlefish
the faeces of the moon.

An estimated 80% of people in southern Africa rely on a system of traditional medicine and healing as their primary source of health care. Maputaland is the epicentre of traditional healing and magic in South Africa, and the most skilled and renowned herbalists, *izinyanga*, and diviners, *izangoma*, come from this region. Traditionally, the herbalist uses *muthi*, a medicine made from plants, animals and/or minerals, to treat physical ailments, whereas the diviner consults on psychological and spiritual issues. Today, however, the definitions of herbalist and diviner have become blurred and many carry out both duties. The *izangoma* uses various methods of divination, the most common being *ukushaya amathambo*, the throwing of sets of bones and seashells to establish a diagnosis and prescribe the correct *muthi* for a cure.

In the coastal regions of Maputaland, many *izinyanga* and *izangoma* prescribe *muthi* made from marine animals. To the Tembe-Thonga of Kosi Bay, the ocean and lakes are an ancient, well-stocked pharmacy.

● Seaweeds, *amakhukhula*, cast ashore by wind and waves are boiled up and rubbed onto the skin to alleviate skin conditions.

● The spines of sea urchins, *amanungu*, are ground into a fine powder and combined with pieces of sea cucumbers, *umnyisa*, to help irregular periods and difficult pregnancies.

● The bleached backbone of the cuttlefish, which washes out onto Maputaland's beaches in great quantities, is believed by some of the local people to be the faeces of the moon. They call it *amasimba 'nyanga'* and crush it into a fine powder used to cure a variety of eye ailments.

Most animal *muthi*, though, including marine creatures, are used for 'magical' purposes and have great symbolic and spiritual value to the patient. Marine animals are used as charms for cattle, crops, love, protection, stick fighting and witchcraft. For example, many marine *muthi* are used to exact revenge on an unfaithful wife and her lovers.

● Chitons, *imfinyezi*, have a habit of curling up tightly and are therefore given to an unfaithful wife to cause vaginal spasm, which traps the lover so that the couple cannot separate.

● A sea cucumber, *umnyisa*, avoids being eaten by expelling a small portion of its intestine through its anus to distract attacking predators. *Umnyisa muthi* is therefore said to make an unfaithful wife's lover's stomach fall out.

● The puffer fish, *isibofa*, gulps water or air, inflating itself to look bigger and frighten off potential enemies. *Isibofa muthi* will cause the wife's lover's stomach to swell; the Tembe-Thonga say that he will have high tide in his stomach.

All of this *muthi* is administered as *insizi*, the traditional medicine equivalent of the hypodermic needle. The powdered and often charred mix of *muthi* is rubbed into cuts made into the skin with porcupine quills or a razor blade.

Izangoma throw marine shells and bones
to establish the cause of a patient's illness
and to prescribe the correct cure.

The harvest of traditional medicines has changed dramatically over the past century — from a specialist activity carried out only by herbalists and diviners, to a thriving trade involving commercial gatherers and hawkers. Some Tembe-Thonga women now specialize in collecting marine *muthi*, taking up to 400 chitons and many long-spined sea urchins and live cowries per day. Once a month, they take their *muthi* collections to the city of Durban, where they sell them on the traditional medicine market. The rare python chiton, *Chiton salihafui*, which has its southernmost range in Maputaland, may already have suffered over-exploitation because of the *muthi* harvest.

Traditional healer associations are currently addressing the issue of unsustainable harvesting of medicines. Having realized the importance of a sustainable yield, they plan to train their members in how to harvest in a sustainable manner and how to use alternatives to rare and endangered species.

Nomathemba digs with great ferocity until the crab is caught and subdued.

Winter is also the time of the equinox, which brings the lowest tides of the year. The tide goes out so far that the upper reaches of the vast subtidal red bait stocks become accessible. It is therefore during August that people from all over Kosi Bay venture to the shore, and up to 50 harvesters congregate on a single ledge in what has been termed the annual red bait festival. When the tide begins to turn and waves start licking at the heels of the harvesters, they leave the shore and head up the dune slope to process their catches.

SANDY SHORES

The vast expanse of beaches in this region yields fairly few food items for the Tembe-Thonga. The three species of ghost crab are the exception. *Ocypode ryderi*, *O. madagascariensis* and *O. ceratophthalmus* occur in vast armies of up to 15 200 individuals per kilometre of sandy shore. These crustacean scavengers scuttle up, down and along the beach on a mission to find washed-up animals such as fish, mussels or – perhaps the greatest windfall of them all – a decaying whale.

During high tide and times of danger, ghost crabs retreat into their burrows, which protect them from predators such as the palmnut vulture, *Gypohierax angolensis*, a bird with a penchant for crabs. But their burrows are no defence against the Tembe-Thonga, who enjoy the crabs almost as much as the vultures do. On an incoming tide during late afternoon and early evening, women and children venture onto the beach to harvest these crabs, which they call *inkalankala*. On a typical harvesting excursion women walk up to 6 km along the beach and collect around 30 crabs each.

There are two ways to catch ghost crabs. Experienced harvesters can tell which holes are occupied. Crouching down, they dig with great ferocity until the crab is caught and subdued. Girls and young women often practise an even more energetic method, though there are also some senior specialists of this technique. As a group, the women charge onto the beach and into the sea, grabbing crabs with hands and feet. With an agility that would make any cricketer proud, they fling themselves at any crab that moves.

When handling ghost crabs, harvesters have to be careful not to get nipped by their powerful pincers. Freshly caught crabs are cooked on an open fire and consumed almost immediately.

FOLLOWING THE MOON

The Tembe-Thonga believe that every time a waning moon sets, it dies, and when the first sliver of the new moon reappears on the horizon several days later, another moon has been born. The moon is central to their lives, telling them when and where to find food, providing them with medicine, and being the subject of many of their ceremonies and rituals.

Dusk falls quickly on the shores of Lake Nhlange and a homestead situated on a dune crest high above the lake is awash with activity. Some 30 people, mainly women from the surrounding homesteads, have gathered around a fire. The sky in the west darkens quickly and all eyes scan the heavens for the first sign of the new moon. When the thin sliver is finally spotted, there is shouting and rejoicing. This is the sign that the ceremony can begin and Thulile, the leader of the proceedings, begins to sing and dance. The fire roars as it is stocked with dry tinder-like brush, transforming the women into dancing silhouettes.

From outside the circle of light, a young woman cradling a baby girl approaches. The singing and dancing grows more frenzied and stomping feet propel dust high into the air. Thulile takes the baby and the mother braves the intense heat of the fire to grab a burning stick. She arches backward and launches it into the air. The trailing embers show the stick's flight path across the night sky as it streaks up towards the moon.

The singing and dancing calms and a cracked pot of cold ash is brought close to the fire, where it is poured into a large heap. The baby is placed onto the heap of ash and rolled gently from side to side. She is patient and does not cry, her wide eyes staring calmly back at Thulile. The baby is taken from the ashes and lifted towards the heavens, then gently thrown upward towards the moon as fevered cries of 'this is your moon' echo over the dunes of eNkovukeni.

As the moon begins its descent below the horizon, the fire dies and the women return home, some chased by hippos that have come ashore to graze. They all reunite the next morning on the shores of the Indian Ocean to finish what they started the previous night. The baby girl has to undergo one last rite — to be presented to the sea. As the women begin dancing, the infant is laid down alone before the mercy of the ocean. As a wave curls up, about to break and wash the child away, she is snatched from death. The ceremony is complete: child and ocean have met.

CURRENTS of
CONTRAST

The beaches of Kosi Bay yield as many as 146 000 harvested ghost crabs every year, but the Tembe-Thonga also regularly cross the border into Mozambique. The women say the crabs there are easier to harvest because they are not used to people trying to catch them. Apart from ghost crabs, another two species of sandy shore crustaceans are also harvested – the mole crabs *Emerita austroafricana* and *Hippa ovalis*. Mole crabs are only harvested at night, dug out by hand from the swash zone as the waves recede. About 129 000 mole crabs are harvested every year at Kosi Bay. Almost all the crabs caught are eaten by the harvesters and their families, but some are sold in the form of crab kebabs – crab on a stick – at markets, celebrations and other gatherings.

The Tembe-Thonga's harvesting of sandy shore organisms is a unique representation of the use of sandy beaches in southern Africa, where the bulk of fishing is carried out on rocky shores and reefs.

THE LAKES

The term Kosi Bay is a misnomer, as the bay is actually the estuarine mouth of a much vaster lake system formed during the late Pleistocene when the sea level was much higher than it is today. The lakebeds are ancient submarine canyons carved out of the Earth by the relentless forces of the ocean. Salt water intrudes into the system every high tide at its northernmost end, through Kosi mouth, a 30 m wide channel linking the ocean and the lakes. It flows through the estuarine basin known as Enkovukeni (meaning the up-and-down action of water), as far south as Lake Makhlawulani and Lake Mpungwini.

The shores of the estuary are lined with mangrove forests that thrive in these saline conditions (*see* 'The realm of dancing crabs and walking fish', page 148). The ocean's influence is felt less and less the further south the Kosi system is penetrated, and the waters of Lake Nhlange and Lake Amanzimnyama are completely fresh, fed by the Sihadhla and Nswamanzi rivers. During low tide, their fresh waters flow towards the sea through the deep reed-lined channels and during times of flood can even reach the mouth. The never-ending battle between the rivers and the ocean for control of the lakes creates a seesaw of salty and fresh water, an estuarine environment that is ever changing. The Kosi system is southern Africa's most pristine estuary and its silt-free nature and peat-stained waters make it unique in KwaZulu-Natal.

TRADITIONAL FISH TRAPS

The Kosi system is inhabited by 133 species of fish, some of which – like perch, *Acanthopagrus berda*, and pouter, *Gerres acinaces* – spend their entire lives in the estuary and only return to the ocean for a short time to spawn. Marine fishes such as spotted grunter, *Pomadasys commersonnii*, and flathead mullet, *Mugil cephalus*, enter the estuary during their juvenile stages to escape the intense predation on the reefs, and migrate back out to the sea on reaching maturity.

The Tembe-Thonga have known about this interestuarine-marine movement of fish for more than 500 years and have devised an ingenious fishing strategy to take advantage of it. They build elaborate, permanent fish kraals designed to trap the fish as they swim back to the sea. On the southern banks of Lake Makhlawulani up to 100 fish traps crisscross the shallows for miles in a seemingly endless maze of sticks and reeds. Almost every available site has a fish kraal on it, each owned by a particular household. Fish-trap sites are jealously guarded as they are valuable commodities passed down from father to son.

Travel on the lakes is still largely in reed boats made from Kosi palms *Raphia australis*.

Fish traps are mostly made out of wood from red-heart, *Hymencardia ulmoides*, and white mangrove, *Avicennia marina*, trees. A single trap can consist of over 1 000 kg of wood. The guide fences, known as *umtamana*, are constructed at right angles to the water flow. Each consists of a line of closely spaced poles with horizontally interwoven brushwood and saplings. Fish swimming downstream during nocturnal high tides will reach the fences and be guided towards the heart-shaped palisade. This leads into the circular enclosure, known as *ijele*, where the fish are finally trapped. In the morning during low tide, the fisherman will check his trap and spear any fish in it.

Grunter and mullet are the most commonly caught fish, making up 50% and 30% of the catch respectively. Research has shown that fish kraals trap less than 10% of the migrating fish, as long as a 30 m-wide channel of inflowing and outflowing tidal water is left free of obstructions. The use of traditional fish traps is a very sustainable way of exploiting the riches of the Kosi system.

SPEARFISHING

Many generations of men have taken the straightest branch they could find from an *umpahla* tree, *Brachylaena discolor*, broken it off at its base, hardened its tip over a fire and inserted a sharpened iron rod into the end of the stick. Brandishing these spears, groups of boys and young men walk along the edges of the reed-flanked lakes Makhlawulani and Mpungwini, stalking individual fish in the clear water and throwing the spears at them. They also blindly thrust their spears deep into the reeds where tilapia, *Oreochromis mossambicus*, hide during the day.

Records of Portuguese mariners who sailed along this coast in 1554 make reference to fish traps at Kosi Bay, confirming that this truly ancient art of fishing has been practised for at least 450 years.

Another form of spearing, less widespread, but one that was very common 80 years ago, is underwater spearfishing. Using the same type of spear, men free-dive in the channels between the lakes. When a fish comes within range, it is speared with an underarm forward thrust and threaded onto a piece of creeper vine, which is passed through the gills and mouth of the fish. The other end of the creeper is tied to the fisherman's waist, trailing in the water behind him as he continues hunting. In the past up to 50 spear fishermen would gather if conditions were right, but today only a handful of old men are keeping alive Africa's only estuarine underwater spearfishery.

GILL NETS

A present-day Kosi Bay fishery that does not have its roots in the ancient hunter-gatherer traditions of the Tembe-Thonga is the industry making use of gill nets. Gill nets were developed in India and first used at Kosi Bay in the 1950s. The use of gill nets reached epidemic proportions in the 1980s when over 40 km of illegally set nets were confiscated. Gill nets are especially damaging when they are set over channels, decimating fish populations within a very short period. During fish migrations they catch over 90% of the fish compared with the 10% caught by traditional fish traps.

Only a handful of old men are keeping alive Africa's only estuarine spearfishery.

THE REALM OF DANCING CRABS AND WALKING FISH

The mudskipper is a fish equally at home on land as in water.

Kosi Bay's mangrove forests are made up of six species of trees: the black mangrove, *Bruguiera gymnorrhiza*, white mangrove, *Avicennia marina*, red mangrove, *Rhizophora mucronata*, Indian mangrove, *Ceriops tagal*, and the Kosi or spring-tide mangrove, *Lumnitzera racemosa*. The last species of this sextet is the Mozambique mangrove, *Heritiera littoralis*, which is represented by only a single specimen.

At Kosi Bay, mangrove forests thrive along the intertidal fringes of the estuary and are exposed to a continually changing environment of varying salinity, temperature, nutrients and oxygen levels. Only the surface layer of the muddy soil is well oxygenated. Below that conditions are anoxic (oxygen deficient) due to bacterial decomposition of plant material. Survival is only possible with sophisticated root systems, such as arching prop roots that find a firm grip in the loose and unstable soil. Some trees also send up vertical root extensions called pneumatophores, which rise from the mud to create a dense carpet of spiky breathing appendages.

Living in these estuarine conditions raises the overall salt concentrations in plant tissues and this can easily disrupt vital internal chemical reactions. Mangrove trees have evolved an array of coping mechanisms, ranging from preventing the salts entering the roots in the first place, to specialized glands that secrete excess salt onto the surface of the leaves, where it is washed away by the next rains.

Mangroves produce elongated conical pods harbouring a single seed each. Once ripened, the pods fall away from the tree and if release occurs when the tide is high, the seedpods disperse by remaining afloat for several weeks. If the seedlings fall during low tide, they will become embedded in oozing mud and roots will sprout almost immediately.

Mangrove swamps offer a wide range of animals a near-seamless interface between a terrestrial and a marine environment. Birds, monkeys and snakes are at home in the terrestrial tree canopy, while many marine species occupy the roots and muddy flats between the trees. The mudskipper, *Periophthalmus* spp., is a fish that can walk on land. During low tide it hobbles along on its pectoral fins, searching for prey. It can breathe on land because it retains oxygenated water in its gill chambers. At the first signs of an encroaching tide, it seeks shelter in a burrow with a raised turret several centimetres high. These homes are excavated by the male one mouthful at a time, and are fiercely defended against other intruding males.

Sharing the muddy forest floor with the mudskipper is a wide variety of crabs. Some migrate up and down the roots and tree trunks to graze on fresh succulent leaves, while others never leave the forest floor, living in burrows and feeding on fallen and decaying leaves.

The Tembe-Thonga tribe has a long history of exploiting both the mangrove fauna and flora. Women dig out the mangrove crabs, *Sesarma meinerti*, from their burrows, collecting almost half a million annually — one of the largest crab fisheries in southern Africa. The mangrove whelk, *Terebralia palustris*, is used as bait in fishing baskets. Mangrove wood is very popular as it is resistant to rot and termites, making it the prime material for the construction of traditional fish traps.

Mangrove crabs, *Sesarma meinerti*, are harvested on the banks of the estuary near Kosi mouth and are sometimes sold in the nearby town of Manguzi.

In 1992, gill net fishing at Kosi was re-evaluated and the use of these nets manipulated to target less-exploited species of fish. In an experiment, fishermen were allowed to set 30 m gill nets only in the shallows around the edges of Lake Nhlange. Careful monitoring revealed that these nets did not impact on fish migrations and caught primarily common fish such as barbel, *Plotosus lineatus*, pouter and tilapia.

As long as gill nets are not set over or near channels, and are kept to the specified length and gap size, this type of fishing can be sustainable as it does not compete for the same resource niches as other traditional fisheries, such as the fish traps.

CONSERVATION

The Tembe-Thonga have harvested the marine and estuarine resources of Kosi Bay for well over 500 years. Until fairly recently, the rest of South Africa seemed unaware of their activities. The entire region lay hidden behind a curtain of malaria-infested swamps and foreboding clouds of tsetse flies, and nobody ventured to Kosi Bay unless they had to. With the eradication of the tsetse fly, the draining of the swamps, the building of roads and the more recent proclamation of the Maputaland Marine and the Kosi Bay Nature reserves in the 1980s, the curtain was drawn back, and the harvesting activities of the Tembe-Thonga became a contentious issue.

Their marine and estuarine harvests were allowed to continue while awaiting the results of a scientific study. In order to assess whether the harvests were sustainable or not, researchers began to monitor the quantities fished. Between 1988 and 1994, catch per unit effort (CPUE) data were collected for the main Tembe-Thonga marine

and estuarine fisheries and the results initially led scientists to suggest that the harvest was sustainable across the board. Without having conducted direct surveys of the resources, though, and lacking pristine benchmarks for areas where no harvesting was taking place, further lines of evidence were needed before sustainability could be confirmed.

THE MARINE LIVING RESOURCES ACT AND SUBSISTENCE FISHING

With the democratic elections in 1994 heralding the end of the apartheid state, a new National Fisheries policy needed to be developed, as the old one was tainted by unequal sharing of marine and estuarine resources. Fishing activities carried out by rural indigenous peoples like the Tembe-Thonga were almost always unrecognized and in many cases were deemed illegal.

With the promulgation of the new Marine Living Resources Act in 1998, indigenous, so-called subsistence fishermen were for the first time regarded as holding important rights to the marine and estuarine resources alongside their commercial and recreational counterparts. The act defines subsistence fishermen and women as poor people who personally harvest marine resources as a source of food or to sell locally, thereby meeting the basic need for food security. They operate on, or near to, the shore or in estuaries, live close to the resources and use low technology/traditional gear.

In some places along the coast steep dunes, covered in lush forests, plunge straight into the sea.

To implement the Act and make the subsistence fishermen legal entities, several steps were necessary, including the introduction of a permit system, management measures such as bag and size limits, as well as closed seasons and areas. For almost two decades, Dr Scotty Kyle, resource ecologist with Ezemvelo KZN Wildlife, based in Kosi Bay, has been pioneering co-management principles in the region, forging trust and mutual respect between a few select Tembe-Thonga communities and the nature conservation authorities. In 1999, building on this foundation, the Nedbank Green Trust (a subsidiary trust of WWF-SA), Ezemvelo KZN Wildlife and the University of Cape Town, spearheaded by Ronnie Brereton-Stiles and Dr Jean Harris, implemented a project to arrange for subsistence co-management structures to be put in place at Kosi Bay.

The essence of co-management is that local fisherpeople and the conservation authorities share the responsibility for managing the resource within the framework of the law. The harvesters become part of the decision-making process that will ultimately lead to their becoming legal resource users. This process was initiated by an information campaign, including road shows and a succession of community meetings where all the facets of co-management and the new Marine Living Resources Act were explained.

But not all the Tembe-Thonga communities shared the authorities' enthusiasm for the new Act. 'Why must we buy a permit, a piece of paper giving us permission to harvest what has belonged to us since the time of our ancestors?' was the most common sentiment expressed. 'We have been taking care of our nature for hundreds of years, we do not need you to do it for us; you just want to steal our land,' was another.

These misgivings resulted in riotous protests and the disruption of public meetings and information campaigns. Despite these initial hostilities, two dedicated conservation field workers persisted, slowly gaining the trust and respect of the Tembe-Thonga. Three years later, the tables began to turn and many communities became less opposed to the implications of the Marine Living Resources Act.

CO-MANAGEMENT AT WORK

Today, 10 Tembe-Thonga women of the Enkovukeni community sit on a patch of dusty earth, drenched in the shade of a Natal mahogany tree. Together with a number of conservation managers and researchers, they are the Songimvelo ('Let us conserve together') Mussel Committee, one of the first groups of Tembe-Thonga harvesters to embrace co-management. In monthly meetings, they discuss and address conservation and resource management issues and other dilemmas.

Among the first items on the committee's agenda was the implementation of conservation measures to safeguard the resource. While things had moved slowly on the co-management front, the newly implemented resource survey programme yielded results

fairly quickly. Surveys revealed an 80% reduction of mussel stocks at Black Rock over the past 20 years, restricting them to the lower reaches of the shore. Anecdotal evidence also showed that mussels were much more abundant in the past on rock ledges at Bhanga Neck and Dog Point. The densities of the Natal bearded limpet, *Scutellastra pica*, were also substantially lower than in 1997. 'The tide just does not go out as far as it used to,' one of the older residents lamented. 'Every year we get wetter and wetter harvesting the mussels.'

The monitoring of shellfish harvests between 1988 and 1994 had missed this steep decline in mussels and limpets because it relied exclusively on the monitoring of catches – and this measure is often not a reliable indicator of stock size and sustainability until the stocks have almost completely disappeared. The loss of the brown mussel, *Perna perna*, in particular not only spells the loss of the Tembe-Thonga tribe's favourite shellfish item, it has led to changes in the rocky shore ecosystem and its ecological functioning. Rocky ledges once dominated by mussels were quickly invaded by algae, on which few mussel larvae could settle. The results were large areas of rock remaining devoid of mussels for long periods of time, perhaps even forever.

One of the most destructive and unsustainable practices is the use of broad-bladed tools such as spades, hoes and axes to remove large quantities of rocky shore organisms. These tools clear gaps too large for recolonisation to occur quickly, and there are substantial quantities of unwanted bycatch, such as juvenile mussels and red bait. The Songimvelo committee decided to impose an outright ban on such tools. In conjunction with marine biologists, the Tembe-Thonga harvesters set up the first no-take areas to serve as benchmarks for future research in assessing human impact. Highly visible flags demarcated these areas, and community monitors made sure no harvesting occurred. The indigenous owners of the rock platforms were thus now directly involved in conserving them, a major breakthrough for the establishment of a co-operative relationship between the Tembe-Thonga and the conservation authorities. They also became involved in the research by helping to monitor the state of the mussel beds and install experimental plates to assess mussel and barnacle larvae recruitment.

With the progress shown by the Songimvelo committee, the remaining communities agreed to establish both fishing and harvesting committees in the marine reserve, as well as in the other, non-rocky shore fisheries of Kosi Bay. The fish kraal committee has made some tough conservation and management decisions of its own. The use of traditional fish traps is only sustainable if a wide enough channel is left free of any obstacles. Over time people had been breaking this rule, building their traps further into the channel to catch more and more fish. The committee, in liaison with the communities, decided to stop this unsustainable practice, encouraging the authorities to remove the offending fish traps with their blessing.

THE RETURN OF THE MUSSEL

In the south of KwaZulu-Natal brown mussels occur in large, dense beds, but in Maputaland they aggregate only in small clumps. Scientists are currently testing whether this pattern is caused by over-exploitation or underlying differences in environmental conditions.

The Tembe-Thonga used to believe that new mussels were brought with the rains, and that as long as it kept raining mussels would be available in great numbers on the rocky ledges. In reality, though, mussels shed their eggs and sperm into the water column and fertilized eggs become free-swimming larvae that drift for weeks in ocean currents before finding a suitable place to settle. Larvae prefer to settle in a clump of already established mussels, so if mussels are absent from a rocky platform, larval recruitment will be very low.

As part of a scientific experiment to find out if mussels can survive at Maputaland sites in larger numbers, mussels from Cape Vidal are being transplanted onto rocky shores with little or no mussel cover. If these translocations are successful, this method could be used to re-establish mussel beds and increase larvae settlement rates, thereby allowing more women to sustainably harvest brown mussels in the Kosi Bay region.

Ronnie Brereton-Stiles and Gugu Zama prepare to transplant mussels onto a denuded rocky shore. Dense clumps of these bivalves are secured to the platform with a plastic mesh, which is only removed once the mussels have reattached themselves after several weeks.

The people of Kosi Bay, the conservation authorities and researchers have turned the tide of environmental destruction in the face of burning swamp forests, banana plantations and widespread poaching. The Tembe-Thonga have begun to take responsibility for their marine and estuarine resources, thereby safeguarding them for their children and their children's children.

SEA TURTLES

prehistoric survivors

bulldozer-like track comes to an abrupt end where the exposed sandy slope of the dune meets the base of thick subtropical forest. The silhouettes of spindly casuarina trees on the dune crest, the white expanse of beach lit up under a full moon, and the pounding sea give the setting a timeless, almost prehistoric feel. Less than an hour ago, a female leatherback turtle, weighing nearly as much as a small car, crawled out of the sea to lay her eggs. In about 60 days, on a night similar to this one, a brood of hatchlings will emerge from a nest deep beneath the sand and scramble for the sea. In the process, they perpetuate a marine reptilian life cycle that has been re-enacted millions of times since its inception. The leatherback turtle is a species so ancient that it was already roaming the oceans in pursuit of now long-vanished jelly-fish during the heyday of the dinosaurs. However, unlike the dinosaurs, which went extinct, this turtle species has survived largely unchanged to the present.

TURTLE MECCA

The oceans around southern Africa are home to five of the world's seven marine turtles: the leatherback, *Dermochelys coriacea*, the loggerhead, *Caretta caretta*, the green, *Chelonia mydas*, the hawksbill, *Eretmochelys imbricata*, and the olive Ridley, *Lepidochelys olivacea*. Leatherbacks and loggerheads nest in large numbers along the coast, while greens, hawks-bills and olive Ridleys nest only in small numbers in northern Mozambique.

The leatherback is the world's largest living sea turtle, reaching up to 2.5 m in length and regularly weighing over half a ton. Its carapace is distinct from that of all other marine turtles in that it lacks external horny plates; instead, it is covered by a brown to black leathery skin with seven raised longitudinal ridges. Its head is without scales, the upper jaw has an exaggerated tooth-like projection and the foreflippers are almost 1 m long. The slightly smaller logger-head turtle can still reach an impressive length of up to 1.2 m and has a distinctive broad reddish-brown carapace and a yellowish underside.

Southern Africa's turtle Mecca is without doubt a 56 km-long stretch of sandy beach in the northeastern corner of South Africa, a place called Maputaland, which is interrupted periodically by rocky headlands and wave-cut platforms. This is the only major turtle-nesting site in south-ern Africa and the location of one of the longest-running turtle research programmes in the world. Since 1963, under the leadership of Dr George Hughes, the beaches here have been intensively patrolled and surveyed almost every night during the nesting season.

Sandy beaches free from development and human disturbance make ideal nesting grounds for sea turtles.

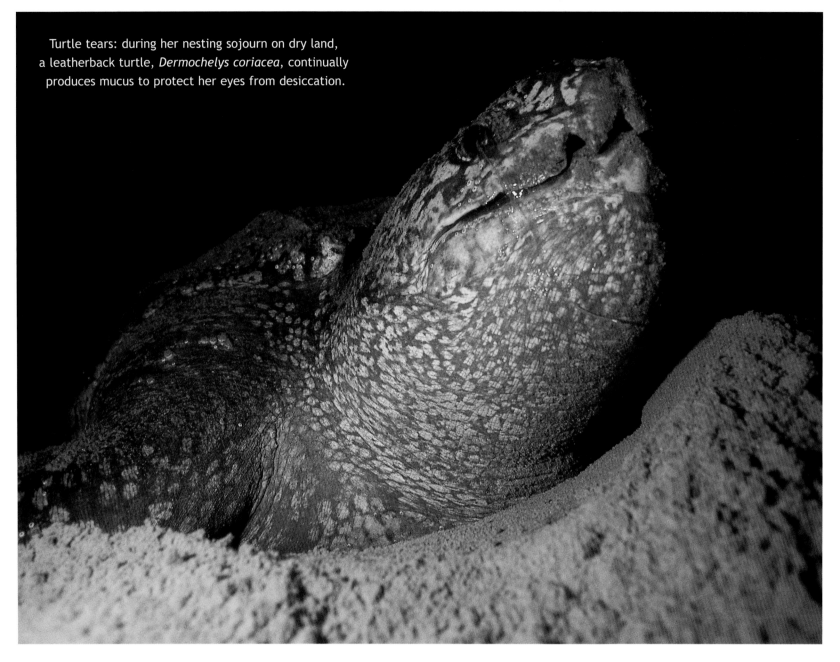

Turtle tears: during her nesting sojourn on dry land, a leatherback turtle, *Dermochelys coriacea*, continually produces mucus to protect her eyes from desiccation.

LIFE ON LAND

From October onwards, males and females of two species arrive off the Maputaland coast. Loggerhead turtles are drawn here from the entire western Indian Ocean region, but it is not known from which region the leatherbacks come to breed.

In both species, mating is believed to occur some 1–2 km offshore, mainly in water 15–20 m deep. Claws on the male's front flippers are specifically designed to hang on tightly to the front of the female's carapace during copulation. The male's penis spends most of its time in a small pouch at the end of the tail, only becoming everted once it is near the female's cloaca. It is thought that female turtles only mate once per season and that the male's copious sperm production is enough to fertilize up to 10 batches of over 100 eggs during the coming months. Males, however, probably mate with multiple females during a single breeding season.

When the female's oviduct is filled to capacity with ripe eggs, she approaches the coast and rests in the swash (surf) zone, now and then lifting her head as if scanning the beach for signs of danger. She leaves the ocean moments later and clumsily clambers ashore under cover of darkness. The leatherback hauls her huge body across the sand by simultaneously moving both flippers, while the loggerhead uses alternate flipper movements.

Loggerheads, in particular, are often seen thrusting their beaks into the wet sand immediately after stranding. This is called tactile tasting or sand smelling and is believed to play an important role in turtles' ability to relocate their preferred nesting beaches year after year. The exact nature of this olfactory cue is as yet unknown, but it could be the smell of freshwater seepages that drain through the dunes from the adjacent Kosi lake system. Alternatively, the nesting activities themselves could be providing navigation beacons.

The nest cavity is scooped out, one flipper at a time. Once egg laying commences sea turtles enter a trance-like state. They become oblivious to their surroundings, ignoring researchers, photographers and even poachers.

BELOW AND RIGHT: Each female turtle lays over 100 billiard ball-sized eggs in her nest.

Normally nesting only under the cover of darkness, this loggerhead turtle left the beach well after sunrise.

After many decades, it is likely that frequently used nesting beaches have become impregnated with the smell of the mucus exuded by females while laying eggs. Rains and drainage could even carry this scent into the sea, allowing it to linger in the nearshore zone.

The strength of this cue decreases abruptly above the high-tide mark, potentially giving the nesting turtles an indication of how high up the shore they must climb to avoid having their nests washed away or becoming waterlogged. The turtles probably become imprinted with the smell of their nesting beach while still in the egg chamber and are able to recall it during their first nesting migration many years later.

Loggerhead turtles nest high on the dune slopes, while leatherbacks generally prefer to lay their eggs close to the high-water mark. Other distinct spatial differences in their nesting habits also exist. Loggerheads tend to emerge more frequently than leatherbacks onto beaches near intertidal reefs, and two sections of beach consistently boast the highest number of nesting females year after year. Both sites lie in the northern half of Maputaland, between Castle Rock and Kosi mouth, one between Dog Point and Bhanga Neck, the

other between the N22 rock ledge and Kosi mouth. Leatherback turtles generally only nest on beaches with heavy surf and ready access to deep water. Nesting females are more commonly seen to the south of the prime loggerhead nesting hot spots, peaking in the Manzengwenya, Rocktail Bay and Mabibi regions.

Having found a suitable nest site, the females of both species first dig a body cavity with their foreflippers until their carapaces are level with the surrounding beach. Then they dig the egg cavity, scooping out the sand with one hind flipper at a time. The flask-shaped nest is dug as deep as the flippers can reach. Both species lay over 100 soft-shelled eggs the size of billiard balls. The eggs need to be soft and pliable so as not to damage each other as they fall in quick bursts of one to four onto the mass of eggs already in the nest. When finished, the females gently fill the egg cavity with sand and compact it with the weight of their bodies. Finally, they throw sand over the disturbed site, taking great care and time to disguise it. The whole procedure can last as long as three hours, after which the female turtle returns to the sea.

Leatherbacks nest up to 10 times a season at intervals of 9–10 days and loggerheads about four times at 14–17 day intervals. They both return to the same stretch of coast at two- to four-year intervals but what governs the extent of the 'remigration' period is, as yet, unknown. Over a single breeding season, however, a nesting female can lose up to a quarter of her body weight and much of her fat reserve producing eggs. Since egg production and nesting behaviour place considerable strain on the turtles, it can be presumed that the abundance and quality of prey are important factors. The poorer the feeding conditions, the longer the remigration nesting interval will be, for it will take the turtle longer to regain condition and build up fat reserves.

HATCHING

The eggs remain underground for about 60 days and hatching occurs between January and March, reaching a peak in February. During that time, predation can occur and feral dogs, honey badgers and monitor lizards have been known to dig up nests and destroy entire clutches. If the nest remains intact, the young turtles will chisel their way out of the egg using the specialized egg tooth at the end of their beaks. Once out, it will take them almost a day to unfold from the foetal position adopted inside the egg.

This ghost crab may have bitten off a little bit more than it can chew. Attempts to drag this leatherback hatchling underground to escape competition from other crabs failed repeatedly.

BELOW: Hatchlings, like this loggerhead, *Caretta caretta*, find their way to the sea by instinctively crawling away from the dunes and towards the much brighter ocean horizon.

The sex composition of the nest group depends on the nest temperature. A cool nest of below 25 °C will almost certainly result in all turtles being male, while higher temperatures exceeding 29 °C will produce an all-female clutch. Intermediate temperatures ensure more balanced mixed-sex ratios.

Soon after the bulk of the eggs have hatched, an extraordinary display of teamwork begins. Together, all the hatchlings begin digging away at the sides and roof of the nest chamber. Sand cascades down and passes through the seething mass of hatchlings to the bottom of the egg chamber, forming a new floor. By moving constantly, the hatchlings avoid getting covered by the falling sand and are slowly carried to the surface by the continually rising floor of the nest chamber – a sand elevator, so to speak. Those that do not move vigorously enough are buried and are rarely able to make their own way to the surface. If the hatchlings approach the surface during the day and the sand is still too hot, they await nightfall before emerging from the final centimetres of sand.

On leaving the nest, both loggerhead and leatherback hatchlings begin to crawl immediately towards the ocean. They orientate themselves by moving away from the dark shadows and silhouettes of the dune slope and towards the bright oceanic horizon. Light is such an overriding factor in orientation that hatchlings have been known to follow the torches of fishermen up the dunes and along the beach.

While about 80% of the young turtles successfully emerge from the nest, only two individuals in every thousand survive to full maturity. The moment the hatchlings leave their nest, they face the most treacherous part of their journey. As they scramble towards the sea *en masse*, they are targeted by side-striped jackals, honey badgers, larger spotted genets and water mongooses. Those turtles unfortunate enough to attempt to run the gauntlet during the day are picked off by palmnut vultures, egrets and yellow-billed kites. The turtles' main predators, however, are the much smaller ghost crabs *Ocypode ceratophthalmus* and *O. kuhlii*. These have been known to kill up to 12% of the hatchlings of a single clutch and are responsible for the death of some 4% of hatchlings in any given nesting season. Large ghost crabs are formidable predators and are particularly active on moonless nights. They easily disable and kill hatchlings with their large claws, and then attempt to drag them into their holes. They have the greatest impact when the clutch is small and the tide is low as the hatchlings have a much longer distance to travel before reaching the sea.

LIFE AT SEA

Upon leaving the beach, the young turtles quickly embrace their new home in the ocean.

HATCHLINGS AND JUVENILES

On reaching the ocean, the turtles immediately head in an offshore direction, orientating themselves by swimming directly into the waves. Hatchlings detect the direction of wave travel not by vision, but by the movement of their bodies as the waves pass over them. Experiments have shown that hatchlings swim with a so-called orbital movement, the sequence of which differs depending on wave direction. By monitoring the sequence of acceleration and movement as each wave passes, the hatchling can detect wave direction. A turtle swimming in an offshore direction will move in the following sequence as the waves pass: upward, forward, downward and backward. If it is swimming towards the shore, however, it will move upward, backward, downward and forward.

The hatchlings now undertake a swimming frenzy that lasts at least 20 hours, in which they can travel up to 28 km offshore. Predation by fish decreases as hatchlings distance themselves from their natal nests. They suffer a mortality rate of 40–60% within the first two hours at sea, the majority of which occurs before crossing the 10 m depth contour. When the hatchlings make it past the reef and reach deeper water, predation rates drop by two-thirds and their swimming speed decreases.

The young turtles reach the outskirts of the Agulhas current after several days. In deeper water, far from land, waves no longer move exclusively in any one direction relative to the coastline, yet the turtles maintain their offshore course, swimming in a straight track out to sea until they join the main stream of the current. Experiments have shown that by using magnetic inclination and reading the strength of the Earth's magnetic field, sea turtles can orientate themselves without the aid of any coastal and seabed landmarks. Further experiments have revealed that hatchlings can switch from following a course initiated on the basis of wave cues to maintaining one based on magnetism.

Loggerhead and leatherback juveniles live a pelagic lifestyle for at least the first three to five years, are at the mercy of the currents and feed primarily on bluebottles, storm snails and other small free-floating organisms with gas-filled bladders or floats. At full speed, the Agulhas current can carry hatchlings from Maputaland to Cape Agulhas in 30–50 days, and loggerhead hatchlings of up to six months of age (10 cm) regularly wash up on beaches between Cape Point and Cape Agulhas, mainly during gale-force onshore winds. However, very few loggerheads between 10 cm and 60 cm are ever encountered and to date it is not known where they spend their time, but presumably they are either carried back into the Indian Ocean via the Agulhas return current or into the Atlantic, where they drift in offshore gyres.

SUB-ADULTS AND ADULTS

At around 70 cm, loggerheads abandon their oceanic existence and move into the nearshore zone along the east coast of southern Africa. There seems to be a distinct segregation of adults and sub-adults. Sub-adults are mostly encountered to the south of the nesting beaches, while 97% of tagged adult recoveries come from Mozambique, Madagascar, Tanzania and Kenya. Sub-adults do not hold distinct feeding territories and need to remain on the move until they come across an unclaimed territory or are in a position to oust a territory holder.

GREEN, HAWKSBILL AND OLIVE RIDLEY TURTLES

Apart from the leatherback and loggerhead turtles, another three species occur in southern African waters, including the green, olive Ridley and hawksbill turtles. The green turtle is the second largest after the leatherback, attaining a length of up to 1.5 m. Its shell is heart-shaped and dark greenish-brown to olive in colour, though its common name is derived from the green colour of the turtle's fat.

It nests only sporadically in southern Africa, with the nearest major nesting areas located on Europe Island in the Mozambique Channel, where between 5 000 and 10 000 females come ashore annually to lay their eggs. The green turtle is also known in some parts of the world as the edible turtle and continues to be heavily exploited for eggs and its high-quality meat. Hatchlings are carnivorous during the first 6 to 12 months of their lives, but as adults they become herbivores that graze predominantly on seagrass and green algae. The green turtle is probably the slowest-growing turtle, only reaching sexual maturity at somewhere between 20 and 50 years.

The hawksbill is a medium-sized turtle that grows up to 90 cm long. It has a distinctive amber carapace with radiating streaks of brown and black, and a strongly serrated posterior margin. The name hawksbill comes from the species' narrow head and tapering beak. It is probably the most tropical of all turtles and is most frequently seen foraging on coral reefs, where it feeds predominantly on encrusting organisms such as sponges. It is believed that hawksbill turtles occupy more or less permanent feeding territories. Sub-adults, which are most often encountered by divers, occur mainly in the shallower regions, while adults hold territories in deeper water. Here, presumably, the stock of encrusting organisms is higher due to lower light levels, resulting in less competition with seaweed and hard corals. The species has been harvested since antiquity for its beautiful shell, and to this day it is made into polished jewellery, combs and fans.

The olive Ridley turtle, *Lepidochelys olivacea*, is probably the world's most abundant sea turtle. It grows fairly quickly, attains a maximum length of 80 cm and reaches maturity much earlier than other species. It nests sporadically in northern Mozambique, but the nearest major nesting areas lie in India. As an adult it feeds predominantly on benthic invertebrates and, occasionally, on fish.

Hawksbill turtles, *Eretmochelys imbricata*, are most frequently associated with coral reefs where they feed predominantly on sponges.

Loggerheads appear to reach maturity at between 12 and 13 years of age, when they begin to migrate regularly between nesting beaches and their northern tropical feeding grounds. This migration seems to be fairly fast and purposeful: one loggerhead turtle travelled between Maputaland and Zanzibar in just 66 days.

Both adults and sub-adults feed mainly on benthic invertebrates such as clams and crabs, their strong jaws allowing them to crush shells and carapaces with ease. Tiger and Zambezi sharks are their most important predators, the former able to cut through any carapace with their saw-shaped teeth. In some areas, sharks have become turtle specialists and many nesting females sport the telltale marks of an attempted attack – crescent-shaped bite marks on the carapace or injuries to the flippers.

In stark contrast with loggerheads and all other turtles, leatherbacks maintain a wholly pelagic existence and diet throughout their lives. Their formidable-looking jaws are, in fact, rather weak and really only lend themselves to crushing soft-bodied prey, for which they have been known to dive for nine minutes and to depths of over 1 500 m. Their main food source is jellyfish, whose floats are caught and punctured by a special notch on the turtles' beaks.

Adults are present throughout the Indian Ocean and females tagged in Maputaland have been recovered in central Mozambique and along the east coast of Madagascar. In 1996 a female leatherback turtle was fitted with a satellite transmitter after nesting on one of Maputaland's beaches. During the first nine days of tracking, she spent her time in the nearshore waters around the nesting beaches, but on the tenth day she went offshore and entered the Agulhas current, swimming quickly on a straight southerly course parallel to the coast. Near Port Elizabeth she moved offshore and headed towards the cold Southern Ocean, where she spent the next three months, crisscrossing and presumably feeding in the vicinity of the sub-Antarctic convergence, an area rich in pelagic food. She then moved due southeast, and by the time the transmitter unit stopped operating on 18 May, she was at 40 degrees South, 600 km south of the coast, heading in the direction of western Australia. It was a great revelation that this turtle travelled more than 7 000 km in only a few months, but even more unexpected was the fact that she penetrated the Southern Ocean as far as the convergence.

There are striking physiological differences between leatherbacks and other marine turtles. They are partially warm-blooded creatures, which have thick layers of insulating fat under their leathery skin and a vascular system designed to minimize heat loss. Their ability to regulate heat exchange with the environment allows them to travel regularly to – and survive in – sub-Antarctic and Arctic habitats. Northern hemisphere leatherbacks have been sighted as far north as Greenland.

TURTLE CONSERVATION

In 1982 the world's population of leatherback turtles numbered about 115 000 females. By 1996 there were only 34 500 left, a 70% decline in under 15 years. Leatherbacks are classified as endangered throughout their global range and almost all populations have declined in recent years or are close to extinction.

THE BEACH: BATTLEGROUND OF SAND AND WAVES

Beaches or sandy shores are more than just nesting habitats for sea turtles — they are complex and fascinating marine ecosystems in their own right. Beaches are either dissipative or reflective in nature. A broad and expansive surf zone characterizes dissipative beaches, where waves spill gently a long way from the shore. Reflective beaches, however, almost lack a surf zone and waves often surge directly up a steep and short beach face. Here, the ocean's full fury is unleashed on the shore.

Unlike rocky shores and coral reefs, where much of the life exists on a base of hard substrate and is often opulent and colourful, sandy shore organisms are a lot less obvious. They have to cope with an environment of constantly shifting sand grains and have adapted to life in very different ways. In fact, at first glance beaches appear like lifeless wastelands, attached plants are nowhere to be seen and the macrofauna are only represented by the occasional fleeting glimpse of ghost crabs, surfing whelks on the prowl, or the burrow openings of the Donax clam.

External appearances are deceiving because sandy beaches are a marine habitat as rich in both plant and animal life as any other. Living creatures here are incredibly small, on average less than 1 mm long, and remain largely hidden beneath the surface, spending their days living and travelling between the sand grains. The animals here are called meiofauna, while the plants are referred to as microflora.

The microflora consists of both benthic microalgae, which are attached to the grains of sand, and phytoplankton, mainly diatoms, resident in the nearshore water column. Benthic microalgae dominate on sheltered beaches, while phytoplankton appear to be more prominent at exposed beaches. Worms dominate the meiofauna that lives interstitially (between the grains of sand) on sandy beaches. From free-living flat and ribbon worms, to nematodes and polychaetes, worms of all shapes and guises are the rulers of this battleground between sea and sand.

The ecology and biology of life on sandy beaches appears to be primarily controlled by oceanography, with wave energy being the driving force for most processes. However, recent research has shown that biological interactions like competition and predation are a lot more important in structuring sandy shore fauna and flora than previously believed.

The South African population is one of the few exceptions: its numbers have been steadily increasing since the 1960s. In the 1963/64 nesting season only five leatherback turtles nested on Maputaland's beaches, while the present-day record count is over 168 individuals in a single year.

In South Africa, the status of loggerhead turtles has never been quite as precarious as that of leatherbacks and just under 100 females nested here in the early 1960s. Loggerheads also showed a remarkable population increase, doubling over 30 years from an average of 200 females per season to well over 400. Such a drastic improvement of the species' conservation status in fewer than 40 years was only possible as a result of protective measures introduced by conservation authorities with the full co-operation of the local communities.

Growth in the numbers of nesting females over the years has resulted in a parallel rise in the popularity of turtle watching, which plays an important role in the local eco-tourism industry today, when community guides lead hundreds of tourists annually on turtle-nesting safaris. This has not only made poaching turtle eggs more difficult because of the greater presence of people on the beaches, but has also created a greater awareness of, and interest in, turtle conservation among the general public who have been able to witness nesting and hatching turtles themselves.

THREATS TO TURTLES ON THE BEACH

Historically, the collecting of eggs and killing of breeding females have been the greatest causes of sea turtle population demises around the world. Before 1963, egg collecting was rife in Maputaland and many older people along this coast can remember regularly collecting turtle eggs with their parents when they were younger. Some people used to feed turtle eggs to their chickens to increase their egg-laying capabilities.

Egg theft is rare in South Africa today, but alarm bells sounded recently when it was heard that turtle eggs were being sold for high prices in traditional medicine markets as a cure for HIV/Aids. Soon afterwards, many turtle nests were found dug up within the Maputaland marine protected area and entire clutches of eggs were stolen. On a single night 24 nests were raided, probably by people from outside the area, who took more than 2 500 eggs. A number of adult turtles were also removed from the beach while they were laying and were presumably slaughtered. Turtle shells and skin are also frequently used in the traditional medicines of South Africa, Swaziland and Mozambique.

In many parts of the world, the modification of beachfront habitat through unregulated coastal development has had a severe impact on sea turtle populations. Artificial lights on, and adjacent to, the beaches have discouraged females from nesting and have interfered with the nocturnal sea-finding behaviour of the hatchlings. The presence of people, dogs, boats and vehicles has also

Turtle products, including skin, shells and skulls, are used in traditional medicines and are frequently offered for sale in markets across South Africa, Swaziland and Mozambique.

been known to discourage turtles from nesting. Such developments are not presently a problem in southern Africa, but vast stretches of picture-perfect beaches in Mozambique have been earmarked for various tourism developments.

Hatchling mortality also results from tyre ruts left by 4x4 vehicles travelling on the beaches. These have been known to entrap hatchlings for long periods, causing them to become exhausted before reaching the sea and increasing their chances of being taken by predators. While 4x4 driving on South African beaches was banned in 2000, it is still fairly prevalent in Mozambique.

Yet another danger facing turtle populations is global warming. Since the sex ratio of hatchlings is determined by nest temperature, global warming could wreak havoc on turtle populations across the globe. Higher air and sea temperatures would translate into a higher sand temperature, resulting in an unnatural majority of female hatchlings.

The protection of turtles during their nesting stage is important, since their populations require a very large number of eggs, hatchlings, juveniles and sub-adults to maintain a relatively small number of reproductively active adults. For example, in the United States more than half a million female eggs and immature turtles are necessary just to maintain an adult population of female loggerhead turtles of 1 277 animals. However, less than 0.01% of the turtle's life cycle is spent nesting on South Africa's well-protected beaches and the biggest threat to these turtles today comes when they leave our shores and travel out to sea and to other countries. It is, therefore, important to protect not only nesting areas, but feeding grounds and oceanic migration corridors as well.

DANGER AT SEA

A recent study followed the fate of 50 green, loggerhead and leatherback turtles carrying satellite tags. Alarmingly, 31% perished as a result of fishing activities. Some tagged turtles were recorded moving inland from fishing villages on the backs of trucks, and on one occasion a tourist was able to provide photographs of a turtle being barbecued – with the transmitter still firmly attached to the shell. Of the turtles that were killed, two (one loggerhead and one leatherback) perished off the coast of southern Africa.

Thousands of sea turtles die annually in pelagic long-line fisheries, in which thousands of baited hooks are attached to long lines. Loggerheads are especially prone to swallowing the hooks, which can become internally embedded. In some fisheries, 40% of hooked turtles die *in situ* and many of those released perish later due to internal injuries. In 2001, turtle carcasses that had been decapitated or had their throats slit washed up in alarming numbers on the beaches of southern Mozambique. This is believed to be the handiwork of unlicensed Asian long-liners catching sharks; any turtles landed alive are killed and unceremoniously dumped.

In addition to the pressure from long-line fisheries, turtle populations are under threat from the shrimp-trawling industry, which

Eggs are extracted from the ovaries of a freshly killed loggerhead.

A hatchling struggles through the tyre tracks of a 4x4 vehicle.

Turtles, like this loggerhead, accidentally caught in gill nets almost always end up being killed for their meat.

kills more sea turtles than all other causes of mortality combined. A global estimate puts the figure at over 150 000 annually. In Mozambique, shrimp trawlers operate extensively on the Sofala Bank off the central coast, and it is estimated that each year between 1 900 and 5 400 turtles die as bycatch.

There is, however, a simple way to prevent the needless deaths of many sea turtles and reduce the volumes of unwanted bycatch by up to 60% – the Turtle Excluder Device (TED). Consisting of a simple and relatively cheap trap-door mechanism, this was developed in the United States in the early 1980s. When TEDs are fitted to shrimp trawl nets, up to 97% of all turtles caught in the nets are able to escape unharmed. Their use has been a legal requirement for shrimp trawlers in the United States and several other western-hemisphere countries for a long time. Currently, however, TEDs are not legally required under Mozambican fishing regulations and it is not known when or if they will become mandatory.

The ingestion of plastics and other non-biodegradable debris is responsible for high levels of mortality in many species of sea turtles, but it appears that leatherbacks, whose diet consists predominantly of jellyfish, have particular problems in distinguishing between the plastic fare and their natural food. It seems that a hungry leatherback will swallow almost anything. In one study, 44% of stomachs examined contained items made from plastic, which can cause fatal blockages of the gut.

CORAL REEFS

rainforests of the sea

CURRENTS *of*
CONTRAST

ABOVE LEFT: A coral community dominated by staghorn coral, *Acropora* spp., in shallow water off Sodwana Bay.

ABOVE RIGHT: During low tide a coral reef off the coast of northern Mozambique endures prolonged exposure to the air and searing tropical heat.

he ocean's sprawling, homogenous surface belies the riots of splendour that lie hidden beneath, such as Africa's southernmost coral reefs off South Africa's subtropical east coast. To slip into the water and submerge oneself beneath the waves is to step through a portal into a world of unrivalled complexity.

Soft coral-encrusted pinnacles erupt from the gently sloping, hard coral-studded seabed. Drawn to these summits like rain clouds to craggy peaks are vast, gyrating schools of fish that dart back to the safety of their coral fortress every time a shark rushes in from the blue. In deeper water, where low light levels allow for only a sparse covering of coral, myriad sponges dominate the landscape. Here only turtles manage to glean nutrition from such a spike-studded meal.

Coral reefs are overflowing with life, which is why they are often referred to as the rainforests of the sea. While the total number of plants and animals is higher in tropical forests, in terms of species diversity per unit of global area, coral reefs are the most diverse biome on the planet. In addition, the reef's exuberance of life is evenly distributed across more than 28 phyla, or classification groups, while tropical rainforest biodiversity emanates mainly from just two groups of organisms: plants and insects. Unlike the world's tropical rainforests, where the majority of life remains hidden in the canopy, the coral reef delivers a slap-in-the-face kind of biodiversity experience.

CORAL REEFS
rainforests of the sea

CORAL REEF BASICS

While coral reefs are complex in character and grand in size, the architects responsible for their construction are not. The parties responsible for producing the largest biogenic structures of our planet are no more than elongated, tubular blob-like creatures, each with a single opening at its apex, adorned with a ring of mobile tentacles. These tiny animals are polyps, the living entities that secrete the coral.

Polyps of scleractinian, or hard corals, are similar in appearance to the more familiar sea anemones. Lacking the support of a stiff body wall, they secrete a calcium carbonate skeleton around themselves, in which they lie embedded. As they multiply, so the coral reef develops and grows. Hard corals are polytrophic feeders, meaning they get their nutrition in a variety of different ways. In addition to absorbing dissolved organic matter through their cell walls, they are also ravenous carnivores. While most coral polyps remain withdrawn into their calyces, or skeletal cups, during the day, at night the stage is set for a concert of tentacles. Each polyp takes in water and swells up to such an extent that the cilia-crowned mouths are pushed outwards; then hunting for zooplankton begins.

Gardens of coral polyps are habitats in themselves, offering refuge and feeding opportunities to small fishes such as gobies and blennies.

Due to the low nutrient status of the clear warm water in which coral reefs thrive, however, these two foraging methods contribute to only half of the coral's energy needs. The rest comes courtesy of a mutually beneficial relationship between each coral polyp and a tiny algae that the polyp harbours within its gastrodermal cells. These algae, or zooxanthellae, are so tiny and prolific that one square centimetre of coral surface can accommodate more than one million of them.

The entire functioning of the coral reef depends on this symbiotic relationship. The algae carry out photosynthesis and provide the corals with sugars and amino acids that gradually diffuse into their cell walls and are used for energy. They also provide calcium carbonate, which the coral uses to lay down its skeleton. The coral's symbiotic partners do not go unrewarded; they receive ammonia and phosphates, the waste products of the coral's metabolism, which are important nutrients. The zooxanthellae are also provided with a refuge from planktivorous predators and the luxury of being suspended in the photic zone – where light penetrates – at all times without having to expend energy through swimming.

For this crucial symbiotic relationship to flourish and the reef to function optimally, a certain set of environmental conditions is required. The optimal water temperature for growth is between 26 °C and 28 °C. Although most of the world's coral reefs live in the upper ranges of their thermal limits, southern Africa is slightly unusual in this respect: its reefs experience much cooler conditions and water temperatures can drop to lows of 21 °C during winter.

Light, too, is an essential ingredient without which the zooxanthellae cannot photosynthesize. In very clear water, light levels can be sufficient for photosynthesis to depths of up to 100 m, but under normal conditions the limit is about 40–50 m. In areas of high turbidity, where heavy river discharge and sediment drastically cut down on the amount of available light, coral cannot grow even at the most shallow depths.

Salinity also plays an important role in coral reef health. Levels must range between 32–40 parts per million as prolonged influxes of fresh water have been known to kill corals.

ORIGINS

Corals have a long fossil record that can be traced back about 250 million years and their prehistory is characterized by many cycles of extinction and rebirth. During the dawn of coral reef evolution, the continents were still fused into a single giant landmass and prehistoric coral reefs lined the warm shallows of the Tethys Sea. As the ancient landmasses broke apart, ocean basins formed between the various retreating continents and their fringing reefs. In some cases barriers appeared, cutting off the coral faunas of the various continents from each other by preventing larval exchange and thus spurring on evolution in isolation.

This is how some scientists explain the innate differences between, for example, East African, Australian, Caribbean and Red Sea coral reefs. Other scientists cite an origin-dispersal hypothesis, where the present-day coral species hotspots – Indonesia and the Philippines – represent the epicentre of coral evolution, from which all coral species radiated to other parts of the world's oceans over time. Close relatives of today's reef-building coral evolved during the Mesozoic and Cenozoic eras and have existed more or less in their current state for almost 250 million years, but it was only during the Tertiary era that reefs were for the first time dominated by hard corals. During the Ecocene, modern-day genera like *Acropora*, *Porites* and *Pocillopora* appeared – and with them the first signs of today's coral reef fish fauna.

The exact location of a coral reef's birth often depends on the bottom topography of the seabed, where rocky ridges and other topographic highs are frequently the most favoured starting points. Corals can reproduce either sexually or asexually. The former can involve either the brooding of internally fertilized eggs or the

As day turns to dusk and the reef is plunged

into darkness, coral polyps open and begin their

hunt for zooplankton in a nocturnal sea.

external fertilization of the eggs, followed by their development into planktonic larvae. All that is needed for a coral reef to begin life is for a single coral larva to settle on a favourable substrate, where it almost immediately transforms itself into a sessile polyp resembling a sea anemone and secretes its limestone skeleton.

Asexual reproduction comes into its own in the creation of the colonial organism known as a coral colony, which is built through self-cloning by repeated budding and fission. As each colony grows, more and more coral larvae settle. Over thousands of years, a network of three-dimensional coral creations becomes a mature coral reef. On a human timescale, they grow incredibly slowly – just 4 m every 1 000 years on average. Over time the lower reaches of each coral colony die off and form compact coral rubble, which later turns to a near-solid mass of coral rock, upon which sits the present-day veneer of living coral.

During Earth's turbulent history, sea levels rose and fell as the Earth cooled and warmed. At times the sea level dropped significantly, exposing many coral reefs to the air, so that they subsequently died. As the sea level rose again, new coral larvae settled on the remains of the long-dead reefs. Thus, most coral reefs have been built on the remains of many predecessors, and present-day reefs are simply the latest participants in this cycle of death and rebirth.

BIOGEOGRAPHY

In southern Africa the warm Mozambique and Agulhas currents create subtropical and tropical conditions that allow coral communities and coral reefs to thrive at relatively low latitudes along the eastern seaboard of the subcontinent, from St Lucia in the south to the Rio Rovuma in northern Mozambique and beyond. Southern Africa's subtropical and tropical coast can be divided into two distinct regions: that of South Africa and southern Mozambique, dominated by coral communities or so-called coral-encrusted reefs; and northern Mozambique, dominated by extensive true tropical coral reefs.

THE SOUTH
Maputaland
The coral reefs that lie off the Maputaland coast are not true coral reefs, but coral communities or what are called coral-encrusted reefs. They differ in that their foundations are not coral but rather 140 000-year-old fossilised, submerged dunes and beach-rock, which is then covered by a thin veneer of coral. True coral reefs sit on a base of coral hundreds, if not thousands, of metres thick. For example, drilling operations on the remote Pacific atoll Entewak have revealed coral rock descending to a depth of more than a kilometre. South Africa's coral communities lie several miles from the shore, generally at fairly great depths, and nowhere do they reach the surface. Scientists do not yet understand why these reefs are not more extensive and better developed when the growth rate of many coral species is similar to that in other coral reef locations around the world.

Maputaland's coral communities are the most southerly on the African continent. They can be divided into three groups: the Northern, Central and Southern reef complexes. The Northern complex consists of the Kosi Reef system, the Central complex of Nine-Mile, Four-Mile and Two-Mile reefs, and the Southern complex of Red Sands Reef and Leadsman Shoal. These subtropical coral communities are characterized by their relatively homogenous topography, often being very flat, with some gullies, ridges and short drop-offs adding relief.

Coral community structure differs distinctly on each of these topographical features, with soft corals such as *Lobophyton* and *Sinularia* dominating the tops of ridges and outcrops, whereas hard corals such as *Faviidae* and *Pocilloporidae* dominate the gullies. This difference in community structure is believed to be related to the high rates of sedimentation that occur in the gullies. Hard coral is far more tolerant of this than soft coral.

On some reefs at depths of around 20 m staghorn corals, *Acropora*, begin to dominate by forming large, open arborescent, or branch-like, colonies. Below 30 m, where light intensity drops to very low levels, a low-density community of sponges, gorgonians and ascidians occurs. In total, the Maputaland reefs are home to 43 hard corals and at least 11 genera of soft corals, together making up no less than 132 species. Recent genetic research on certain hard coral species across all the Maputaland reef complexes has shown that the gene frequencies are very homogenous. This indicates that the coral communities in the Southern and Central reef complexes are highly connected in terms of larval flow and can therefore be considered part of a single population.

Inhaca Island and the Bazaruto Archipelago
Africa's southernmost true coral reefs lie at Inhaca Island in southern Mozambique. Here three small fringing reefs 3–4 km long occur on the limestone substrate of previous reefs. However, they lack many features characteristic of mature tropical reefs, as they are thought to be in a constant state of turnover linked to cyclonic destruction and burial with sand. Offshore patch reefs occur at depths of 5–15 m along the island's east coast, as well as opposite the mainland coast near Santa Maria. The structure of Inhaca's coral reefs closely resembles the edges of the inner fringing reefs on sheltered shores further north, and coral species' composition is also similar but somewhat impoverished. Corals belonging to 45 genera from 16 families occur here, with over 30 species of *Acropora* alone.

To the north of Inhaca Island lies Mozambique's dune coast, which stretches northwards for over 700 km to Vilanculos. Some 30–35 km offshore from here lies the Bazaruto Archipelago, consisting of the five islands of Bazaruto, Santa Carolina, Benguérua, Mararuque and Bangue. The bulk of southern Mozambique's coral reefs lie here. In 2001 the archipelago was declared a protected area that now ranks as one of the largest marine national parks in

The lionfish, *Pterois miles*, as deadly as it is beautiful, uses its poison-tipped pectoral fins to corral small fish into corners before eating them.

southern and eastern Africa. To the north of the islands lies an extensive 1 000 km stretch of swamp coast, where the silt-laden discharges of 24 rivers, including the mighty Zambezi, prevent any coral reef growth.

THE NORTH

Strictly biogeographically speaking, southern Africa ends at the banks of the Zambezi, but for the sake of completeness the coverage of coral reefs in this book extends a further 800 km north to the Rovuma River, which forms the natural border with Tanzania. This stretch of coast is called the coralline coast, and it is here in the true tropics that the most prolific and well-developed coral reefs occur.

Fringing reefs occur close to shore along exposed sections of the mainland at Pemba, Mecufi and Nacala, but are most prolific on the seaward sides of three groups of islands, the Primeras, Segundas and Quirimbas. The Ilhas Primeras and Segundas lie off the coast of

Angoche and the more northerly Segundas consist of four islands surrounded by three large reef complexes. These are poor in hard corals, while soft coral dominates the shallows and algae dominates the deeper reaches. Only in south-facing shallow water is there an abundant low-lying cover of branching and encrusting hard corals. To date, nothing is known about the coral reefs and marine habitats of the Ilhas Primeras.

The Ilhas Quirimbas (*see* 'The forgotten isles of Mozambique', page 175) that lie to the north of Pemba are home to southern Africa's most well-developed and extensive coral reefs. Here reef zonation is more conventional than that further south, being of the classic exposed fringing reef type. Sandy beaches or rocky platforms give way to intertidal rock and sand flats, where coral growth is limited to isolated outcrops alongside many species of seagrass and algae. In a seaward direction, coral cover increases as the lagoon becomes shallower and transforms into the reef flat, an area that is often laid bare by spring tides. Species diversity here is usually low due to torturous temperatures and frequent exposure to air.

The crest of the coral reef is most exposed to the heavy onslaught of Indian Ocean swell, which regularly reduces much of the coral to rubble. Hard coral species that do survive here tend to be short, robust and stunted *Acropora*, and soft corals are abundant. The reef crest slopes steeply into deeper water, often in the form of vertical walls. At 20 m, life on these reefs really begins to flourish and the highest diversity of both hard and soft coral occurs amid calmer conditions. Hard corals of the genera *Montipora* and *Echinopora*, as well as soft corals such as *Sarcophyton* and *Lithophyton*, dominate. At least 55 coral genera occur in northern Mozambique, putting the region on a par with the most diverse coral reefs of East Africa, although the exact number of coral species is not yet known.

CORAL REEF FAUNA AND FLORA

The high diversity of animal and plant species co-existing on coral reefs is well documented. The likely key to this richness is that it has perhaps the highest spatial and temporal diversity of microhabitats of any shallow-water system. The complex three-dimensional coral reef matrix offers many different kinds of shelter and provides a food supply that is incredibly varied. On the coral reef the notions of co-existence and resource partitioning have been pushed to their limits. Intense competition for shelter, food and territory has resulted in the evolution of a pool of specialized organisms occupying very narrow and specific niches, and exhibiting a great variety of unique morphological and behavioural differences.

Some coral reef organisms have taken specialization to extremes. For instance, cleaner fish feed exclusively on the parasites of larger fish, and one species of shrimp occurs only among the tube feet and spines of one particular species of venomous sea urchin. There is even a fish that spends much of its life sheltering in the anus and water lungs of a sea cucumber.

Due to overfishing, in particular unscrupulous spear fishing, the potato bass, *Epinephelus tukula*, has become rare outside of protected areas. This one lives on a reef inside the Maputaland Marine Reserve and is so tame and trusting of divers that it follows them around like a pet dog.

ALGAE

Coral reef algae are nowhere near as dominant or obvious as the seaweeds of the temperate regions. This is mainly because herbivorous fish populations here are much more diverse and so levels of grazing pressure are much higher. The algae that do survive here are either inedible or unpalatable, or they persist by being able to recover quickly from grazing damage. Coral reefs are therefore usually dominated, alongside the coral's own symbiotic zooxanthellae, by heavily calcified encrusting red and upright green algae, as well as turf-forming, or grass-like, algae species that owe their persistence to their incredibly high growth rates and the fact that herbivores can only crop the upper layers, leaving the inaccessible bases intact.

A clear shift from algal turfs to crustose, or calcified, algae can be seen along gradients of grazing pressure on most coral reefs. The calcified species help to stabilize and cement the reef framework, while the turf-forming species are important traps for detritus and other organic material that would otherwise be lost, carried away by currents and wave action. Apart from making important contributions to the food web as primary producers, some species like the green algae *Halimeda* are major sand producers; at some locations 50% of all beach sand is derived from this alga.

INVERTEBRATES

In addition to the hard and soft corals and calcareous seaweeds that make up the reef matrix, sessile invertebrates, which are attached to the rock, also contribute significantly to the reef's three-dimensional structure. Filter feeders – such as sponges, gorgonians, ascidians and bryozoans among others – play an important role, especially in deeper water, where lower light levels are less favourable to hard coral and seaweed growth. Lacking the ability to escape predation by fleeing, many of these sessile organisms are usually well-defended by toxic compounds, which are not essential for their growth, called secondary metabolites, so grazing pressure on them tends to be quite low.

There is also an abundance of mobile invertebrates. Sea urchins are among the most visible and dominant on some parts of the reef. They graze primarily on algae, which grow on dead coral skeletons, in the process also removing large amounts of calcium carbonate. In the absence of their predators they can become destructive eroders that significantly decrease live coral cover and the topographic complexity. This can eventually lead to a negative calcium budget, which occurs when more calcium is being eroded than the corals are able to produce.

This psychedelically coloured mantis shrimp, *Odontodactylus scyallarus,* is a ferocious predator and extremely fierce for its size.

THE FORGOTTEN ISLES OF MOZAMBIQUE

The Ilhas Quirimbas consist of 31 low coral islands that stretch from just north of Pemba to the delta of the Rovuma River, which forms the natural border between Mozambique and Tanzania. These islands harbour one of the planet's last unexplored regions of coastal and marine biodiversity. The range of different marine habitats found here is staggering — tropical coral reefs, dense and diverse seagrass meadows, extensive mangrove forests and several different kinds of intertidal shores.

The livelihood and survival of the island's indigenous inhabitants is closely linked to the ocean. Due to the highly exposed nature of these coral reefs, their exploitation using canoes and traditional sailing vessels is extremely limited. As a result, they were until recently in pristine condition, with large resident reef fish still plentiful. It was the Ilhas Quirimbas' remoteness, the complete absence of transport infrastructure and the civil war that was the key to their preservation.

While the end of the civil war in 1992 was a blessing for Mozambique's tormented people, it also heralded the beginning of a critical episode for the islands. By the late 1990s, the rich marine life started coming under threat from a burgeoning human population that grew exponentially as more and more refugees returned from their inland hideouts. The arrival of modern fishing gear meant the outer reef could be harvested more regularly. In 1996 two fishing operations had already taken up residence on Ilha Ibo and Ilha Mefunvo, exploiting and exporting sea cucumbers and shark fins to Asia. As teams of divers began to harvest sea cucumbers using scuba gear, signs of over-exploitation soon became apparent. Localized depletion, if not downright extinction in some areas, is almost certainly a sad reality today.

The use of long-line fishing in the channels at night also seems to have caused a dramatic decrease in the resident shark population. In addition, the population on the adjacent mainland practises slash-and-burn cultivation and during the heavy rains of the cyclone season the soil is no longer held together by the vegetation, but begins slipping away into the rivers that surge towards the sea. If such practices are allowed to continue, even the densely tangled maze of mangrove forests and seagrass beds will be unable to halt the advancing avalanche of silt. At the ocean's edge the rivers will haemorrhage sediment plumes into the sea. The coral reef will starve to death as its filter-feeding coral polyps become clogged and the turbid water robs their zooxanthellae of life-giving sunlight.

The Quirimbas National Park was proclaimed in 2002. Apart from 11 of the islands, it also includes a vast area of mainland where elephant, lion and hyena still roam free. While the creation of this protected area is encouraging, it is only the first step. The most difficult step — trying to enforce the all-important conservation legislation — is still ahead.

Other mobile invertebrate species include spiny lobsters (Palinuridae) that inhabit crevices on the deeper parts of the reef, an almost endless variety of colourful nudibranchs, which are marine snails without shells, a mantis shrimp, *Odontodactylus scyallarus*, with claws powerful enough to cut a human finger to the bone, and the geographer cone, *Conus geographus*, a marine snail that hunts small fish with a poison-tipped harpoon so potent that several human fatalities are attributed to it every year.

FISH

Fish are the most plentiful, conspicuous and well-known vertebrate inhabitants of coral reefs. Several hundred species varying in shape, colour and size can co-exist on a single small reef, from the tiny 4 cm two-stripe blenny, *Plagiotremus rhinorhynchos*, to the 3 m brindle bass, *Epinephelus lanceolatus*. The reefs off Maputaland are home to over 399 fish species in 74 families, 96% of which have an Indo-Pacific distribution. The remaining 4% are endemic to southern Africa. Just as the number of species of coral differs between the different reef complexes along the southern African coast, so does the number of fish, with diversity increasing in a northerly direction.

Fish interact with the coral reef habitat in two ways. First, there is the direct relationship between reef structure and mainly smaller fish, which seek shelter in coral recesses, among coral branches or inside tubular sponges. Second, there are the feeding interactions that occur between reef fish and hard corals, seaweeds, sponges, as well as the sessile and mobile invertebrate fauna that live within the reef matrix.

Based on their feeding habits, fishes on coral reefs can be grouped into distinct guilds.

Herbivorous fish make up nearly 25% of the coral reef fish fauna. The most common are surgeonfish (Acathuridae), damselfish (Pomacentridae), parrotfish (Scaridae) and rabbitfish (Siganidae). Herbivorous reef fish are most abundant on the shallow fore-reef and are the main consumers of primary productivity, channelling this energy to other members of the food chain. Herbivorous fish can consume 50–100% of algal production and one patient and meticulous reef fish researcher has concluded that one square metre of reef algae can be exposed to as many as 156 000 bites per day.

It is the vast schools of so-called denuders, such as the convict surgeonfish, *Acanthurus triostegus*, and the aptly named rabbitfish that significantly control the growth of turf-forming algae. They are

A school of fusiliers swimming high above the reef, filtering microscopic planktonic organisms from the water.

INSET LEFT: Frogfish are territorial ambush hunters who choose their perches wisely. This one has picked a throne of coral from which to engulf small fishes that stray too close.

INSET RIGHT: Like a silver bullet, a kingfish rushes from out of the blue, speeding towards the reef hoping to catch its prey off guard.

Fish are the most plentiful, conspicuous and well-known vertebrate inhabitants of coral reefs.

A school of humpback snappers, *Lutjanus gibbus*, swimming above a coral pinnacle on Two-mile Reef off Sodwana Bay.

also important mediators in the competition between coral and algae. Parrotfish are scrapers and excavators and are the most diverse group of herbivores in the Indo-Pacific. By vigorously grazing turf and heavily calcified algae with their fused teeth, they erode calcareous structures and produce vast amounts of sediment as a by-product. Damselfish are a group of non-algae-denuding species that can even enhance algal growth. Their strongly territorial behaviour excludes all other grazers from their algal carpets and they have been known to kill coral directly by removing polyps, opening up substrata for the growth of their algal mats.

Planktivorous fish are a visible and prominent component of the reef fish fauna. Members of almost all major reef fish families feed on zooplankton. Most fish are planktivorous during their larval stages but the anthias (Anthiinae), the fusiliers (Caesionidae) and the chromis (Pomacentridae) retain this foraging strategy into adulthood. During the day, diurnal planktivores swim along the reef edge where densities of zooplankton are highest. Diurnal planktivores feed predominantly on so-called transient zooplankton, which are swept over the reef by the currents, making them an important nutrition/feeding link between the coral reef and the open ocean. Without the recycling capabilities of this guild of fishes, the nutrients in the plankton would not be made available to the reef's other inhabitants. During feeding, planktivores produce copious amounts of faeces, which rain down onto the reef and become food for reef-dwelling herbivores and detritivores. As the day winds down, diurnal planktivores descend towards the reef and by about 30 minutes before sunset they will have retired to the crevices and cracks in the reef.

Nocturnal planktivorous fish, which spend the day sheltering in the same crevices as the dayshift, soon appear to take their place. Soldierfish (Holocentridae) and cardinal fish (Apongoniidae) are the most prominent nighttime plankton feeders on southern African reefs, but they do not rise as high into the water column as their daytime counterparts and feed mainly on resident zooplankton such as mysid shrimps.

Carnivores include benthic invertebrate predators, often the most numerous of all reef fish. Making up 30–60% of the fish fauna, these include coral polyp feeders and predators of both sessile and mobile invertebrates. Butterflyfish are the main vertebrate corralivores in southern Africa. Feeding exclusively on coral are five species – archers *Chaetodon bennetti*, maypole *C. meyeri*, chevron *C. madagascariensis*, redfin *C. trifasciatus* and Zanzibar butterflyfish *C. zanzibariensis*. The long-nose filefish, *Oxymoncanthus longirostris*, and large star puffer, *Arothron stellatus*, also feed on coral. With its elongated mouth, the filefish – like the butterflyfish – extracts individual polyps from their coral skeletons, while the beak-like mouth of the puffer operates with much less precision.

Sessile invertebrates without shells, such as sponges, soft corals and bryozoans, are usually very well chemically or structurally defended, and the amount of predation tends to be low, but angelfish (Pomcanthidae) are among the few exceptions: they are specialist sponge feeders.

Second only to the sharks, the barracuda *Sphyraena barracuda*

is a formidable predator in Africa's tropical oceans.

For the predators of mobile invertebrates the main challenge lies in catching their food. Not only is their prey often highly mobile, it is equipped with a wide range of behaviours designed specifically to escape predation. In response, the fish have evolved what are probably among the most diverse and varied approaches in feeding behaviour and apparatus. Wrasses (Labridae), sweetlips (Haemulidae), emperors (Letherinidae) and triggerfish (Balistidae) are all mobile invertebrate feeders.

Piscivores, that is, fish that specialize in feeding on other fish, are at the top of the coral reef food chain. They include groupers (Serranidae), jacks (Carangidae), barracudas (Sphyraenidae), lionfish (Scorpaenidae) and sharks.

REPTILES AND MARINE MAMMALS

While turtles are an important component of southern Africa's coral reefs, they are covered in great detail in Chapter 10 and will not be the subject of further discussion here.

Mammals are mostly non-resident and only pass through the reef briefly to feed, rest or to use the water column above as a travel corridor. There is, however, one animal that makes its permanent home in the tropical seagrass beds so closely linked to the coral reef. This is the endangered and elusive dugong, *Dugong dugon*. Dugongs, also called sea cows, are classified in the order Sirenia and are pro-lific seagrass feeders, playing an important role in nutrient recycling. They used to be widely distributed across the Indo-Pacific and also ranged across southern and eastern Africa.

Surveys in the 1930s and 1960s showed relatively healthy dugong populations in the seagrass beds around Inhaca Island, Inhambane, the Bazaruto Archipelago and Angoche. They also seem to have been plentiful in the Quirimbas in the 1950s. Today, how-ever, they are absent from much of their past range, primarily due to the high volume of boat traffic and fishing activities that take place in seagrass beds. Only the population in the Bazaruto Archipelago somehow managed to sustain itself at up to 110 individuals. However, when the civil war ended in 1992, the dugong population also crashed, and there are currently fewer than 20 individuals. One of the main causes of dugong mortality today is the vast number of gill nets that are set for the burgeoning shark fishery.

THREATS TO CORAL REEFS

Among the threats facing coral reefs are climate change, scuba diving and crown of thorns starfish.

CORAL BLEACHING AND CLIMATE CHANGE

The year 1998 was the hottest single year on record and sea surface temperatures over much of the world's oceans were at an all-time high. During this temperature anomaly, coral reefs across the globe began los-ing their natural colours as shades of green, purple and yellow turned a ghostly white so that corals looked as if they had been bleached.

This loss of colour was the result of coral polyps expelling their zooxanthellae, a phenomenon believed to be triggered by a significant and prolonged increase in water temperature. At high temperatures, the zooxanthellae produce excess energy, which can lead to a build-up of toxins in the coral polyp. The expulsion of their symbiotic partners is a safeguard against being poisoned. Without their key energy producers, however, the corals cannot sustain themselves indefinitely, and recovery from a bleaching event depends on how long higher temperatures prevail.

If the increase is only short-lived, corals are able to reacquire their zooxanthellae from the water column or regrow them from leftover remnants within their tissues, regaining their normal coloration. If the temperature remains too high for too long, the corals will begin to die, and a reef tract killed by bleaching is rapidly overgrown by algae, preventing new coral larvae from settling. Weakened by the presence of algae, the bleached coral skeletons usually crumble during the subsequent heavy storms, reducing a vibrant, living reef to unstable coral rubble.

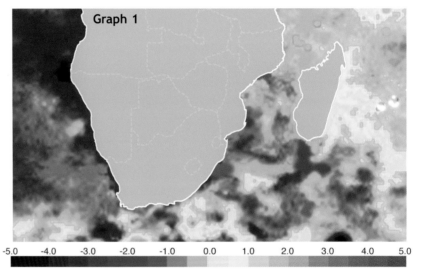

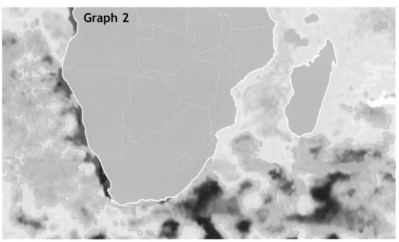

Sea surface temperature maps for April 1997 (Graph 1) and April 1998 (Graph 2). April 1998 was the peak of the Indian Ocean-wide coral bleaching event. The colour key indicates sea surface temperatures that are above or below the expected norms.

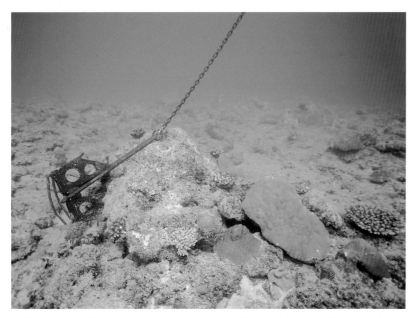

Anchors can lay waste to many acres of branching corals, reducing thousands of years of growth to rubble in mere minutes.

Bleaching-induced coral mortality also has profound effects on other reef organisms, with vertebrate and invertebrate populations becoming severely depleted. Species that feed directly on polyps or rely on thick, branching coral gardens as a habitat are usually those that are affected almost immediately and most severely.

In the last 100 years, the mean global sea temperature has increased by at least 1 °C and the latest predictions suggest it will rise by approximately 2 °C within the next 50 years. This brings the sea temperature in some regions close to the upper limits of many coral species' tolerance. What at present appear to be only sporadic bleaching events could become more frequent and more prolonged episodes, eventually leading to the extinction of many coral species and the disappearance of entire coral reef communities.

Coral reefs as we know them today can only survive if they are able to adapt physiologically to such high temperatures. This is unlikely, since most coral species that were tolerant of such temperatures are believed to have been wiped out during past ice ages. The bulk of the species we encounter on the reefs today are the descendants of their replacements – coral with an affinity for lower temperatures.

The 1998 bleaching event was of a magnitude never before recorded. During its March/April peak, the epicentre, or bleaching hotspot, ravaged the western reaches of the Indian Ocean. Extremely high coral mortalities were recorded in the Seychelles, where virtually all shallow water species were killed and in some places 95% of coral died down to a depth of more than 23 m. The coral reefs of northern Mozambique were also hard hit, but the destruction was not as wholesale as in the Seychelles, Madagascar and East Africa. On the reefs off the Quirimbas, coral mortality was around 30% onaverage, although some spots lost almost 99% of their coral cover.

The coral communities and reefs of South Africa and parts of southern Mozambique were the only ones in the western Indian Ocean to be spared the devastation. Only minor bleaching was reported, primarily because they lie at much more southerly latitudes and thus live in an environment with far lower average temperatures. In addition, the South African coral communities, in particular, occur in relatively deep water where temperatures are always cooler. Since many of the coral communities and reefs of southern Africa occur in a low temperate belt, a shift towards a more tropical community consisting of species with more warm water affinities is more likely than a massive die-off. These increases in sea temperature due to global climate change will inevitably result in the melting of the polar ice caps, causing a dramatic rise in the sea level. To survive this, coral reefs will have to keep pace with rising sea levels in order to maintain themselves at depths with enough light for photosynthesis. Only time and further research will tell whether the reef will sink or swim.

SCUBA DIVING

The invention of the aqualung in the 1960s opened a magical portal to the oceans and it was its use by diving scientists that rapidly advanced our knowledge of coral reefs. Scuba diving is generally regarded ecologically as a non-destructive activity that actually benefits the coral reef by providing local communities with economic benefits beyond the more traditional exploitation such as fishing. Diving tourists who pay for the privilege provide local communities with an incentive to keep their coral reefs healthy and brimming with fish and marine invertebrate life.

Divers have visited the coral communities and coral reefs of southern Africa since the 1960s, but their numbers have begun to grow exponentially only during the past decade. In 1986, approximately 25 000 dives were conducted on the Central Reef complex near Sodwana Bay but by 1992 that figure had rocketed to 80 000. The two biggest centres of dive tourism in southern Africa are Sodwana Bay and Ponta d'Ouro, which lie close to one another along the continent's southernmost reef complexes – the former in South Africa and the latter just across the border in Mozambique. Established dive resorts are also found in the Bazaruto Archipelago, while the country's tropical northern coral coast is still a diving frontier where scuba tourists are a very recent phenomenon.

Today, more and more studies have shown that divers can cause significant damage to the coral reef habitat and even impair its ecological functioning. In some places, coral reefs are in danger of being dived to death. It is primarily the direct contact between divers and the corals that causes damage; a carelessly placed fin, a dragging pressure gauge or a knock from a dive cylinder can easily break off entire branches that have taken thousands of years to grow. Studies in the Red Sea have shown that on average each diver has potentially damaging contact with live coral six times during a single 45-minute dive. On a heavily dived reef this can work out to 500 such contacts per day. In South Africa, on the most heavily dived sections of Two-Mile Reef, about 9 250 diver contacts per year result in damage.

Not only does intensive fishing impact negatively on reef fish populations but recent research has shown that coral colonies that become heavily entangled in monofilament fishing line exhibit higher levels of mortality than normal.

have been obtained for the Red Sea reefs. Surprisingly, the annual number of dives at South Africa's Two-Mile Reef is already four to five times higher, but coral damage appears to be lower at Sodwana Bay. On the whole, less than 5.9% of the hard corals and 4% of the soft corals show signs of diver damage, compared to the northern Red Sea where up to 10% of coral colonies have been broken by divers.

In southern Africa, dive tourism has been zoned with the fragility of the reef in mind. The coral species known to be the most susceptible to diver damage, *Acropora austere*, occurs at great densities in deep water of 18–24 m. These are found mainly at Four-Mile and Kosi Mouth reefs, both of which have been declared off limits to divers.

CROWN OF THORNS STARFISH

The crown of thorns, *Acanthaster planci*, is a large predatory starfish that can reach a diameter of 60 cm. It has up to 21 arms, each lined with a formidable array of poisonous spines. This armour protects it from all but one predator: only the very large triton snail, *Charonia tritonis*, is capable of consuming it.

They are broadcast spawners and females can release up to 250 million eggs in a single spawning season. This starfish's larvae are pelagic in nature, drifting at the mercy of the currents for up to one month before settling on the reef. In their juvenile stage, they feed predominantly on encrusting coralline algae; only when they are about a year old does their diet change. Adults feed almost exclusively on the tissue of living hard corals. As their many tube feet propel them over the reef, their extruded stomachs hug the coral tightly, digesting each polyp, leaving only the white bleached coral skeleton in their wake.

At normal population densities of about one starfish per hectare, crown of thorns are exclusively nocturnal, feeding selectively only on branching corals. However, at what seems to be regular intervals, densities increase from one per hectare to several per square metre and, at such high densities, competition for coral food increases. When this happens, these starfish become much less selective feeders, foraging both during the day and night.

At some places on Australia's Great Barrier Reef outbreaks of crown of thorns have damaged up to 90% of hard corals, while in the Comoros Islands they have laid waste to a pristine tract of reef in just 17 months. Recovery is slow; it can take more than a decade for the signs of the devastation to disappear. Many reasons have been

Although not all coral species are equally susceptible to diver damage, branching and plate-like species in the genus *Acropora* are particularly susceptible. It is no coincidence that these show the highest amount of damage on frequently dived sites, with 33% of diver damage inflicted on a single species, *Acropora austere*, a delicately branching coral. Calculations have shown that diver contacts in the most heavily dived sections of the reef reduce every fourth branch by 10 cm annually. The key to reducing and controlling damage seems to be increasing diver awareness by means of thorough briefings from dive masters. Studies have shown that divers who were given detailed briefings were 10 times less likely to come into contact with the reef.

The diver-carrying capacity – the number of dives and divers a coral reef can sustain without resulting in serious damage – has been calculated for some diving hotspots around the world. For example, off the Caribbean island of Bonaire each dive site is said to have a carrying capacity of 4 000 to 6 000 dives per year. Similar figures

THE CORAL REEF PHARMACY

For hundreds of years, coral reefs have provided the coastal tribes of southern and eastern Africa with ingredients for their traditional medicines. Everything from *Acropora* and organ-pipe corals to porcupine fish and sea cucumbers have been used to cure a variety of ailments.

Today western medicine is also looking to coral reefs to provide it with the chemical compounds needed to develop new medicines. Marine pharmacologists and biochemists are screening the sessile coral reef fauna for often-toxic secondary metabolites, which are believed to be the prime candidates for yielding anti-tumour or anti-viral agents. Secondary metabolites are compounds that organisms usually produce under stress. Since stress levels on the coral reefs are very high due to intense competition for food and shelter and the constant threat of becoming a meal, its organisms produce a ready supply.

Chemical compounds isolated from sponges have already led to the development of the drugs ara-A, an anti-viral agent, and ara-C to treat leukaemia. Anti-inflammatory properties have been discovered in a Caribbean gorgonian, and the neurotoxins in pacific cone shells have been shown to have powerful painkilling properties. In southern Africa, too, coral reef animals are being screened for secondary metabolites, and some ascidians, sponges and seaweeds are already showing some biomedical potential.

suggested to explain these outbreaks, and although there is no universally accepted conclusion at present, science does offer three theories. They may be the result of over-harvesting of the starfish's key predator, the triton snail, for the curio trade; they may be caused by increased levels of nutrients from human activities that provide favourable feeding conditions for crown of thorns larvae, significantly increasing their survival rate; or they may be the result of natural cyclical events. The last two theories are the most likely candidates, whereas the first is doubtful since it was recently discovered that a triton could eat only about one crown of thorns per day – far too few to control a full-blown outbreak.

In 1995 above-average densities of crown of thorns, i.e. over 1 000 individuals per hectare, were noticed on Kosi Bay and Two-Mile Reef, but these aggregations dispersed after several months and were believed to have been natural spawning groups. Cores drilled into the coral communities off Sodwana Bay have showed no signs of past crown of thorns impacts and some scientists concluded that this was the first outbreak of these starfish in the 137-year recorded history of the South African reefs.

The question many scientists are posing is how much of a risk an outbreak of crown of thorns poses to a South African reef. While little is known about them in this region, it is likely that the South African coral communities are very vulnerable because they consist of only a 30–40 cm layer of coral sitting on top of a fossilized dune. In addition, the total area of these reefs is quite small and could easily be devastated by an outbreak of crown of thorns in a short time.

'It has up to 21 arms, each lined with a formidable array of poisonous spines.'

THE COELACANTH

a fish that time forgot

'From Africa comes always something new.'

This is how Professor J.L.B. Smith began his 1939 article for the prestigious scientific journal *Nature*. Smith, then South Africa's foremost ichthyologist, was about to announce to the world the zoological find of the century – a revelation of such magnitude that today it would be akin to the discovery of a *Tyrannosaurus rex* wandering the back roads of the Kruger National Park.

On 22 December 1938 Captain Hendrick Goosen caught a very strange fish in the nets of his fishing trawler near the Chalumnae River mouth in the eastern Cape. The fish was 1.5 m long, metallic blue in colour, its body was encased in hard mottled scales covered in tiny spines, and its large eyes are said to have glowed like burning coals. It had unusual lobed fins, as well as a small fin that protruded from the tail. Despite his 30 years of experience he was unable to identify the fish.

OPPOSITE: After a search of nearly 14 years, Prof. J.L.B. Smith finally found a second coelacanth specimen in the Comoros Islands, 2 000 km to the north of the Chalumnae River mouth, where the first specimen was caught in 1938.

BELOW: The sketch that Marjorie Courtenay-Latimer made of the first coelacanth in 1938 and subsequently sent to Prof. J.L.B. Smith.

RIGHT: A variety of postcards and stamps commemorating the discovery of the coelacanth.

Neither was the then-curator of the East London Museum Miss Marjorie Courtenay-Latimer. She took it into safekeeping and sent a sketch and description to Professor Smith, asking for his help in identifying it. However, almost two months passed before Smith managed to see the fish. By that time the soft tissues had long since spoilt and the specimen had been stuffed and mounted. Nevertheless, he was able to identify it as a coelacanth, a fish belonging to a group that had thrived in the oceans around 400 million years ago and then became extinct – or so everyone thought.

Astonishingly, although these fish had disappeared from the fossil record 70 million years ago, it seemed that some had survived. In 1939 Smith announced to the world that the coelacanth had come back from the dead. He christened it *Latimeria chalumnae* after Marjorie Courtenay-Latimer and the location where it was captured.

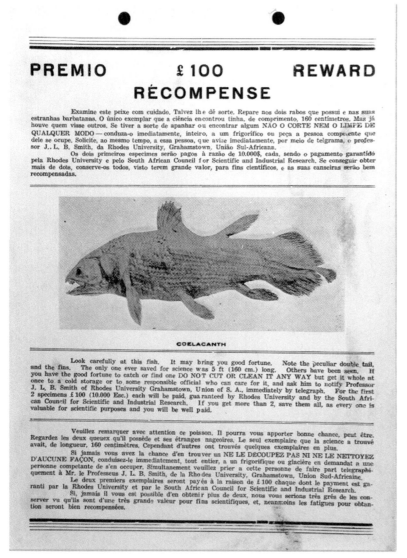

PREMIO   £100   REWARD
RÉCOMPENSE

Examine este peixe com cuidado. Talvez lhe dê sorte. Repare nos dois rabos que possui e nas suas estranhas barbatanas. O único exemplar que a ciência encontrou tinha, de comprimento, 160 centímetros. Mas já houve quem visse outros. Se tiver a sorte de apanhar ou encontrar algum NÃO O CORTE NEM O LIMPE DE QUALQUER MODO — conduza-o imediatamente, inteiro, a um frigorífico ou peça a pessoa competente que dele se ocupe. Solicite, ao mesmo tempo, a essa pessoa, que avise imediatamente, por meio de telegrama, o professor J. L. B. Smith, da Rhodes University, Grahamstown, União Sul-Africana.
Os dois primeiros specimens serão pagos à razão de 10.000$, cada, sendo o pagamento garantido pela Rhodes University e pelo South African Council for Scientific and Industrial Research. Se conseguir obter mais de dois, conserve-os todos, visto terem grande valor, para fins científicos, e as suas canseiras serão bem recompensadas.

COELACANTH

Look carefully at this fish. It may bring you good fortune. Note the peculiar double tail, and the fins. The only one ever saved for science was 5 ft (160 cm.) long. Others have been seen. If you have the good fortune to catch or find one DO NOT CUT OR CLEAN IT ANY WAY but get it whole at once to a cold storage or to some responsible official who can care for it, and ask him to notify Professor J. L. B. Smith of Rhodes University Grahamstown, Union of S. A., immediately by telegram. For the first 2 specimens £100 (10.000 Esc.) each will be paid, guaranteed by Rhodes University and by the South African Council for Scientific and Industrial Research. If you get more than 2, save them all, as every one is valuable for scientific purposes and you will be well paid.

Veuillez remarquer avec attention ce poisson. Il pourra vous apporter bonne chance, peut être. Regardez les deux queues qu'il possède et ses étranges nageoires. Le seul exemplaire que la science a trouvé avait, de longueur, 160 centimètres. Cependant d'autres ont trouvés quelques exemplaires en plus.
Si jamais vous avez la chance d'en trouver un NE LE DECOUPEZ PAS NI NE LE NETTOYEZ D'AUCUNE FAÇON, conduisez-le immédiatement, tout entier, a un frigorifique ou glacière en demandant a une personne competente de s'en occuper. Simultanement veuillez prier a cette personne de faire part télégraphiquement à Mr. le Professeur J. L. B. Smith, de la Rhodes University, Grahamstown, Union Sud-Africaine.
Le deux premiers exemplaires seront payés à la raison de £100 chaque dont le payment est garanti par la Rhodes University et par le South African Council for Scientific and Industrial Research.
Si, jamais il vous est possible d'en obtenir plus de deux, nous vous serions très grés de les conserver vu qu'ils sont d'une très grande valeur pour fins scientifiques, et, neanmoins les fatigues pour obtention seront bien recompensées.

Between 1939 and 1952 Prof. J.L.B. Smith distributed thousands of these reward posters all over the western Indian Ocean in the hope of locating a second specimen.

THE COMOROS COELACANTHS

Smith was troubled by the loss of the fish's soft anatomy and clearly frustrated by the missing parts of this ancient and important puzzle. Determined to obtain a complete specimen, he launched a search in the western Indian Ocean. For 14 long years his efforts bore no fruit, until 1952 when his persistence was rewarded with a second specimen.

This coelacanth was caught more than 2 000 km to the north of the first, in the Comoros, an archipelago of islands that lies at the northern entrance to the Mozambique Channel, about 300 km from both the African mainland and the northern tip of Madagascar to the east. After much waiting and political wrangling, Smith finally found himself in a borrowed South African military aircraft heading for the Comoros to claim the fish before the French authorities, who administered the islands at that time, became wise to its importance and claimed it for French scientists.

He succeeded in bringing the specimen safely back to South Africa and was finally able to begin to study the coelacanth's internal structure and anatomy. Instead of a backbone or rib cage, the coelacanth had a notochord made from cartilage – in effect a hollow spinal column filled with a unique oily fluid. Its gills resembled jawbones and the swim bladder was slender, tubular and filled with fat and other non-compressible body fluids.

The French, clearly upset by the whole 'fishnapping' incident, declared that from now on only their own scientists would be allowed to remove and study coelacanths. So the third specimen, caught on 24 September 1953, and another dozen that followed, went to French scientists. They began a meticulous investigation into the internal morphology and biochemistry of the coelacanth that lasted 10 years and filled three scholarly volumes.

It became apparent that the coelacanth was a fish with a unique combination of characteristics, sharing some traits with amphibians, some with bony fishes and others with sharks. The inner workings of a coelacanth's ear, for example, resemble those of a frog, while its urea-rich blood is not unlike that of a shark.

Between 1952 and 1996 a further 180 coelacanths were caught in the Comoros and studied by scientists. With the fish's anatomical and biochemical secrets almost all revealed, it was now time for someone to observe live coelacanths in their deep-water habitat and record their behaviour in situ.

FACE TO FACE WITH COELACANTHS

In 1987 Juergen Schauer and Dr Hans Fricke of Germany's Max Planck Institute were the first people ever to observe a coelacanth in its natural habitat. After many frustrating weeks of searching the steep drop-offs of Grand Comoros their research submersible, named Geo, finally drifted alongside two coelacanths as they hovered off a steep lava slope at a depth of 200 m.

The first-ever video footage of this animal in the wild revealed that coelacanths swim by moving their lobed pectoral and pelvic fins: the left pectoral fin moves up at the same time as the right pelvic fin, and the right pectoral fin is raised in unison with the left pelvic fin. Some have said that coelacanths swim as if they are dancing and there are few animal movements as beautiful as a coelacanth ballet. The anal fin, tailfin and second dorsal fins are used as rudders and the large caudal fin is only used when rapid escape is necessary. During this first expedition in 1987, the team was frustrated by Geo's 200 m depth limit, which prevented them from following the fish to greater depths for observation. It was there that the team presumed these nocturnal hunters spent their days. Two years later, the team returned with a new submarine called Jago, which had an extended depth range of up to 400 m.

Daytime searches for coelacanths at these depths yielded nothing, but an exploratory glance into one of the many deep, dark lava caves at 200 m revealed all they were searching for. During the day, groups of up to 10 coelacanths were seen to occupy lava caves, perhaps to escape predation from an abundance of deep-sea sharks or to conserve energy by seeking shelter from the currents. The subsequent use of acoustic tags, which allowed scientists to track them, showed that shortly before dusk the fishes left the safety of the caves to forage. As drift hunters they ride the deep ocean currents just as vultures ride the grassland thermals.

It is believed that coelacanths detect their prey in the ink-black waters by using a complex electro-detection system consisting of six jelly-filled cavities embedded in the fish's snout, the so-called rostral organ. Analysis of their stomach contents suggests they are primarily piscivorous (fish eaters) and prey on lanternfish, deepwater cardinal fish and snapper, as well as the occasional squid. They appear to swallow their prey whole, using the sink-suck method, in which the mouth is opened rapidly, creating negative pressure, and causing the prey to be sucked in with the surrounding water. The skull of the coelacanth has a strange joint separating the front portion from the back, and this allows the fish to open its mouth very wide and very rapidly to create this suction effect. The coelacanth's stomach contains a spiral valve allowing it to digest its food very slowly and completely. This means that coelacanths can probably go for long periods between meals, perhaps an adaptation to life in food-poor areas.

THE HUNT FOR NEW COELACANTH POPULATIONS

As the years passed, many believed that the coelacanths of the Comoros were a relict population – the only one to have survived – and that the Chalumnae River mouth specimen was probably a stray swept southwards from the Comoros by the swift-flowing currents. Nonetheless, the search in other areas continued unabated and in 1991 a survey was carried out around the Eastern Cape, including the site where the original fish was caught. However, it yielded no trace of the fish or suitable habitat, as the friable sandstone near the river mouth was not conducive to producing caves and overhangs.

Then the unexpected occurred. In the same year, a large pregnant female was trawled from a depth of 40–45 m off Pebane in central Mozambique. Coelacanth reproduction had remained a mystery for many years because some fossilized remains harboured eggs, while others showed the skeletons of small coelacanths within the adults. Today we know that they are live bearers: the young hatch from grapefruit-sized eggs while still inside the mother and grow inside the womb by gaining nourishment from a large external yolk sac. Female coelacanths give birth to a few very large, well-developed young, thus avoiding a larval stage, which is usually associated with high mortality rates.

In August 1995 another coelacanth was captured in the western Indian Ocean, this time hauled up in a deep-set shark net off the southwest coast of Madagascar. Two years later, another specimen was caught in the same area. These discoveries indicated the likely existence of other viable populations, but until they were found, any specimens discovered outside the Comoros would continue to be classified as strays by the sceptics.

If Earth history is closely examined, though, the whole notion of the Comoros as the coelacanth's ancestral, and only, home must be called into question. The coelacanth disappeared from the fossil record 65 million years before the volcanic creation of the Comoros. With the African mainland and Madagascar being of much more ancient origins, it is more likely that the coelacanth's ancestral home is Africa and that only later did a population take up residence in the Comoros.

In 2001 the nets of a commercial prawn trawler operating off the Kenyan coastal resort town of Malindi captured a 1.7 m coelacanth weighing 77 kg. This was the first confirmed find north of the Comoros and one that could not be explained by the notion that it, too, had 'drifted' south in the current. In 2002 a further coelacanth population, probably of a different species, was discovered in Indonesia, and in 2003 another specimen of *Latimeria chalumnae* was caught off Songa Mamora, an island off the southern coast of Tanzania.

SOUTH AFRICAN COELACANTHS AT LAST

On 28 October 2000, Peter Timm, Pieter Venter and Etienne le Roux were on a Trimix training dive in Jesser Canyon off Sodwana Bay on the KwaZulu-Natal coast, when they discovered three long fish about 2 m long, underneath an overhang at a depth of 104 m. The very limited bottom time on a dive at such great depths only allowed them a few minutes with the fish, but they were convinced that they had seen coelacanths. A month later, the team returned to the site and discovered

A rare image of one of the Sodwana coelacanths, photographed from the *Jago* submarine at a depth of around 120 m.

another coelacanth at a depth of 108 m, which cameramen Chris Serfontein and Dennis Harding managed to film. During the ascent, however, triumph turned to tragedy when Harding died as a result of an uncontrolled ascent to the surface.

Despite the tragedy, a further expedition was organized for May 2001, but initial dives in Wright Canyon failed to yield more coelacanths. Only when the expedition returned to Jesser Canyon, the site of the initial discovery, were more of the fish seen. In total, the May 2001 expeditions' successes amounted to the sighting and filming of nine different coelacanths. Using the white markings on the fishes' sides, the team was able positively to identity one of the fish as the one they had seen the previous year.

After this dive team's spectacular discovery, the South African Coelacanth Conservation & Genome Resource Programme was born, a multi-disciplinary project that incorporates scientists from various South African institutes and universities, as well as coelacanth experts from Germany's Max Planck Institute.

After a thorough mapping survey of all potential coelacanth habitats off the Maputaland coast, a submersible expedition using the tried-and-tested *Jago* was planned for April 2002. Mapping of the seabed resulted in the discovery of 24 submarine canyons in addition to the 12 already known. During that first submersible expedition, surveys concentrated on searching cave habitats for coelacanths during the day. In 13 dives, *Jago* had 15 coelacanth sightings – 12 in Jesser and three in Wright Canyon, making up an estimated population of between 9 and 10 individuals. One fish encountered in Wright Canyon was identified as having previously been seen at Jesser, indicating that these fish are capable of moving more than 4 km against prevailing currents. Three coelacanths seen by divers in 2000 were also resighted in 2002, showing that at least some are permanent residents in the canyons.

All coelacanths at Sodwana were encountered at depths of 70–140 m. This range correlates well with the species' known preferred temperature range of 14–20 °C, which occurs at the deeper depth of between 200 m and 250 m in the Comoros. It is believed that this specific temperature range is important to the coelacanth because it possesses a gill area smaller than any other fish of comparable size – 100 times smaller than that of a tuna. Therefore, because it absorbs oxygen at a much lower rate, it is probably restricted to living in the deeper, cooler areas where water has a higher concentration of oxygen.

Just as in the Comoros, cave shelters seem to play a crucial role in the lives of Sodwana coelacanth populations, and the majority of them seem to spend their days seeking refuge here in groups of up to seven fish. However, two individuals were observed swimming over open ground during the daytime. In 2003 one individual was acoustically tracked; it spent the day in the shelter of caves and emerged at night, presumably to hunt. In contrast to the Comoros coelacanths, which descend into deeper water to forage, at Sodwana the tagged individual remained at the canyon edge and even ascended to a depth of 70 m. In the Comoros, a more prolific population of fish occurs in deeper water, but in South Africa the opposite is true, with potential prey more abundant in shallower water. In March 2004, divers encountered a coelacanth off Sodwana at just 54 m, the shallowest depth at which this fish has ever been seen.

One month later a third population was discovered by the *Jago* during the fourth expedition of the African Coelacanth Ecosystem Programme (ACEP), 45 km to the south of the Jesser and Wright coelacanths in Chaka canyon. During this expedition a total of nine different coelacanths were sighted, five of which were new, thereby increasing the known South African population to a minimum of 18.

CONSERVING THE COELACANTH

Before its discovery by western scientists, local Comoros islanders knew the coelacanth as 'Gombessa'. While they did not target it directly, it was landed occasionally as bycatch while fishing for the oil fish *Ruvettus pretiosus*. Coelacanths were not sought after, as their oily flesh caused diarrhoea, but the fish had been used medically as a purgative.

After the coelacanth was thrust from its deep dark lair into the international limelight, it became a valuable commodity. Stuffed or frozen coelacanths became favourite gifts to visiting heads of state and other dignitaries. All coelacanths caught by fishermen had to be sold to the government, and the small island nation also did a roaring trade selling these fish to museums and institutions all over the world. Coelacanth specimens can fetch up to US$2 000.

A coelacanth ballet. These clumsy looking fish are in fact elegant swimmers and those privileged enough to have observed them in their natural surroundings say that they swim as if they were dancing.

THE TWILIGHT ZONE

In addition to being the title of a science fiction TV show dealing with unexplained and strange phenomena, the twilight zone is also the scientific term for an unknown and unexplored marine habitat. The discovery of coelacanths in the submarine canyons off Sodwana has sparked scientific interest in the twilight zone. The deep reefs at between 50 and 120 m receive too little light to support conventional reef-building corals or seaweeds, but are also much richer and more productive than the deep dark zone below.

Dr Kerry Sink, the Marine Ecology Coordinator for the African Coelacanth Ecosystem Programme, leads research aimed at unlocking the mysteries of these deep reefs. Utilizing experienced Trimix dive teams and the *Jago* submarine to carry out surveys, she also dons scuba gear herself to sample the biodiversity at the edge of the twilight zone between 50 and 60 m. To date she has described seven new habitat types, or so called biotopes: canyon drop-offs, rocky canyon walls, sandy slopes, caves and overhangs, rooftops, mixed substrate and sandy plains.

The *canyon drop-offs* lie at depths of between 90 and 110 m and have the highest diversity of any twilight zone biotope. Sponges, black corals and many other soft corals are well represented and the cover of living organisms can be as high as 90%. Below the drop-off, steep and highly eroded *rocky canyon walls* descend into the depths and are encrusted by a diverse assemblage of black coral trees, sea whips and gorgonians. Canyon walls that form *sandy slopes* are blanketed by silt, sand or mud and compared with the steep walls harbour an impoverished animal community. *Caves and overhangs* host encrusting invertebrates, including lace and cup corals, delicate bryozoans and sea fans. The mobile fauna inside the caves includes rock cod, pineapple fish and, of course, the coelacanths themselves. The rocky ledges above the caves and overhangs, the *rooftops*, are, in addition to supporting many invertebrates, also home to an abundant fish community that includes slinger, scotsmen and yellowtail fusiliers. *Mixed substrates* combine types, while the *sandy plains* that meander around the canyon heads are comparatively barren — home only to a low-density assemblage of sea pens, club sponges and sea squirts. The canyon bottom is covered in thick sediment and is the realm of spider crabs and deep-water rock lobsters.

Following on from these very valuable and long overdue descriptive habitat classifications, the next step will be to establish exactly how Sodwana's coelacanths fit into the twilight zone communities. Which prey species are they eating, what trophic level do they occupy and what impact, if any, are the coelacanths having on twilight zone community structure?

The hunt for a live specimen was kick-started when, in addition to a substantial monetary reward, an aquarium offered a trip to Mecca – all-expenses-paid – in an effort to spur on the mainly Muslim population of the islands. Others have offered up to US$40 000 for a live specimen. There are also rumours that coelacanths have entered Chinese medicine and mythology. A drop of notochord fluid is reputed to be worth US$1 000 and to impart immortality.

Between 1952 and 1990 more than 172 coelacanths were caught in the Comoros. Professor Smith first raised concerns about the potential over-exploitation of the species in 1956; in his opinion there were already sufficient specimens available for study. He was particularly concerned since the coelacanth possesses many characteristics that predispose it to premature extinction: it is rare, it grows to a large size, it sits on top of the food chain, it has low dispersal capabilities, it gives birth to few live offspring, and it lives in a very specialized niche.

It was to be many years before the rest of the world shared Professor Smith's concerns. Only in October 1989 did CITES (Convention On International Trade in Endangered Species) place its strongest protection order on the coelacanth, and it now sits alongside the blue whale, the black rhino and the Sumatran tiger on Appendix I, which prohibits all trade in these creatures. To date all countries where coelacanths have been caught or observed have ratified this convention.

A survey of the coelacanth population on Grande Comoro Island in the early 1990s estimated that up to 650 individuals occurred there. Further surveys in 1994 and 1995 noted a dramatic reduction in the number of fish seen in their daytime resting caves, and a population decline down to 300 individuals was estimated. A further survey in 1998 showed that the number in the caves had risen again to normal levels, but the overall population estimate was much lower than initial figures due to an overestimation of the available habitat.

One of the most important recent developments in coelacanth conservation is the establishment of a pelagic fishery in the Comoros through the use of fish aggregation devices (which attract fish) and motorized boats funded by donor agencies. This new fishery was designed to relieve pressure on the inshore reef and could also lead to a dramatic decrease in the coelacanth bycatch.

Finding a population of *Latimeria chalumnae* in South Africa that incidentally occurs within the boundaries of a well-established marine protected area was a conservation triumph. The submarine canyons off Sodwana lie within the boundaries of the Greater St Lucia Wetland Park, a World Heritage Site where all forms of bottom fishing are prohibited. Nonetheless, shortly after their discovery, additional regulations to protect the coelacanths in all of South Africa's territorial waters were swiftly promulgated.

Since the coelacanth was first rediscovered in South Africa in 1938, scientific research has provided many answers, but has also yielded many more questions. How many other undiscovered populations are out there in the seas off southern Africa? Is this fish perhaps more widely distributed and common than previously thought? This fish has surprised many scientists of the past and present, and will, in all likelihood, continue to do so well into the future.

The 4x4 from hell. The engine of this Land Cruiser broke down nearly twelve times in the space of just eight short weeks.

Tom (second from left) and Claudio (middle) in the Namib Desert on a wildlife documentary film shoot.

After six expeditions to the Tembe-Thonga, travelling to Maputaland is almost like coming home for Tom. In one village he has even been offered a place to build his own hut.

The research vessel EDNA cruises the waters of northern Mozambique. Tom was part of a team that carried out the first-ever marine biodiversity study of the remote Quirimba Islands.

The organized chaos of the scientific research camp in the Quirimbas, Mozambique.

Cape Cross seal colony, the smelliest place on Earth. After weeks of photographing there, most clothes were beyond redemption and had to be burned.

A close encounter of the otter kind.

When this dead sperm whale washed up on a beach near Hawston, it gave Tom the unique opportunity to examine the fierce business end of this formidable predator.

Tom eye-to-eye with the ocean's greatest predator.

Claudio on Malgas Island evading, often unsuccessfully, gannet nutrient contributions.

Roads are few and far between in Kosi Bay, and often getting from one village to another means wading for kilometres across shallow lakes, keeping an eye out for hippos.

A curious great white shark, about to 'investigate' Tom's underwater camera housing.

While in Botswana, searching for rock art depicting whales, the 4x4 was attacked by a tree.

Correct exposure and focus were the least of Tom's worries in the confined space of this Kosi Bay fish trap. Surrounded by murky water, he was more concerned that this harvester might mistakenly spear him, instead of the trapped fish.

Fully laden in northern Botswana. Tom lived in this Land Rover for almost 200 days, while photographing and writing Currents of Contrast.

Glossary

AMPHIPOD Small crustacean with laterally compressed body

ANOXIC Devoid of oxygen

ASCIDIAN Sea squirt

BENTHOS Fauna and flora living on the seabed

BIOGENIC Made by living organisms

BIVALVE Class of molluscs with two bilaterally symmetrical valves

BRYOZOAN Colonial moss animal

CETACEAN Order of aquatic mammals: whales, dolphins and porpoises

COPEPOD Small pelagic crustacean

CORRALIVORE Coral eater

CRETACEOUS Geological period about 135 million years ago, at the end of which the dinosaurs died out

DETRITIVORE Detritus eater

DEVONIAN Geological period about 405 million years ago

DUIKER A small antelope occurring throughout Africa south of the Sahara

EOCENE Epoch of geological time about 55 million years ago

EPIPELAGIC Oceanic zone from the surface to 200 m

EPIPHYTE Plant that grows on a host but does not feed on it

GAMETOPHYTE Male/female gamete-forming organism

GASTROPOD Marine snail

GENERA Taxonomic groups of closely related species

GYRE Circular ocean current

HOLOCENE Most recent geologic age, including all time since last glaciation approximately 12 000 years ago

INFRATIDAL Zone between the intertidal and subtidal zones

INTERTIDAL Zone between the high- and low-water marks

ISOPOD Small dorso-vertically flattened crustacean

PALAEOCENE Epoch of geological time about 65 million years ago

PELAGIC Living in the ocean at middle or surface level

PHOTIC ZONE Surface water penetrated by sunlight

PHYTOPLANKTON Microscopic free-floating plants

PLANKTIVORE Plankton eater

PLANKTON Small marine plants and animals that drift with the water

PLEISTOCENE The epoch of geological time about 16 000 000 years ago

PLEUSTONIC FAUNA Small free-floating organisms with gas-filled bladders or floats

PNEUMATOPHORE Aerial root of mangrove tree that rises above level of water or soil

POLYTROPHIC Ability to obtain food from more than one source

PRIMARY PRODUCTIVITY The rate at which new plant biomass is formed by photosynthesis. Primary productivity is the start of the food chain, which in the oceans consists of phytoplankton and seaweed.

RADULA Rasping feeding organ in mouth of most gastropods

SCLERACTINIAN Hard coral

SESSILE Attached to the rock

SPOROPHYTE Asexual spore-forming organism

STIPE Stalk or stem

SUBTIDAL Permanently covered by water

SWASH ZONE Surf zone

THERMOCLINE Boundary layer between waters of different temperatures

TUBE FEET Rows of tiny flexible appendages equipped with suction cups that are located on the underside of starfish. To move, the animal grips the substrate with its tube feet and pulls itself forward

VIVIPAROUS Young are born live

ZOOPLANKTON Small planktonic animals

ZOOXANTHELLAE Symbiotic algae living with marine invertebrates

Humpback whales do battle with the south-flowing Agulhas current as they travel northwards to their breeding grounds off Madagascar.

Selected bibliography

GENERAL AND INTRODUCTION

Adnan, A., Griffiths, C.L. and Turpie, J.K. 2002. 'Distribution of South African marine benthic invertebrates applied to the selection of priority conservation areas.' *Diversity and Distributions.* 8(3):129–146.

Branch, G.M. and Branch, M.L. 1981. *The Living Shores of Southern Africa.* Struik, Cape Town. 272 pp.

Branch, G.M., Griffiths, C.L., Branch, M. and Beckley, L. 1994. *Two Oceans: A guide to the marine life of southern Africa.* David Phillip, Cape Town. 360 pp.

Griffiths, C.L. and Branch, G.M. 1997. 'The exploitation of coastal invertebrates and seaweeds in South Africa: Historical trends, ecological impacts and implications for management.' *Transactions of the Royal Society of South Africa.* 52(1):121–148.

Lubke, R. and de Moor, I. 1998. *Field guide to the eastern & southern Cape coasts.* UCT Press, Cape Town. 559 pp.

Payne, A.I. L., Crawford, R.J.M., and van Dalsen, A.P. 1989. *Oceans of Life off Southern Africa.* Vlaeberg, Johannesburg. 380 pp.

Richmond, M.D. 1997. *A guide to the seashores of eastern Africa and the western Indian Ocean islands.* SIDA/Department for Research Cooperation, SAREC, Zanzibar. 448 pp.

Siegfried, W.R. (ed.) 1994. *Rocky Shores: Exploitation in Chile and South Africa.* Springer-Verlag, Berlin. 177 pp.

Singer, R. and Wymer, J. 1982. *The Middle Stone Age at Klasies River Mouth in South Africa.* University of Chicago Press, Chicago and London. 234 pp.

Smith, M.M. and Heemstra, P.C. 1986. *Sea Fishes of Southern Africa.* Southern Book Publishers, Johannesburg. 1 047 pp.

Turpie, J.K., Beckley, L.E. and Katua, S.M. 2000. 'Biogeography and the selection of priority areas for conservation of South African coastal fishes.' *Biological Conservation.* 92:59–72.

THE REALM OF THE BENGUELA
GREAT WHITE SHARK: MISUNDERSTOOD PREDATOR

Cliff, G., Dudley, S.F.J. and Davies, B. 1989. 'Sharks caught in the protective gill nets of Natal, South Africa. 2. The great white shark *Carcharodon carcharias* (Linnaeus).' *South African Journal of Marine Science.* 8:131–144.

Compagno, L.V.J., Ebert, D.A. and Smale, M.J. 1989. *Guide to the Sharks and Rays of Southern Africa.* Struik, Cape Town. 160 pp.

Ellis, R. and McCosker, J.E. 1991. *Great White Shark.* Stanford University Press, Stanford. 270 pp.

Fallows, C. and Fallows, M. 2001. 'Depth chargers.' *BBC Wildlife.* 19(4):49–55.

Klimley, A.P. and Ainley, D.G. 1996. *Great White Sharks: The Biology of Carcharodon carcharias.* Academic Press, California. 517 pp.

Pardini, A.T., Jones, C.S., Noble, L.R., Kreiser, B., Malcom, H., Bruce, B.D., Stevens, J.D., Cliff, G., Scholl, M.C., Francis, M., Duffy, C.A.J. and Martin, A.P. 2001. 'Sex-biased dispersal of great white sharks.' *Nature.* 412:139–140.

Peschak, T.P. 2004. 'Poachers target Great White: Illegal fishing puts pressure on ocean's top predator.' *BBC Wildlife.* 22(1):19.

Wallet, T.S. 1983. *Shark Attack and Treatment of Victims in Southern African Waters.* Struik, Cape Town. 184 pp.

KELP: THE GOLDEN FOREST

Anderson, R.J., Carrick, P., Levitt, G.J. and Share, A. 1997. 'Holdfasts of adult kelp *Ecklonia maxima* provide refuges from grazing for recruitment of juvenile kelps.' *Marine Ecology Progress Series.* 159:254–273.

Barkai, A. and McQuaid, C.D. 1988. 'Predator-prey role reversal in a marine benthic ecosystem'. *Science* 242:62–64.

Bolton, J.J. and Anderson, R.J. 1994. 'Ecklonia.' In: *Biology of Economic Algae* (I. Akatsuka, ed.) SPB Academic Publishing, The Hague. 385–406.

Day, E.G. and Branch, G.M. 2002. 'Effects of sea urchins (*Parechinus angulosus*) on recruits and juveniles of abalone (*Haliotis midae*).' *Ecological Monographs.* 72(1):133–149.

Day, E.G. and Peschak, T.P. 2001. 'Prickly triangles: Sea urchins, abalone and rock lobster.' *Africa Geographic.* October: 71–81.

Estes, J.A. and Steinberg, P.D. 1988. 'Predation, herbivory, and kelp evolution.' *Paleobiology.* 14(1):19–36.

Field, J.G., Jarman, N.G., Dieckmann, G.S., Griffiths, C.L., Velimirov, B. and Zoutendyk, P. 1977. 'Sun, waves, seaweed and lobsters: the dynamics of a West Coast kelp bed.' *South African Journal of Science.* 73(1):7–10.

Mayfield, S. and Branch, G.M. 2000. 'Interrelations among rock lobsters, sea urchins, and juvenile abalone: implications for community management.' *Canadian Journal of Fisheries and Aquatic Science.* 57:2175–2185.

Peschak, T.P. 2000. 'Poachers Paradise.' *Africa Geographic.* August: 22–23.

Peschak, T.P. 2003. 'Chinese takeaways: Abalone poaching in South Africa.' *BBC Wildlife Magazine* September: 64–66 pp.

Tarr, R.J.Q., Williams, P.V.G. and Mackenzie, A.J. 1996. 'Abalone, sea urchins and rock lobster: a possible ecological shift that may affect traditional fisheries.' *South African Journal of Marine Science.* 17:319–323.

JACKALS, LIONS AND HYENAS: FISHING FOR A LIVING

Avery, G., Avery, D.M., Braine, S. and Loutit, R. 1987. 'Prey of coastal black-backed jackal *Canis mesomelas* (Mammalia: Canidae) in the Skeleton Coast Park, Namibia.' *Journal of Zoology* (London). 213:81–94.

Bartlett, D. and Bartlett, J. 1992. 'Africa's Skeleton Coast.' *National Geographic.* 181(1): 55–85.

Berry, H.H. and Lenssen, J. 1997. 'Cape fur seal predation by brown hyena in the Namib-Naukluft Park, Namibia.' *Madoqua.* 19(2):115–116.

Bridgeford, P.A. 1985. 'Unusual diet of the lion *Panthera leo* in the Skeleton Coast Park.' *Madoqua.* 14(2):187–188.

Hall-Martin, A., Walker, C. and Bothma, J. du P. 1988. *Kaokoveld – The last wilderness.* Southern Book Publishers, Johannesburg. 146 pp.

Nel, J.A.J., Loutit, R. and Bothma, J.P. 1997. 'Prey use by black-backed jackals along a desert coast.' *South African Journal of Wildlife Research.* 27(3):101–103.

Schoeman, A. 1996. *The Skeleton Coast.* Southern Books, Johannesburg.

Skinner, J.D., van Aarde, R.J. and Goss, R. 1995. 'Behavioural ecology of brown hyaenas *Hyaena brunnea* in the central Namib desert.' *Journal of Zoology* (London). 237:123–131.

Stander, P.E. and Hansen, L. 2003. 'Population ecology of desert adapted lions in the Kunene region, Namibia.' *Predator Conservation Trust.* 1–13.

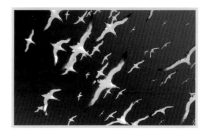

SEABIRDS: DWELLERS OF THE OCEAN SKY

Aupiais, L. and Glenn, I. 2000. *Spill. The story of the world's worst coastal bird disaster.* Inyati Publishing, Kenilworth. 96 pp.

Avery, G. and Underhill, L.G. 1986. 'Seasonal exploitation of seabirds by late Holocene coastal foragers: Analysis of modern and archaeological data from the western Cape.' *Journal of Archaeological Science.* 13:339–360.

Crawford, R.J.M., David, J.H.M., Williams, A.J. and Dyer, B.M. 1989. 'Competition for space: Recolonising seals displace endangered, endemic seabirds off Namibia.' *Biological Conservation.* 48:59–72.

Crawford, R.J.M., Williams, A.J., Hofmeyer, J.H., Klages, N.T., Randall, R.M., Cooper, J., Dyer, B.M. and Chesselet, Y. 1995. 'Trends of African Penguin *Spheniscus demersus* populations in the 20th century.' *South African Journal of Marine Science.* 16:101–118.

David, J.H.M., Cury, P., Crawford, R.J.M., Randall, R.M., Underhill, L.G. and Meyer, M.A. 2003. 'Assessing conservation priorities in the Benguela ecosystem, South Africa: Analyzing predation by seals on threatened seabirds.' *Biological Conservation.* 114(2):289–292.

Ginn, P.J., McIlleron, W.G. and Milstein, P. le S. 1990. *The Complete Book of Southern African Birds.* Struik/Winchester, Cape Town. 760 pp.

Hockey, P.A.R. 2001. *The African Penguin – A Natural History.* Struik, Cape Town. 72 pp.

Nelson, B. 1978. *The Gannet.* T. & A.D. Poyser, Hertfordshire. 336 pp.

SOUTHERN RIGHT WHALE: THE JOURNEY

Best, P.B. 1981. 'The Status of Right Whales (*Eubalaena glacialis*) off South Africa, 1969–1979.' Investigational Report 123, Sea Fisheries Institute: 1–43.

Best, P.B. 2000. 'Coastal distribution, movements and site fidelity of Right Whales *Eubalaena australis* off South Africa, 1969–1998.' *South African Journal of Marine Science* 22:43–55.

Best, P.B., Peddemors, V.M., Cockcroft, V.G. and Rice, N. 2001. 'Mortalities of right whales and related anthropogenic factors in South African waters, 1963 – 1998.' *Journal of Cetacean Research and Management.* (Special Issue) 2:171–176.

Chadwick, D.H. 2001. 'Evolution of Whales.' *National Geographic.* November: 64–77.

Cockcroft, V. and Joyce, P. 1998. *Whale Watch. A guide to whales and other marine mammals of southern Africa.* Struik, Cape Town. 104 pp.

Jeradino, A. and Parkington, J. 1993. 'New evidence for whales on archaeological sites in the south-western Cape.' *South African Journal of Science.* 89:6–7.

Smith, A.B. and Kinahan, J. 1984. 'The invisible whale.' *World Archaeology.* 16(1):89–97.

LIMPETS: A LIFE BETWEEN THE TIDES

Branch, G.M. 1981. 'The biology of limpets: Physical factors, energy flow and ecological interactions.' *Oceanography and Marine Biology Annual Review.* 19:235–379.

Branch, G.M. 2001. 'Rocky Shore.' In: *Encyclopedia of Ocean Science.* Steel, J.A., Thorpe, S.A. & Turekian, K.K. (eds). Academic Press, Orlando. 2427–2434.

Branch, G.M., Harris, J.M., Parkins, C., Bustamante, R.H. and Eekhout, S. 1992. 'Algal gardening by grazers: A comparison of the ecological effects of territorial fish and limpets.' In: *Plant-Animal interactions in the Marine Benthos* (eds. John,D.M., Hawkins, S.J. and Price, J.H), Clarendon Press, Oxford. 405–423.

Bustamante, R.H., Branch, G.M. and Eekhout, S. 1995. 'Maintenance of an exceptional intertidal grazer biomass in South Africa: Subsidy by subtidal kelps.' *Ecology.* 76: 2314–2329.

Herbert, D.G. 1999. '*Siphonaria compressa*, South Africa's most endangered marine mollusk.' *South African Journal of Science.* 95, February 77–79.

Hockey, P.A.R. and G.M. Branch. 1983. 'Do Oystercatchers influence limpet shells?' *The Veliger.* 26(2):139–141.

Peschak, T.P. 2001. 'Life between the tides: Marine resource use by chacma baboons at Cape Point.' *Africa Geographic.* October: 20–21.

Peschak, T.P. 2004. 'Chacma Baboons: Fishing for a Living'. *BBC Wildlife Magazine.* August: 50–55.

Steffani, C.N. and Branch, G.M. 2003. 'Spatial comparison of populations of an indigenous limpet *Scutellastra argenvillei* and an alien mussel *Mytilus galloprovincialis* along a gradient of wave energy.' *African Journal of Marine Science.* 25:195–212.

THE REALM OF THE AGULHAS
THE SARDINE RUN: THE GREATEST SHOAL ON EARTH

Beckley, L.E. and van der Lingen, C.D. 1999. 'Biology, fishery and management of sardines (*Sardinops sagax*) in southern African waters.' *Marine and Freshwater Research.* 50:955–78.

Cockcroft, V.G. and Peddemors, V.M. 1990. 'Seasonal distribution and density of common dolphins *Delphinus delphis* off the south-east coast of southern Africa.' *South African Journal of Marine Science.* 9.371–377.

Peddemors, V.M., Cockcroft, V.G. and Wilson, R.B. 1990. 'Incidental dolphin mortality in the Natal shark nets: A preliminary report on prevention measures.' In: Cetaceans and cetacean research in the Indian Ocean Sanctuary. Leatherwood, S. and Donovan, G.P. (eds.). United Nations Environment Programme (UNEP) Marine Mammal Technical Report No.3:129–137.

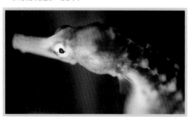

KNYSNA SEAHORSE: CREATURE OF THE BLUE LAGOON

Allanson, B.R. and Baird, D. 1999. *Estuaries of South Africa.* Cambridge University Press. Cambridge. 340 pp.

Bell, E.M., Lockyear, J.F., McPherson, J.M., Marsden, A.D. and Vincent, A.C.J. 2003. 'First field studies of an endangered south African seahorse, *Hippocampus capensis.*' *Environmental Biology of Fishes.* 67:35–46.

Lourie, S.A., Vincent, A.C.J. and Hall, H.J. 1999. *Seahorses. An identification guide to the world's species and their conservation.* Project Seahorse. 214 pp.

Teske, P.R., Cherry, M.I. and Matthee, C.A. 2003. 'Population genetics of the endangered Knysna seahorse, *Hippocampus capensis.*' *Molecular Ecology.* 12(7):1703–1715.

Vincent, A.C.J. 1996. *The International Trade in Seahorses.* TRAFFIC International, Cambridge, UK. 163 pp.

THE TEMBE-THONGA: PEOPLE OF THE SEA AND LAKES

Branch, G.M. (ed.) 2002. 'Developing subsistence fisheries in South Africa: Marrying human needs and biological sustainability.' *South African Journal of Marine Science.* 24:403–523.

Cunningham, A.B. and Zondi, A.S. 1991. 'Use of animal parts for the commercial trade in traditional medicines.' Working paper No. 76. Institute of Natural Resources, University of Natal. 42 pp.

Felgate, W.S. 1982. *The Tembe Thonga of Natal and Mozambique: An Ecological Approach.* Occasional Publications No. 1. Department of African Studies, University of Natal. 182 pp.

Kyle, R., Pearson, B., Fielding, P.J. and Robertson, W.D. 1997a. 'Subsistence shell-fish harvesting in the Maputaland marine reserve in northern KwaZulu-Natal, South Africa: rocky shore organisms.' *Biological Conservation* 82:183–192.

Kyle, R., Robertson, W.D. and Birnie, S.L. 1997b. 'Subsistence shell-fish harvesting in the Maputaland marine reserve in northern KwaZulu-Natal, South Africa: sandy beach organisms.' *Biological Conservation.* 82:173–182.

Junod, H.A. 1962. *The Life of an African Tribe. Volume I. Social Life.* University Books, New York. 560 pp.

Junod, H.A. 1962. *The Life of an African Tribe. Volume II. Mental Life.* University Books, New York. 660 pp.

Mountain, A. 1990. *Paradise under Pressure.* Southern Book Publishers, Johannesburg. 149pp.

SEA TURTLES: PREHISTORIC SURVIVORS

Hays, G.C., Broderick, A.C., Godley, B.J, Luschi, P. and Nichols, W.J. 2003. 'Satellite telemetry suggests high levels of fishing induced mortality in marine turtles.' *Marine Ecology Progress Series.* 262:305–309.

Hughes, G.R. 1989. 'Sea turtles.' In: *Oceans of Life of southern Africa.* Crawford, R., Payne, A. (eds). Vlaeberg, Cape Town:230–242.

Hughes, G.R., Luschi, P., Menacacci, R. and Papi, F. 1998. 'The 7000 km oceanic journey of a leatherback turtle tracked by satellite.' *Journal of Experimental Marine Biology and Ecology.* 229:209–217.

Lohmann, K.J. 1992. 'How sea turtles navigate.' *Scientific American.* 266(1):100–106.

Lohmann, K.J., and Lohmann, C.M.F. 1996. 'Detection of magnetic field intensity by sea turtles.' *Nature.* 380:59–61.

Mortimer, J.A., Donnelly, M. and Plotkin, P.T. 2000. 'Sea turtles.' In: *Seas at the Millennium: An environmental evaluation.* Sheppard, C. (ed.) Elsevier Science Ltd, Amsterdam:59–71.

Perrine, D. 2003. *Sea turtles of the world.* Voyageur Press:1–144.

CORAL REEFS: RAINFORESTS OF THE SEA

Birkland, C. 1997. *The Life and Death of Coral Reefs.* Chapman and Hall, New York. 536 pp.

Goreau, T., McClanahan, T., Hayes, R. and Strong, A. 2000. 'Conservation of coral reefs after the 1998 global bleaching event.' *Conservation Biology.* 14(1):5–15.

Riegl, B. 2003. 'Climate change and coral reefs: different effects in two high-latitude areas (Arabian gulf, South Africa).' *Coral Reefs.* 22:433–446.

Riegl, B. and Riegl, A. 1996. 'Studies on coral community structure and damage as a basis for zoning marine reserves.' *Biological Conservation.* 77:269–277.

Riegl, B., Schleyer, M.H., Cook, P.J. & Branch, G.M. 1995. 'Structure of Africa's southernmost coral communities.' *Bulletin of Marine Science.* 56(2):676–691.

Sale, P.F. 1991. *The Ecology of Fishes on Coral Reefs.* Academic Press, San Diego. 754 pp.

Schleyer, M.H. 1999. 'A Synthesis of Kwazulu-Natal Coral Research.' Oceanographic Research Institute Special Publication. No. 5. 36 pp.

Spalding, M.D., Ravilious, C. and Green, E.P. 2001. *World Atlas of Coral Reefs.* University of California Press, Berkeley. 424 pp.

Walters, R.D.M. and Samways, M.J. 2001. 'Sustainable dive ecotourism on a South African coral reef.' *Biodiversity and Conservation.* 10:2167–2179

Index

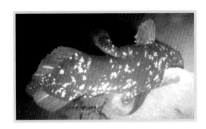

THE COELACANTH: A FISH THAT TIME FORGOT

Fricke, H., Reinicke, O., Hofer, J.H. and Nachtigall, W. 1987. 'Locomotion of the coelacanth in its natural environment.' *Nature.* 329:24.

Fricke, H., Schauer, J., Hissmann, K., Kasang, L. and Plante, R. 1991. 'Coelacanth *Latimeria chalumnae* aggregates in caves: First observations on their resting habitat and social behavior.' *Environmental Biology of Fishes.* 30:281–285.

Hissmann, K., Fricke, H. and Schauer, J. 1998. 'Population Monitoring of the Coelacanth (*Latimeria chalumnae*).' *Conservation Biology* 12 (4):759–765.

Smith, J.L.B. 1939. 'A living fish of Mesozoic type.' *Nature.* 3620: 455–456.

Thompson, K.S. 1991. *Living Fossil. The Story of the Coelacanth.* W.W. Norton & Company, New York. 252 pp.

Venter, P., Timm, P., Gunn, G., Le Roux, E., Serfontein, C., Smith, P., Smith, E., Bensch, M., Harding, D. and Heemstra, P.C. 2000. 'Discovery of a viable population of coelacanths (*Latimeria chalumnae*, Smith, 1939) at Sodwana Bay, South Africa.' *South African Journal of Science.* 96:567–8.

Weinberg, S. 1999. *A Fish Caught in Time.* Fourth Estate, London. 239 pp.

LATEST RESEARCH RESULTS

A complete listing of all scientific and popular references can be found at www.currentsofcontrast.com

For the latest research results, post-May 2004, the following scientific and popular publications can be consulted, either at university and museum libraries or on the internet.

Scientific journals: *African Journal of Marine Science, African Zoology, Biological Conservation, Conservation Biology, Journal of Experimental Marine Biology and Ecology, Marine Biology, Marine Ecology Progress Series, Nature, South African Journal of Science, Science.*

Popular publications: *Africa Geographic, African Wildlife, BBC Wildlife, Divestyle, Earthyear.*

Page numbers in *italics* indicate illustrations.

A

abalone 53, 55, *55*, 58, 59-61, *60*, *61*
Acanthaster planci 182-183, *183*
Acanthopagrus berda 145
Acanthurus triostegus 176
Acropora austere 182
Acropora spp. *167*, 170, 171, 182
Agulhas current 13, *15*, 19, *19*, *20*, 21, *21*
algae 52, 110, 168-169, 174, 176, 180
green algae 131, 174
alikreukel 53
amphipods 22, 81
kelp curler 52
Ampithoe humeralis 52
anchovies 88
angelfish 178
anthias 178
Aonyx capensis 57, *57*
archers 178
Arctocephalus pusillus 123
Argobuccinum pustulosum 56
Arothron stellatus 178
Atlantic Ocean 13, *14*, 17, 21, 49, 63, 64, 70, 93, 114
Atractoscion aequidens 123
Aulacomya ater 53, 116
Avicennia marina 146, 148

B

baboons *see* chacma baboon
badger, honey 160
Balaenoptera edeni 123
barbel 149
barnacle, Natal volcano 138
Barnard, Keppel 26
barracuda *179*, 180
bass
brindle bass 176
potato bass *172-173*
Bazaruto Archipelago *20*, 170-171, 180, 181
beaches 162, 163-164
beetle, tenebrionid 69

Benguela current 13, *14*, 16, *16*, *17*, 18, *18*, 21, 69
Best, Peter 27, 92
biodiversity 22
Bird Island (Algoa Bay) 32, 73, 82, 84
Bird Island (Lambert's Bay) 73, 87
blenny, two-stripe 176
Bonfil, Ramon 40, *40*
Brachylaena discolor 146
Branch, George 27, 109
Brereton-Stiles, Ronnie 150, *151*
Brown, Alec 27
Bruguiera gymnorrhiza 148
Burnupena papyracea 56, 57
butterflyfish 178

C

Callianassa kraussi 116
Cape Cross seal colony *18*, 191
Cape Point *13*, 22, 79, 114-115, *114*, *115*
Carcharhinus brachyurus 122-123, *123*
Carcharhinus limbatus 122
Carcharhinus obscurus 122
Carcharodon carcharias 122
cardinal fish 178
Caretta caretta 155, *159*
Carybdea alata 36-37
Caulerpa 131
Ceriops tagal 148
chacma baboon *12*, 79, 114-115, *114*, *115*
Chaetodon bennetti 178
Chaetodon madagascariensis 178
Chaetodon meyeri 178
Chaetodon trifasciatus 178
Chaetodon zanzibariensis 178
Charonia tritonis 182
Chelonia mydas 155
chevron 178
Chiton salihafui 141
Choromytilus meridionalis 57
Choromytilus sp. 53
Chorisochismus dentex 112
chromis 178
chumming 38, 47
CITES (Convention on International

Trade in Endangered Species) 40, 189
clam, Donax 162
climate change 180-181, *180*
clingfish, giant 112-113
Codium 131
coelacanth 26, 27, *184*, 185-189, *185*, *186*, *187*, *188*
commercial fishing 24, 88-89
cone shells 183
Conus geographus 176
coral reefs
biogeography 170-171
description *10*, 22, *166*, 167-169, *167*, *168*, *169*
fauna and flora 171, *172-173*, 174, *174*, 176, *176*, 176-177, 178, *178*, 179, 180
origins 169-170
research 27
threats 180-183, *180*, *181*, *182*, *183*
cormorants 79-81, *79*, *80*, *81*
bank cormorant 54, 79-80, *80*, 86
Cape cormorant *18*, 64, 78, 79, *79*, 80, 86, 88
crowned cormorant 80, *80*
white-breasted cormorant 65, 80, *81*
Courtenay-Latimer, Marjorie 185, *185*
crabs
ghost crab *8*, 142, *142*, *143*, 145, *159*, 160, 162
mangrove crab 148, *148*
mole crab 145
rock crab 115
cuttlefish 141, *141*
Cymbula compressa 112
Cymbula granatina 105,111
Cymbula oculus 112

D

damselfish 176, 178
Dassen Island 79, 82, 83, 85, 87
Day, John 27
Delphinus delphis 122
Dermochelys coriacea 155, *156*
Diadema antillarum 55
dolphins *16*, 22, 39, 121, 122, *122*, 123, 129

bottlenose dolphin *122, 123*, 129
common dolphin 122, 129
Heaviside's dolphin *16*
humpbacked dolphin 39, 129
Dugong dugon 180
Dyer Island 31, 32, 34-35, 38, 40, 57, 78, 79, 84

E

East Madagascar current 19
Eatoniella nigra 52
Echinopora 171
Ecklonia maxima 49, 58, 79, 112
Ecklonia radiata 50
ecotourism 25, 127, *128*, 129, *129*
egg harvesting 86, 87, 163, *164*
elf 123
Emerita austroafricana 145
emperors 180
environmental threats 25-26, 85-89, 116-117, 134-135, 151, 163-165, 180-183
Epinephelus lanceolatus 176
Epinephelus tukula 172-173
Eretmochelys imbricata 155, 161, *161*
Eubalaena australis 91

F

Faviidae 170
Field, John 27
filefish, long-nose 178
fish 55, 176, *176-177*, 178, *178, 179*, 180
fish traps (kraals) *21*, 145-146, *146*, 150, *193*
flamingos *17*, 84
frogfish *176*
fusiliers *176-177*, 178

G

gannet, Cape
decline 86
description 64, 72, 73-75, *73, 74, 75, 76-77, 77*, 88, *192*
predator of sardines 121, 123, 127
threat from seals 78, *78*
gecko, palmato 69, *69*
geelbek 123
genet, larger spotted 160
Gerres acinaces 145

Gilchrist, J.D.F. 26
gill nets 147, 149, 180
global warming 164, 180-181, *180*
gorgonian 183
great white shark
attacks on humans 40-41
biology and ecology 32-35, *33, 34, 35, 36-37*, 38-39, *39*
conservation 43-44
description 10, 31, *31, 32, 192, 193*
distribution 32
migration 40, *40*
predators 41-43, *41*, 122
role in eco-tourism *42-43*, 44, *45, 46-47, 47*
and whales 39, *39*
groupers 180
grunter, spotted 145, 146
guano 81, *81*, 85, 86, *86*, 87
gulls 83-84, *83*
grey-headed gull 83
Hartlaub's gull 83, 84
kelp gull 83-84, *83*, 87
Gypohierax angolensis 142

H

Haematopus moquini 113, *116*
Halimeda 174
Haliotis midae 53, 55, 60, *60*
Harris, Jean 150
Heritiera littoralis 148
Hippa ovalis 145
Hippocampus algiricus 133
Hippocampus borboniensis 133
Hippocampus camelopardalis 133
Hippocampus capensis 131, *131*
Hippocampus histrix 133
Holbaai 32, 35, 38
Hollams Bird Island 79, 82
hottentot 53
Hughes, George 27, 155
hyenas
brown hyena 63, 67, *67*
spotted hyena 67
Hymencardia ulmoides 146

I

Ichaboe Island 73, 79, 87
Ilhas Primeras 171
Ilhas Quirimbas 171, 175, *175*, 180,

190, 191
Ilhas Segundas 171
Indian Ocean 13, *15*, 137, 171, 181, 187
Inhaca Island 170, 180

J

jackals *62*, 63
black-backed jackal 63, *68*, 69, *69*, 71
side-striped jackal 160
jacks 180
Jasus lalandii 54
jellyfish
box jellyfish *36-37*
red-banded jellyfish 81

K

kelp fly 53
kelp
bamboo kelp 49, 53, 58, 79
bladder kelp 50, *51*
description 18, *48*, 49, 50-51, *50, 51*
distribution 49-50
harvesting of organisms 58-61, *58, 59, 60, 61*
kelp industry 58
kelp limpet 52, 112
research 27
role in food web 52-57, *52, 53, 54, 55, 56, 57*
spined kelp 50
split-fan kelp 49, 53, 58
structure 51-52, *51*
Keurbooms Estuary 131, 132
Khoi-Khoi people 23, 25, 98
kingfish *177*
kite, yellow-billed 160
Klassies River mouth 99, 107
klipfish 22, 55
Knysna Estuary 131, 132, 134, *134-135*
Kosi Bay *21*, 22, 23, *192*
see also Tembe-Thonga people
Kyle, Scotty 150

L

Lambert's Bay 73, 78
Laminaria pallida 49
Laminaria schinzii 50
Larus dominicanus 83

Larus hartlaubii 84
Latimeria chalumnae 185
Lepidochara discoidalis 69
Lepidochelys olivacea 155, 161, *161*
limpets
Argenville's limpet *8*, *110*, 111, *111*, 113, 117
bearded limpet 150
behaviours 81, 109-112, *110, 111, 113*
biology 105-106, *105, 106*
Cape false limpet 112
eelgrass limpet 116
goat's eye limpet 112, 117
granite limpet *105*, 111, 113, *113*
granular limpet *106*, 113, 115
habitat 53, *104*, 108-109
kelp limpet 52, 112
long-spined limpet *109*, 110
pear limpet *109*, 110, 112, 113
predators 112-115, *114, 115, 116*
in prehistory 107-108, *107, 108*
research 27
threats 116-117, *117*
lionfish *10, 171*, 180
lions 63, 65-66, *66*
Lithophyton 171
lizard, shovel-snouted 63
Lobophyton 170
lobsters
spiny lobster 176
west coast rock lobster 54, 55, 56-57, *57*, 58-59, *59*
Lottia alveus 116
Lumnitzera racemosa 148
Lutjanus gibbus 178

M

McLachan, Anton 27
Macrocystis angustifolia 50, *51*
Malgas Island 56, *72*, 73, 78, *86*, 87, *87*
mangrove forests *19*, 22, 145, 148, *148*
black mangrove 148
Indian mangrove 148
Kosi mangrove 148
Mozambique mangrove 148
red mangrove 148
white mangrove 146, 148
Maputaland 32, 170
see also sea turtles; Tembe-

CURRENTS of
CONTRAST

Thonga people

Marcus Island 56, 57

mariculture 25

marine conservation 25-26

Marine Living Resources Act (1998)
    149-150

marine research 26-27

marine snails 52, 53, 55, 84
    see also abalone
    chitons 141
    geographer cone *176*
    nudibranchs *176*
    triton snail *182*, *183*

Marthasterias glacialis 112

maypole *178*

medicine
    Asian 135
    traditional medicine 100, 141, *141*,
        163, 163, 183
    Western 27, 183

Mercury Island 73, 78, 79, 80

mole, golden 71

mongoose
    water mongoose 160
    yellow mongoose 71

Montipora 171

Morrell, Benjamin 87

Morus capensis 123

Mozambique current 19

mudskipper 148, *148*

Mugil cephalus 145

mullet, flathead 145, 146

mussels 53, 57, 84
    brown mussel 140, 150-151, *151*
    Mediterranean mussel 24, 115, 116-
        117, *117*
    ribbed mussel 116

Mytilus galloprovincialis 115, 116-117

O

Ochna natalitia 140

octopus *21*, 55, 138

Octopus vulgaris 21, 138

Ocypode ceratophthalmus 142, 160

Ocypode kuhlii 160

Ocypode madagascariensis 142

Ocypode ryderi 142

Odontodactylus scyallarus 174, 176

oil pollution 87, *88*

Onymacris unguicularis 69

Oreochromis mossambicus 146

otter, Cape clawless 54, *56*, 57, *57*, *191*

Oxymoncanthus longirostris 178

Oxystele spp. *83*, 110

oystercatcher, African black 113,
    116, 117

oysters
    Cape oyster 138
    Natal oyster 138

P

Pachymetopon blochii 53

palm, Kosi *145*

Parechinus angulosus 53, 53, 55, *55*

parrotfish 176, 178

Peddemors, Vic 123

Pelecanus onocrotalus 85

pelican, great white 79, *84*, 85, *85*

penguins 57
    African penguin 78, 82, *82*, 85, 86,
        87, 88, 123

Pentacta doliolum 53

perch 145

Periophthalmus spp. 148

Perna perna 140, 150-151, *151*

petrels 89, *89*

Phalacrocorax capensis 79

Phalacrocorax carbo 80

Phalacrocorax coronatus 80

Phalacrocorax neglectus 79

phytoplankton 18, 64, 81, 162

pilchards 88

Plagiotremus rhinorhynchos 176

Plotosus lineatus 149

poaching 44, 60-61, *61*

Pocilloporidae 170

Pomadasys commersonnii 145

Pomatomus saltatrix 123

porcupine 63, 71

pouter 145, 149

Protoreaster lincki 21

Pterois miles 171

puffers 141
    large star puffer 178

Pyura stolonifera 137, 138, 139, 140, 142

R

rabbitfish 176

Ralfsia 109, 110

Raphia australis 145

red bait *137, 138, 139*, 140, 142

redfin 178

red roman 55

Rhizophora mucronata 148

Robben Island 82, 84, 87

S

Saccostrea cucullata 138

St Croix Island 82

Saldanha Bay 87, 98

sandprawn 116

Sandwich Harbour 71

San people 23, 98

Sarcophyton 171

sardine run
    description 121
    distribution of sardines 121
    fishing and tourism 126-127, *126*,
        128, 129, *129*
    predators 122-123, *122*, *123*, 127

Sardinops sagax 121

Sarpa salpa 52, 53

Schaapen Island 83

Scholl, Michael 33, 38

Sclerocarya birrea 140

scuba diving 181-182

Scutellastra argenvillei 110, 111, *111*

Scutellastra cochlear 109, 110

Scutellastra granatina 105, 111

Scutellastra granularis 106

Scutellastra longicosta 109, 110

Scutellastra pica 150

sea cucumbers 53, 138, *138*, 141, 171,
    175

sea fans *10*

seagrass 22, 116, 131, *132*

seahorses 133, *133*
    giraffe seahorse 133
    Knysna seahorse *130*, 131-135, *131*,
        134-135
    Reunion seahorse 133
    thorny seahorse 133
    west African seahorse 133

seal, Cape fur *18*, 64-65, *64*, 65, 78,
    78, 123, *191*

Seal Island 32, 34, 35, 40

sea snakes 22

sea squirts 53
    see also red bait

sea turtles

breeding 156, *156*, 157, 158-160,
    158, 159
    conservation 26, 162-165, *163*,
        164, *165*
    description *154*, 155, *155*
    green turtle 155, 161
    hawksbill turtle 155, 161, *161*
    leatherback turtle 155, 156, *156*,
        158, 159, *159*, 160, 162, 163,
        164, 165
    life in sea 160-162, *161*
    loggerhead turtle 8, 155, 156, 158,
        158, 159, *159*, 160, 162, 163, 164,
        164, 165
    olive Ridley 155, 161, *161*
    research 27

sea urchins 53, *53*, 55, *55*, 141, 171,
    174
    long-spined sea urchin 55

seaweeds (algae) 22, 81, *109*, 141, 183

Seriola lalandi 123

Sesarma meinerti 148, *148*

shark nets 129, *129*

sharks 27, *54*, 89, 162, 175, 180
    see also great white shark
    blacktip shark 122
    bonnet hammerhead 122
    bronze whaler shark 122-123,
        123, 129
    dusky shark 122, 129
    spotted gully shark *54*

shrimp, mantis *174*, 176

Sink, Kerry 189

Sinularia 170

Siphonaria capensis 112

Siphonaria compressa 116

Skeleton Coast 8, *17*, 62, 63, *63*, 65,
    66, *66*, 98

Smith, J.L.B. 26, *184*, 185-186, *185*,
    189

snails *see* marine snails

snakes
    horned adder 69
    sidewinder 69, *69*

snapper, humpback 178

soldierfish 178

southern right whale
    communication 96, *96*, 97
    conservation 25, 26, 102-103, *103*
    description *90*, 91-92, *91*, 92

eco-tourism 102

evolution 92-93

history of whaling 98-100, *99*, *100-101*, 102, *193*

mating and calving 94-95, *94*, 98

migration 93-94, *95*

spearfishing 146-147, *147*

Sperrgebiet 70-71, *70*, *71*

Spheniscus demersus 82, *82*, 123

Sphyraena barracuda 179

Sphyrna zygaena 122

sponges 53, 183

staghorn coral *167*, 170

Stag Island 84

starfish *21*, 112, 182-183, *183*

   crown of thorns starfish 182-183, *183*

   spiny starfish 112

Stephenson, T.A. 26

Sterna balaenarum 84

Sterna bergii 84

Sterna dougallii 84

strandwolf *see* hyenas, brown

strepies *52*, 53

Striostrea margaritacea 138

stumpnose, red 55

suckerfish 52

surgeonfish 176

   convict surgeonfish 176

Swartvlei Estuary 131, 132

sweetlips 180

Tembe-Thonga people

   and conservation 149-151, *151*, *152-153*

   habitat 137

   hunter-gatherers in lakes *23*, 145-149, *145*, *146*, *147*, *148*

   hunter-gatherers in sea 25, *136*, *137*, 138, *138*, *139*, 140, *140*, 142, *142*, *143*, 145, *190*

   importance of moon cycle 138, 140, 144, *144*

   uses of marine organisms *138*, 141, *141*

Terebralia palustris 148

terns 84

   Damara tern 84

   roseate tern 84

swift tern 84

Tetraclitas squamosa rufotincta 138

Thais bufo 138

Thais dubia 112

Thyone aurea 53

tilapia 146, 149

Topnar people *23*, *24*, *58*, *86*

tourism *see* ecotourism

traditional medicine 141, *141*, 163, *163*, 183

trees

   see also mangrove forests

   marula tree 140

   Natal plane tree 140

   red-heart 146

Triakis megalopterus 54

triggerfish 180

Turbo sarmarcticus 53

Tursiops truncatus 122, 123

turtles *see* sea turtles

twilight zone 189

Tylos granulatus 71

vulture, palmnut 142, 160

Walvis Bay 85

whales 22, 39, *39*, 102

   see also southern right whale

   Bryde's whale 123

   humpback whale *39*, 96, 102, *124-125*, 125

   killer whale (orca) 41, 80

   sperm whale *192*

whelks 56, 57, 112

   mangrove whelk 148

   salmon-lipped whelk 138

worms 52, 53, 162

   bristle worm 52

wrasses 180

yellowtail 123

zooanthids *21*

zooplankton 18, 64, 81, 178

zooxanthellae 168-169, 174, 180

Zostera capensis 116, 131, *132*

Struik Publishers
(a division of New Holland Publishing (South Africa) (Pty) Ltd)
Cornelis Struik House
80 McKenzie Street
Cape Town

New Holland Publishing is a member of the Johnnic Publishing Group

www.struik.co.za

Log on to our photographic website

First published in 2005

2 4 6 8 10 9 7 5 3 1

Copyright © text: Thomas P. Peschak, 2005
Copyright © maps: Thomas P. Peschak, 2005
Copyright © published edition: Struik Publishers, 2005

Publishing manager: Pippa Parker
Managing editor: Lynda Harvey
Project manager: Emily Bowles
Editor: Roxanne Reid
Designer: Janice Evans
Cover design: Janice Evans
Cartography and illustrations: David du Plessis
Proofreader: Tessa Kennedy
Indexer: Mary Lennox
Reproduction by Hirt and Carter Cape (Pty) Ltd
Printed and bound by Sing Cheong Printing Co. Ltd, Hong Kong

ISBN 1 77007086 9

All photographs copyright © Thomas P. Peschak, except for:
Claudio Velásquez Rojas copyright ©: pages 1; 16 (top and bottom);
17 (right top and right bottom); 18 (bottom left and bottom right);
19 (top); 20 (main and inset); 21 (inset top middle and bottom); 24 (right);
25; 28; 55 (top left); 58 (bottom); 59; 63 (bottom right); 65; 69 (box top right and
bottom left); 70 (bottom left); 74 (bottom); 75 (top); 104; 105; 106; 107 (main);
108; 109 (both); 110; 111; 114 (top); 117; 155; 158; 164 (top);
165; 194; 195 (seabirds); 196 (limpets and turtle)
Namibian Archive Windhoek copyright ©: page 23 (inset)
Michael C. Scholl copyright ©: pages 33 (fins); 192 (top left and top right);
South African Archives, Cape Town copyright ©: pages 58 (top left); 91 (left)
South African Institute of Aquatic Biodiversity copyright ©: pages 184; 186; 187
South African Post Office ©: page 185 (right top to bottom)
Jürgen Schauer, Jago Team, Germany copyright ©: pages 188; 197 (coelacanth)
Hans Fricke copyright ©: page 5 (coelacanth inset)
John Paterson copyright ©: page 66 (top)
Martin Harvey copyright ©: page 67 (left)

Visit the Currents of Contrast website at www.currentsofcontrast.com